THE NINE LIVES OF A COWBOY

THE NINE LIVES OF A COWBOY

H. "DUDE" LAVINGTON

1982

SONO NIS PRESS

VICTORIA, B.C., CANADA

Canadian Cataloguing in Publication Data

Lavington, Dude, 1907-
   The nine lives of a cowboy

   ISBN 0-919203-20-5

   1. Lavington, Dude.   2. Cowboys — British
Columbia — Biography.   3. Ranchers — British
Columbia — Biography.   4. Ranch life —
British Columbia — Quesnel region.   I. Title.

FC3845.Q48Z49 1982   971.1'2030924
F1089.Q48L39   c82-091327-8

First printing November 1982
Second printing December 1982

This book has been financially assisted by the Canada Council Block Grant Program and the Government of British Columbia through the British Columbia
Cultural Fund and British Columbia Lottery Revenues.

Published by
SONO NIS PRESS
1745 Blanshard Street
Victoria, British Columbia v8w 2j8

Designed and printed in Canada by
MORRISS PRINTING COMPANY LTD.
Victoria, British Columbia

Dedication

To my brother Art, who shared most of these experiences and the trials and accomplishments of building a very isolated ranch, with little but ambition to work with. Twice hypothermia would have got the best of me had he not guessed my whereabouts and fought his way through deep snow in the middle of the night to bring me in.

Acknowledgements

To my late wife Margaret who did a great deal of the original typing after sorting the many incidents into chronological order.

To Nina Wooliams who read my manuscript and gave me a very thorough and constructive criticism to work from.

To my daughter Jean who reorganized and edited all my writing.

To Sheila Nielson who drew the map.

To Carol Rutherford who carried on with the sorting and typing, June Loper for her professional retyping and Karen Kooistra for all the extra bits and pieces to finish.

To the many pioneers who had similar experiences and hardships to contend with but left their stories untold.

Contents

Introduction

Many people have led very dull lives. Certainly mine could not be called dull. I should have been pushing up daisies long ago. All my working life has been that of a pioneer with a pioneer background. My dad had no such background. Raised in the shadow of Wells Cathedral, where his dad was organist for 53 years, he migrated to the States in his late teens — a genuine green Englishman. Working awhile on the railroad and then on ranches in Iowa and Nebraska, he migrated to Alberta in a covered wagon with a bunch of horses in 1896. There, he wintered with a detachment of North West Mounted Police in Southern Alberta. In the spring he worked his way on up to Central Alberta where he homesteaded just north of Big Valley, met and married my mother, Eva Cook, and started cattle and horse ranching there in cahoots with mother's brother Bill.

My brother Art and I saw the light of day in 1906 and 1907 respectively with a sister coming later. Tragedies struck the family very early. When Art was two he was kicked in the face by a colt and was unconscious for four days. This necessitated a nightmare team-and-buggy drive to Stettler, 20 miles away. Then typhoid fever struck and our sister died and I very nearly did. Later our mother became ill and passed away on the train to the coast. Ours become a bachelor outfit for three years. A bad prairie fire and broken and sprained ankles from a runaway team were added to the family's woes. Dad must have wondered just how tough a life he was condemned to live.

Trying to build up a ranch and raise us two hooligans with very little help was beset with difficulties. Dad had to tie us to the bed legs, far enough apart so we couldn't untie each other, so he could go out to feed the cattle in winter. The lack of neighbours, and women being scarcer than hens' teeth, made for a lonely life. Two suicides that I remember were probably directly attributable to these shortages. My early memories include old sod roof shacks, smudge pens for cattle, Dad going away for long periods on round-ups, Harry Simpson the "Hobo Rancher" who ran nearly 400 steers but owned no property and bummed his way from ranch to ranch, and the old Swede hired man who believed that one bath a year was plenty. Then there were the horribly noisy first radios, the first telephone and the first cattle buyer who came around in a car. I also remember throwing a knife at Art and seeing it go through the muscle of his leg, a cow that charged Art and nearly got him, cooking lamb frys (nuts to you, McGinty) over the brandfire, and the runaway in the barnyard with me on top of a load of hay. (The team crashed through one division fence and into another that didn't give way. The last fence didn't give way but my inside works sure did!)

Dad's eldest brother, Charlie, and his two sons, Ralph and Harry, came out and settled near us around 1910. Dad remarried in 1911. Between Uncle Charlie and Dad's new wife, Art and I were doomed to a stricter upbringing — one which we rebelled against as much as possible. Our happiest memories have to do with our neighbours, the Burnstads. Mary Burnstad was the nearest to a mother we ever had and she seemed to be mother to many other boys and girls as well as her own two sons and three daughters. John and Mary's home was our second home.

My story tells a little of Art's and my growing up and school days in Alberta, starting in a one-room school with over 50 pupils in seven grades and finishing my formal education in grade 11 at Crescent Heights in Calgary with about 30 students all in one grade and a teacher for each subject; our migration to B.C. and our 12-year brothers' partnership building up the L^c ranch. We cut more than 75 miles of roads and trails, built bridges, barns, cabins, and fences. We fought high water (and almost drowned), and tangled with horses, moose and wolves. We drove cattle across country, prospected, trapped, packed and freighted into Stanley and Barkerville, got caught in a cattle stampede in Quesnel and got badly injured a few times. One of the yarns also tells how I got my nickname. Several of the episodes I tell of came close to being the end of the road for either Art or myself, hence the title.

So, git down and rest your saddles, folks, and read all about it.

H. "DUDE" LAVINGTON

*A cowboy must be blessed (or cursed) with nine lives
like the proverbial cat, or he would never make
it to the allotted three score and ten —
or even to maturity*

CHAPTER I

School Days

Over the years from the time Dad moved in, Stettler had been build-ing up till it was our main source of supply, so that we were no longer sixty-five miles from a town. In 1910, the railroad went right through Dad's place and the little town of Big Valley sprang up only four miles away. Settlers poured in and the open range was gradually on the way out. Soon there were schools and churches within reach.

Art and I started school together, he at seven and I nearly six. We were four miles from school so had to ride. We used to ride double on an old pony called Babe. He was a smart old cuss. Every once in a while we'd get him jarred into a gallop. Then all of a sudden he would slam on the brakes and stop dead. We would slide over his head and pile up in a heap in front of him. I believe the old devil was smart enough to see the funny side of it and give us the horse laugh. Other times we'd get to laughing and fall off in a heap. Babe always stopped and waited for us to get on again. He was getting old but was still a good stock horse and we could do pretty fair cowboying on him.

We always rode bareback in our younger days as Dad figured that was the surest way to prevent our getting hung up in the stirrups. Consequently, we could ride like Indians before we were very old. We even roped calves and held them with only a mane hold. Old Babe really knew his stuff in that line too. Dad used to let us dehorn the calves on the range. There would be a hundred head or so of them to do every spring and we were to do them around a week old. We would rope them and cut off the little button horns and rub the stump with a caustic stick. So we watched the cows like hawks when they were calving and I don't think we ever missed a calf. One of us would have to stay mounted to keep the cow from taking after the one working on the calf. We had to drive a few of the mean cows into the corrals and separate them to be safe, but all the rest we roped on the range from our bareback cayuses.

We didn't do so well when Art was fourteen and Dad first let us go with saddles. He had bought a couple of old hulls, quite a little the worse for wear, and turned us loose to get a two-year-old steer at a neighbour's with the definite admonition not to rope it. But we didn't listen too well and I got my loop on first. Old Babe set the brakes and the cinch popped and I really went for a ride with the saddle just hitting the ground every fifty feet. I got bruised up quite a little, but the neighbours made a big fuss of me and that seemed to make everything okay. Meanwhile, Art tried the same stunt with the same end result. I don't quite recall the yarn we built to tell the old man, or his reaction, but I do remember I had to put in a day or so in bed from an injured pelvis.

When I was about eight years old, we decided to liven things up at school and entertain the rest of the kids. We weren't allowed spurs so we put shingle nails in our boot heels and made old Babe buck around the schoolyard. The show went over big till the girls told the teacher. The teacher told the folks and Dad grounded us for a year as far as riding to school went. That four-mile walk twice a day was pretty stiff punishment but we sure remembered not to abuse our saddle horses again.

At one time an outfit had gone broke prospecting for oil right in the road allowance close to Ralph's place. They had broken a drill bit and left a drill casing sticking up about four feet above the ground. This was right on our way to school and we would spend time both ways dropping rocks down this pipe and listening to them jingle, jingle all the way down. Years later, oil was discovered on Dad's and Ralph's properties and all up and down the Valley. We were told that at one time there were twenty-six producing wells on Dad's old place (after mineral rights had reverted to the crown).

There was one boy at school who was a real teacher's pet and whenever anyone did any wrong he ran and told the teacher. We figured how to fix him. There were three coal mines close to town and the underground tunnels were mostly fairly close to the surface, and in many places had caved in. There was one of these about a quarter of a mile from the school. That just suited our purpose. It was eight or nine feet deep with steep enough walls that there wasn't a hope of climbing out of it. Several of us boys stayed at school for lunch, as did our victim. So, some way, we enticed him over to the cave-in during the noon hour and ganged up on him and pushed him in. Then we told him the why and wherefore and laid down the law to him.

He had to promise not to ever be a tattletale again or he would have to stay put. He bawled so much we couldn't decide whether he was promising or not. The bell rang so we just left and hit back for school. The teacher asked if any of us boys knew why he was absent from class but we all acted totally ignorant. Art suggested he must have got sick and had to go home and the teacher had to settle for that. We had a pretty guilty feeling by the time school was out and I know I was plumb scared.

To say he was tickled to see us when we raced over would be putting it mildly. At least he could talk now and he pleaded and pleaded to be let out. Seeing him safe and sound we got tough with him again. Knowing if he told on us this time we'd really get the works, we bluffed him into believing that we'd not only leave him for the night, but just plain leave him if he didn't cross his heart and hope to die and promise never to tell a soul this time or ever again. Of course he was willing to promise anything by this time and, after letting him sweat it out for about another half an hour, we hauled him out. He never told on us again but I doubt if any of us slept too well for a night or so after.

I got to be pretty handy on second base in baseball and could easily have been on the team, but being four miles from school I couldn't get in to practices often enough, or even to the regular games. I also got in on football, basketball and hockey games as much as I could. But marbles were my long suit. We used to have a game they called "plunking." One boy would have an alley and he would sit down with his back to a building or backstop of some kind, put the alley between his spread legs, and the game began. There was a line about eight feet back and the rest of us stood toe to the line and plunked our little clay dibs at his alley. Whoever hit it first got the alley. But he got all the dibs plunked at it. Then the new owner took his place and the game went on. The dibs sold for about a nickel a dozen. Another boy went into partnership with me and we cleaned up all the dibs in school. We'd hardly ever have to plunk more than two or three times before hitting the alley, and then we'd rake in the dibs and resell them and go some more. A lot of the kids had more money than skill and we made quite a lot of ice cream money.

Art and I didn't have an awful lot of time at school together. I think after about two years of school our stepmother decided to break up a bad combination and talked Dad into shipping Art away to a boarding school, which was a French convent at Red Deer. We had got into a few mix-ups at school and wouldn't ever tell tales on each other. She decided Art was the leader of the gang and mustn't lead me too far astray (I doubt if I needed much leading).

Art ran away from the school the folks sent him to. There was another boy from town there and together they figured out how to get home. The other boy (Eddie Chapman) knew all about trains as his dad was an engineer. So they decided to "ride the rods," and packed a little of their rigging and got down to the yards in time to catch a freight going to Stettler, and then hooked another one and got home to Big Valley.

Art got quite a little working over, but got nearly a year's respite from boarding school before they sent him to another one at Edmonton. After a couple of years there, they sent him to live with our Uncle Bill who had moved to Vancouver Island. He finished school there and went to work in logging camps on the coast where he got in quite a lot of worthwhile experience handling rigging of all kinds. He learned a lot about logging, which was to be pretty handy later out in B.C., when we went into ranching on our own.

I can vaguely remember Dad riding away for weeks at a time on spring and fall roundups. There were two epidemics of mange in the area, entailing extra roundups. Of the first, I can only remember Dad riding away with two saddle horses, one with a light pack on, as on spring and fall roundups. But the second mange epidemic produced one of my most vivid memories. I was seven years old at the time. Art was away at boarding school.

Every hoof of stock on the range had to be rounded up and dipped. The dipping vat was about forty miles away at Sam Savage's ranch. Being summer time I was out of school and allowed to go on this roundup. A lot of the ranchers in the area pooled their stock and drove together. Dad had close to four hundred head then and Ralph, my cousin, had about one hundred and fifty. Roy Seeley and Ralph and Dad and I went with our drive. We were soon joined by seven or eight of our neighbours, and their stock, and quite a few more riders.

My memory completely fails me on an important part of the outfit — the chuckwagon or pack outfit carrying grub, cooking outfit and blanket rolls. That would seem to be the most important part of the whole expedition to a seven-year-old boy, always hungry, but the excitement of being a cowboy on a drive like that faded everything else into insignificance.

The nearer we got to the dipping vat the more cattle we came in contact with, till, toward the last, the whole countryside seemed to be a moving mass of cattle. Somehow we had to hold ours separate from other herds till it came our turn to go through the vat. We moved our cattle in closer as other herds ahead of us went through, and the last day or so we had our herd in a fenced holding pasture and didn't have to night herd.

The vat was on the shore of a lake. Sulphur and lime were mixed with water and boiled awhile. A steady stream of the stinking mixture was being pumped into the vat from one side, and lake water was being pumped in from the other side. There were great big holding corrals which funnelled into a chute, and this in turn funnelled into the vat which, I believe, was forty or fifty feet long.

Cattle dived off a platform and went right under for a few seconds, came up snorting and blowing, looking like drowned rats, and then swam to the far end and walked out. This steady stream of cattle went through day after day for weeks and months. I felt very sorry for the poor miserable looking devils. After they had gone through once, we had to hold them again until our turn came around to run them through again.

I vaguely remember our camp. It was hot and clear in the daytime and around the corrals a fog of dust all day. We had no tent and just spread out blankets on the ground at night. I can remember getting mighty chilly before morning, so I reckon our bedroll was pretty skimpy. I even seem to remember having frost one morning.

After the last dipping we started for home and when the herd realized they were not just being held, they really started to line out. There was a lake well over a mile wide right across our general homeward direction. These cattle had been forced to drink horribly dirty, riled up water all the time they had been held. Now they got the smell of this fresh water and a stampede started straight for the lake. What a picture that would have made with any kind of a camera, but especially with a movie camera. But in those days cowboys on the roundup who packed a camera were pretty scarce.

That huge mass of moving, running cattle, with their horns flashing in the sun and their hooves rattling, was really something to thrill anyone. The leaders were pushed a mile or more out into the lake by the very momentum of the herd, and must have caused a small tidal wave on the far shores of the lake. Soon they were all swimming; a sea of swimming cattle, and there was no turning them back. They had to swim all the way across and some of the weaker ones had a tough job making it. That was my longest swim ever on a saddle horse. We all followed them across to bring up the drags. The water was warm and though our legs were immersed all the way across I, at least, enjoyed it immensely and would have liked to get right in and swim a ways on my own. As we neared home, every so often a rancher would have to cut his cattle out of the herd and gradually our trail drive came to an end. Our little bunch looked so insignificant after seeing such masses of cattle.

19

Almost any time stock had to be handled I got a holiday from school, and I always got in on the beef drive. I think I liked school better than most kids and even though I hated to miss any cowboying, I also hated to miss school. That was probably because with Art away I had no one to play with at home. At school I got into all the games the boys played and I never missed a chance to have a wrestling match. Sometimes I rassled all through the hour and a half we got for lunch.

There was one boy in school I got to know pretty well, Jack Bowman was his name. His mother used to make quite a fuss of him. He often took a lunch to school and his lunches were pretty high toned, full of fancy cooking — cakes, cookies and pies. Mine were the opposite, being good, plain grub but no hell for fancy. Well, Jack, or "Porky" as we called him, had got fed up on fancy grub and so we got to trading lunches — "straight across, sight unseen" as the saying goes. I sure got some delicious surprises. The folks used to exchange visits with Jack's family occasionally. Jack and I both got mumps close to exam time at the end of our grade five. So Mrs. Bowman arranged with the folks and the authorities for me to go into quarantine with them and take my exams with Jack at their place. I sure got in on the fancy groceries on that deal.

The same year Mum had to have an operation just before Christmas and was recuperating at Bowman's at Christmas time. So Dad and I were invited to the Christmas dinner there. It was cold and we had to feed three hundred head of stock and do all the ranch chores first. That was a pretty fair day's work and it was definitely time for dinner when we got through. But we had to swop riggin' to our Sunday-go-to-meeting clothes, switch to a driving team on the cutter, drive the four miles to town, put the team in at the livery barn, and walk nearly a half a mile to Bowman's before taking on any nourishment.

Before dinner we had a glass of homemade wine (with a kick to it like a blue mule). Then we put on the nosebag, and in a big way. I could have eaten a horse all by myself — head, tail and all. So I started on my plateful right away and hoisted it in fast as I could to fill the great emptiness. But the drink of wine on such an empty stomach was too much for me, and before I got through the first helping I had to unload the works. Nothing daunted, and just as hungry as ever, I started all over again and made the grade that time. The folks were terribly embarrassed I believe, but I was just a growing boy and awful damn hungry.

Before Art and I were very old we started doing chores before breakfast in the winter. We watered horses that had been in the barn overnight and then fed them. One winter Dad had a shorthorn bull that
was inclined to be a little mean. We didn't like him, and I guess he
didn't appreciate us too much. We figured our best way to work it out
was to keep him afraid of us, so at any opportunity we prodded him
with a pitchfork. That worked okay for awhile but one day the worm
turned. Art took a prod at the bull and it turned on him. Art grabbed
the fence rails and shinnied up. The bull tried to get him on the fence
and Art had to climb up onto the barn roof. The bull ignored his hay
and just kept right after Art. There was a string of sheds joined onto
the barn and Art went from one to the other right to the end, but the
bull followed him right along, giving him no chance to come down and
head for the house and breakfast. We were sure scared. Art told me
to hit for the house and get Dad. The bull never looked at me and I
made my getaway.

We knew we had done wrong prodding the bull with a fork and
I figured the folks would guess that was the reason he had gone after
Art. So I just told them Art had had to go to the toilet and we had
breakfast with Art out in the cold, either on the barn or shed roofs,
trying to get out of sight of the mad and watchful bull. Finally, when
breakfast was all over, the bull relaxed vigilance just long enough for
Art to make his getaway. I saw him coming and told him I'd been
scared to tell the folks and we didn't tell them till years afterwards.
But the bull got meaner and Dad sold him before someone got hurt.

One spring we had a late snowstorm and had to pick up newborn
calves on the feed ground in the late afternoon and take them into the
house to dry and warm up. We brought the mothers into the barnyard and left them there overnight. Mum used to feed the chickens
before breakfast, which entailed going through the barnyard. Those
old range cows didn't like being deprived of their calves and were
pretty ringy in the morning. Mum, Art, and I made the trip across
the big yard to the barn all right, but on her way back one old cow
spotted Mum and pawed the dirt awhile, wrung her tail, and finally
charged. Mum must have been watching out of the corner of her
eye. When the cow charged she also broke into a run and just
barely made the sprint to the fence in time. She grabbed the fence rail
and started up. The old cow hit the fence "smash" between the old
lady's legs. Mum went on up over that fence in nothing flat. Art and
I were watching from the barn and had a little giggle to ourselves, but
we wern't too sure we wouldn't get the same treatment so we went

through a hay-yard and around the buildings to keep out of the old gal's sight.

We had quite a time with that bunch of calves in the house overnight. They were thoroughly chilled and pretty dopey when we brought them in but, as they thawed out, they would start rarin' around the linoleum floor. Their balance is none too good at first anyway and, with this added handicap, they were skidding every which way. Every little while, one would let a blat out and like to scare us to death. They had been fenced in with tables, chairs and anything available. The barricades held for the night but early in the morning with one or two pushing and butting this way and that, the furniture fence gave ground and calves started skidding across country. So come sunup and a little milder day they were all set to tackle any cow in the herd for some milk.

I had the job of cutting water holes half a mile or so from the house one day when it was around 30 below. On the last water hole my axe got away from me, slipping through my icy mitts and down into the water hole. I reached to make a grab for the disappearing handle and slipped into the water hole. I got the axe but also got one leg wet to the hip and the other up to the knee, and one arm up to the shoulder. Panic struck me. I was sure I would freeze to death before I could get home. I started to bawl and run, doing both to the best of my ability.

In no time my pants, boots, and socks were frozen solid and my legs and feet just like encased in splints. This increased my panic. I would never make it. I hollered louder and tried to run faster but it seemed like ages before I made that half mile. I stopped running but forgot to stop bawling. Mum couldn't guess what was wrong and gave me a licking to make me shut up enough so she could find out what was wrong. Imagine my surprise to find out that I was warm as toast and even sweating from all the effort and panic!

I have always had a tough time with my hands in the cold weather and when I was a youngster, I would bawl out "my 'ands are gold" and keep on repeating it. They sure were cold. Actually they hurt more when they were warming up and I would start bawling all over again. If there is a cloud in the sky my hands are apt to be cold even now, yet I hardly ever cover my ears. I wear a Stetson hat the year round and only very occasionally, if there is too much wind when it is lower than 25 below, do I tie a silk scarf over my ears.

Besides Dad's whiskey, Art and I sampled his pipes and smoking tobacco pretty young. But we never really enjoyed either of them. Something we did enjoy, though, was stealing Dad's six-shooter and a little ammunition (as much as we figured we could get away with) and shooting rats and gophers with it. We worked out quite a scheme. On Sundays we would talk Dad into taking the gun out and going gopher hunting and let us get in a shot once in a while. We encouraged him to keep on till he would empty a box of cartridges, then talk him into a few more shots to get him to open a new box and get it started. Then we would pretend to lose interest and go home, so there would be a new box of shells opened. We would steal the gun, an old .45 Colt, and a few shells, and go out and shoot a few gophers or a rat if the fur was good in the spring. Then when the box was getting nearly empty we would put the pressure on Dad to go hunting again and work the same process over. Dad never hinted that he had any idea that there was dirty work at the crossroads, but he must have wondered at times why the ammunition box was always down to the last six or eight cartridges.

We both got to be able to hold our own pretty well in any shooting matches we got into, and there were some good marksmen in the country around.

I didn't do very well on my first two tries with Dad's old 12 gauge, double-barrel shotgun. I spotted a big bunch of ducks landing below a little hill, just perfect for sneaking up on. It took a lot of persuasion to get the old cannon but Dad gave in saying "no sitting shots or you won't get the gun again for a long time." Off I went with two shells, sure I would get several birds.

Stalking was right down my alley, and I got up on them and peeked over the brow of the hill. There were a hundred or more unsuspecting mallards quacking away and diving for weeds. I got the gun up to my shoulder and raised up slowly with the right barrel cocked as I was instructed. Had they flown immediately, I would have been ready. But they started swimming in circles and some took off from one place, some another, and it was some seconds before they all flew. All this rattled me and when the main bunch flew I must have pulled the trigger without aiming, figuring I couldn't miss. None dropped, and that surprised me so much I forgot to get the second barrel away. So, no duck dinner.

The next episode was worse. I saw a flock of Hungarian partridge land not far away and got the shotgun again. As I neared where I had seen the birds land, I brought the gun up to my shoulder and held it right out level and kept on stalking. I went past where the birds had landed, further and further and nothing happened. The old gun got heavier and sagged lower and lower. All of a sudden my birds flew up with a whirr and my cannon went off and blew a great hole in the

23

ground just in front of my foot. I had been holding it ready to shoot with a finger on the trigger. Those little partridges fly so suddenly, so fast and so close that they scare the daylights out of you. I sure learned from that to keep my trigger finger away from the trigger till the gun was pointed right. No birds again.

But I got to be pretty handy with the scatter gun in time. I think where we lived was second to none for flight shooting. We were right on a flyway and didn't have to do more than go outside the house to get in all the shooting we wanted any evening in the fall. I have seen flights of ducks darken the sky and cast a shadow like a heavy cloud on the ground.

We were helping my cousin Ralph cut out his beef on the range one time. The beef steers in those days were mostly three or four years old and nearly all had horns. It didn't take much juggling to rile some of the big steers enough to get 'em on the fight. Mum was riding a little grey pony called Billy and one of these big steers picked her outfit to charge. He hit her just below the knee with a horn on each side of her leg, one in the horse's shoulder and one in the ribs. Dad had his eye on this oily steer and, quick as a flash, he jumped old Buster into the side of the steer and knocked him right off balance and nearly upset him. That took all the fight out of him right away.

Mum had another close call with a bull some neighbours had. We had heard that a gate into our breeding pasture some three miles away was in need of a little fixing. We also knew that a mean bull was on the range so everyone was on the lookout for him. Mum did a lot of riding, and this day decided she would take a hammer and staples and try to patch up the broken gate. She had nearly finished the job when she heard a bull rumbling along towards her. It was the bad bull and as soon as he came in sight he charged her. She left her tools, mounted pronto, and lit out of there just a few jumps ahead of the bull. The little old pony wasn't much for speed ordinarily but with a mad bull right on his tail, and plenty of persuasion with the spurs, he didn't let any grass grow under his feet and the bull gave up the chase. We told the folks who owned the bull, and as others had had the same trouble, and the owners found they couldn't even handle him themselves, they finally shot the bull and we were all relieved.

In haying time Art and I had our jobs as soon as we could handle a fork or axe. While Dad was cutting hay with the mower, Art and I were supposed to cut small clumps of willows that were too tough for the mower. Instead of cutting anything that was anywhere close to the next swath, and doing it systematically, we followed the mower round and round cutting only what we were sure had to be cut to clear the

24

next swath. This way we did far more walking than cutting. But if there was a clear swath we took a rest, never cutting a clump till it was definitely going to be in the way.

This system backfired badly one time. Dad's mower cut a yellow jacket's nest in half just ahead of us. Some of the outraged hornets stung the team and Dad had his hands full trying to avert a runaway, so he couldn't warn us in time and the hornets hit us in a wave. For some strange reason Art seemed to be immune to yellow jackets, hornets and bees. I was not. They stung me all over my face. In no time my face swelled up all over. One eye was almost shut, the other shut tight, and my mouth swelled shut so tight that for more than a week it was very difficult to force even soup between my lips. I think when they first stung me I called Dad everything under the sun except a gentleman. There was no comeback either. Dad was just as sorry for me as I was sorry for myself.

There was an old cowboy, Stuart Clark, who used to come to our place pretty regularly. He had been in Texas working the cow camps for a good many years, in the days of the Texas Rangers and outlaws that the Western story writers tell about. He could tell yarns that were hair-raising as far as Art and I figured; possibly we weren't too critical an audience. Somehow the old boy had got busted up pretty badly in a mix-up with a longhorn steer tied hard and fast to his saddle. He always told us boys never to tie hard and fast. "Take your dallies and you can turn 'em loose if your horse goes down or you get tangled up," was his sound advice.

I remember one awful blizzard we had that lasted for four days with a howling wind all the time, snowing and drifting snow continually. The temperature was never above 20 below day or night. That was when I was around fourteen. We tried to haul hay out to cattle but couldn't get any hay to stay in the rack. We had lots of hay in stacks alongside the barnyards. The wind was from the southeast so we just heaved hay up in the air let it fly and it would scatter away out through the three hundred head of stock. We had to tie sacks over our faces. Twenty below isn't too tough when it is still but it sure is bad medicine in a high wind. Your face will freeze in seconds and the cold seems to penetrate anything you put on.

The drifting was terrible. Roads were all impassable. Some drifts were hard enough to hold a team, but on the lee side of hills they were softer and would bury the whole outfit so trenches had to be shovelled through them. The bulldozers in those days were snow shovels and strong backs, which took a lot of sweat to operate.

There was a deep coulee that went all across Dad's place more or less east to west. The southerly wind drifted both ends full and away out over the southern edge. A few days later we got a northwest blizzard, not lasting as long but much colder. It blew the north side full over the edge. When we fed, not a cow critter showed up. This was bad. We hightailed over to the coulee and there they were fenced in solid, hungry and bawling. During the night the cattle had got into the coulee for shelter as they usually did in a bad storm. They had milled around and kept just enough room to stand in without getting smothered under the drifting snow, as had happened to so many cattle in the winter of the blue snow in 1906-07.

I took my last year of school at Calgary as, at that time, our home town school only went to grade ten. While there I was fortunate enough to be able to see the Lord Strathcona Horse Cavalry Regiment do their musical ride. That, I am sure, was the most wonderful display of horsemanship I am ever apt to see. It was a two-hour show with one hundred of the very best horses, wonderfully trained. There must have been five or six thousand people or more watching and the show was so fascinating that I don't think anyone spoke or even a baby cried all through.

This school term in Calgary was my first ten months completely away from ranch life. During my absence from home the folks decided to dehorn all the cattle. As Art had been away, and I had been at school too much to do the dehorning (as we had done when we were youngsters), the herd had got to be pretty nearly all horned. There was getting to be more and more talk of the damage horns did to beef in transit, and finally a deduction was made at selling time on horned cattle. The folks also knew, from having most of the cattle dehorned before, that the old dehorned cows were much more peaceable around salt licks and water holes and even on the feed ground. So Ralph and the folks bunched their cattle and took them all up to Arthur Wilson's layout where he had a dehorning chute.

They dehorned everything. When I came back they looked like a plumb different bunch of cattle and, somehow, something of the old range days passed. Some people don't dehorn the cattle to this day, but most do. The only horned animals in a dehorned herd now are the registered purebred bulls and cows; and their horns are weighted at an early age to shape them so they are practically harmless. So even the bullfights are not spectacular anymore. Bulls could fight all season and not do any damage to each other. When a bull with natural horns whipped another one, that bull knew for damn sure he was whipped. The victor, immediately he got the vanquished bull to turn

26

and run, would follow him with a mighty thrust of his horns in the rear at every chance he got, and the running bull would beller like he was being eaten alive. He would leave that part of the range for a long time.

One of my most vivid memories of a bullfight happened when we were driving a bunch of cattle alongside a fenced pasture. We were driving along the foot of a steep hill when a bull came down the hill lickety split with blood in his eye. One of our bulls set himself up as the protector of the herd. He went up to the two-strand barbed wire fence, lowered his head, and pawed the dirt. Both bulls were making plenty of war whoops. The oncoming bull came in at full gallop and lowered his head to meet the other right on the fence line. That was unusual as they generally spar around, pawing dirt and bellering for a spell, before clashing. But when they met head on like that, there was a wallop that sounded as though both of them would have broken skulls. The running bull up-ended right over the fence flat onto the other's back, without breaking a strand of wire! Then he rolled off into a most undignified position. Our bull was so stunned by the impact that he failed to follow up his advantage and sock his horns into his opponent. But he didn't need to. The other bull figured he was whipped to a finish, got up shakily and then found his voice. With an unearthly bellow of fear, he lit out of that bunch like seven devils were unloading buckshot into his hind end. The fight was over in one second flat, the shortest I can remember. Most fights go on for hours, days and even weeks, and cowboys packed heavy loaded whips, barbed wire whips and such like to break them up and separate them to other parts of the range. It is mighty dangerous work too and you want to be well mounted before mixing into a bullfight at close quarters.

CHAPTER II

Breaking and Handling Horses

Most of the travelling in those days was done by horse outfit. We used saddle horses or teams, sleighs and cutters in winter, and buggies, democrats and wagons in summer. Some of the buggies and cutters were pretty fancy outfits and a good driving team was a really prized possession and was wonderful trading stock.

My first memory in relation to horses is of Dad's old saddle horse "Buster," a gangling, raw-honed ugly old horse, but a good one. He had been raised and broken by Roy Seeley, a man who was pretty much of an idol to my brother Art and me. Roy was a broncobuster and horseman, but a very rough and severe horseman. He had pretty much broken the spirit of horses he trained instead of merely breaking them to handle. That was what had happened to Buster. He always looked old, but some horses do and are familiarly called "old" much before they are aged. He had an ingrown fear of man, which I think was from his early rough training but, having been handled gently for years, had become very reliable. Dad used to let me sit on him from when I was around three years old and I played around his legs and thought he was a wonderful horse.

I remember a little girl visiting us when we were branding and she sat on the old horse outside the corral all day during the branding and seemed perfectly happy there. Buster never moved although flies must have bothered him quite a lot and he was loose except for his lines being dropped on the ground. Another time I remember Dad roping a bull we wanted to take out of a bunch of cattle. He was on too steep a sidehill to face the bull when the latter headed hell bent down the hill. Buster had to hold him standing broadside. He had to jump all four feet at a time down the hill and catch his footing several times before getting control of the bull. On most horses Dad would either have had to turn the rope lose, or be piled up in a heap.

Another smart old horse I remember was Mac, a work horse Dad had brought up with him from the States. He was part Morgan and part Percheron, as pretty built as they come and always interested and watching what you were doing. But he had found out that he could get away when not watched and was always waiting for his chance. He made several getaways that I recall, and Dad was always the loser in broken wagons or mowers, and twice got a busted ankle from these sessions.

Dad always raised a few colts each year and we got our chance to start breaking colts pretty young, as he was getting past his prime for that kind of deal. Roy Seeley broke several for us and Dad also had a man — McCarthy by name — who was supposed to have a secret system for breaking horses. We always figured he was pretty windy and later found out "Windy" McCarthy was his nickname. The horses he broke for Dad didn't respond to his treatment nearly as well as to the regular range methods, and the horses had to be practically broken all over again.

Somewhere around this time, Roy began to pay quite a little attention to our methods of handling horses. He was a close neighbour and nearly always seemed to be mounted on a green horse of his own or one he was breaking for someone else. Roy started Art off on his first bronc ride at about eight years old. His instructions were pretty tough for a youngster. If he pulled leather, Roy, who rode alongside, would slap his knuckles with a quirt. "Either ride straight up or get piled," were his instructions, and get piled we did on many occasions during our earlier attempts. On one occasion Art was to break a little sorrel mare we called Dolly. When all was ready, Roy held her till Art got loaded on, then rode alongside and whenever Art reached for the old peg, he got a crack from Roy's quirt. It likely made him so mad he forgot to be scared and made the ride straight up that time, and many more since. The little pony didn't do too much fancy stuff and, with Roy's expert instructions and demonstrations, Dolly was soon a gentle-broke, reliable horse.

I think we spoiled a number of horses for Dad by our amateur ways but gradually we acquired the knack, and Dad decided I was old enough to have a horse all my own to break and use as I liked. He picked a four-year-old bay mare, part standard bred and part thoroughbred. She was pretty as a picture and had a kind, gentle eye and disposition, but in my first attempts to handle her she seemed so nervous I didn't make much headway. In breaking her to lead I had got her pretty well warmed up and, being late in the fall and very chilly, I figured I should blanket her when I tied her up to let her learn to stand tied. I had quite a time getting the blanket on her back, but when I succeeded my horse seemed to be three-quarters broken. She lost her nervousness from that point, had no more fear of me, and seemed willing and anxious to learn anything I could teach her. She never bucked, shied very little, and was very soon most reliable, a first-rate stock horse and a good rope horse. I studied quite a time figuring a name for her. It has been one of my superstitions that it is unlucky to name an unbroken horse, and even then I generally stall off the naming till a particular name seems to fit. Jean was a pet name of mine and that seemed to fit okay.

From the time I broke Jean to the time she was retired she was my favourite horse. She carried me many a mile and always willingly. One time I roped a bull that would not cut out of a bunch. When we were trying to drag him out, he threw himself and Jean dragged him at least 100 feet. I don't know how she did it as she only weighed 1,000 pounds and the bull was well over 1,600 pounds. When I let him up he was ready to come my way.

Another time I was going to skin a calf we had lost to make raw-hide hackamores. I tied the calf's head to a tree and, having only one rope, tied the other end on the hide back of the head where I had cut it loose from the head. I took a dally on the saddle horn in the middle. I started Jean away from the calf but when she felt the pull on the horn she swung to face the rope, as a good horse will. She backed up on it and all of a sudden the hide came loose and the faster she backed up the faster the hide came towards her. I had already got a hand burned trying to hold the rope and couldn't get organized to jump her ahead until the hide slapped her in the face going by. Some horses would have torn all hell loose to get out of there. Jean stood and took it but was trembling like a leaf in the wind.

Being such a gentle and reliable horse, she got the honoured task of being my "girl" horse on a number of occasions. At the time I have in mind to relate, I was riding another mare that Art had started to break, but had left when he went out working on a power line project. This mare we called "Calamity" for want of a better-fitting name. She was mostly just a plain knothead. She ducked her head and went to hogging on the least provocation. I was never a very good saddle rider on a bucking bronc. Art was the saddle rider and was better than average, to say the least. When I took over on Calamity she hadn't learned to buck very well and so we learned together. As she did better, so did I. I got unloaded almost as many times as I made it stick. But I was gaining confidence and certainly getting plenty of prac-tice, as she never missed an opportunity.

Getting back to the ladies. I was taking a girl out, a relative of friends of ours, who claimed to have ridden quite a little at riding schools in the east. I mounted her on Jean and we headed down the main drag for Big Valley, as we both wanted to get mail or something in town. I told the lady that Jean was quite reliable, and not in the least afraid of cars, but apparently it didn't register. A truck approached us and she turned Jean around and let out a scream. She grabbed the horn and let the reins loose. Jean was no deadhead and loved to run. Finding no controls in evidence, she headed up the road, gaining speed every jump. I knew something had to be done and quickly or there might be tragic consequences. The best I could hope for was to get my knothead started easily so she didn't begin to buck instead of run, and catch up quickly before Jean really got going. I made it, and reined in as close as possible, reached out and grabbed a rein of Jean's and she stopped quite easily. But Calamity had her opportunity and, catching me off balance, unloaded me in the middle of the road, hooking my chaps on the saddle horn and ripping the leg full length in doing so. The truck passed and repassed us before we got to town after the mishap. It seemed like half the town was there to jeer at me and I betcha my face was red.

Another time I went to visit some neighbours, partly to take a ride with a lady friend and partly for a game of cards. It was a little early when we arrived and the boys were out working. As there were cows to be brought in and milked, after a brief stop and cup of coffee, the lady and I went out to round up the milk cows. Habit had reminded me to loosen Calamity's cinch on arrival, but did not remind me to tighten it on starting out for the short ride. Being at the show-off stage, I had to do a little demonstrating and dabbed my rope on a heifer's hind foot, figuring to let it slack up and fall off and do it over again by way of practice, but mostly for show purposes. But Calamity didn't co-operate. When the rope tightened, she dived her head and went to bucking; saddle and yours truly going over her head and tying her down. Imagine my undignified position in the saddle over her neck, head down and arms around the horse's neck, and almost on the ground on a well-worked, plowed field! I finally got to the ground. The boys were coming in behind us and had seen the works and I got the haw haw some more. I think Jean even gave me a horse laugh that time, she being the lady's mount on this occasion too.

Art rode in local stampedes pretty regularly, and also did a lot of horse-breaking. But at one stampede he didn't do too well. He drew a rawboned gelding around 1,150 pounds that was a real dirty bucker. Art had been working at a place some 40 miles from home and somehow had got strayed from his riding boots and rode in ordinary work boots. He got piled and one foot hung in the stirrups. There were many gasps, groans and "Oh's" from the audience. Was there going to be a fatal tragedy enacted before their eyes? Many a cowboy had

31

been dragged to death. Had Art been wearing his riding boots, they would have either turned in the stirrup or come off to let him loose. Finally, after he was dragged fifty yards or more, his leg broke allowing his foot to turn and let him loose. I had never seen Art in such a jackpot before and I felt so helpless. There was a nurse at the stampede. She put splints on his leg. Then we got him loaded into somebody's car and taken the 55 miles to town to a doctor.

The Doc had been on quite a spree and it would have been much better if we had never located him. But we did and he took the splints off and put on a cast. There was no nurse and he got me to hold Art's leg for about an hour. I was doubled over the high back of a bed and I had a tough time keeping from passing out before the cast was set. I guess the juggling around and the time element and all had caused a lot of swelling. In only a few days the cast was just a loose case and plumb useless. Art went along like that for a couple of weeks before he could get the Doc to do the job over again and then it healed quickly. He was driving a four-horse team a month afterwards, hauling wheat to town. The fellow he was working for would get the outfit lined out and Art would take it from there, a 50-mile round trip. He couldn't keep off horses either and it seemed no time before he started breaking horses again. Some of the boys would protestingly get one rigged out for him and he'd hang up his crutches, climb a fence and get aboard and, with a "let 'er go boys," be away. But he did pick gentle-looking ones and rode tight and got away without any serious damage.

I was a natural bareback rider. I took to riding steers and horses bareback with surcingle and loose rope like a duck takes to water. I never got piled riding horses that way, and only one steer ever piled me though I rode lots of them. It was different with a saddle, though. One saddle ride I made in our home town stampede I drew a real tough horse with a bad reputation. I was scared and my knees shook so I could hardly get down on him. I got unloaded about the fourth jump and one of the pick-up horses stepped on my hand and broke a finger. I won money once at a local stampede in the saddle contest. All the good riders got unloaded and disqualified one way or another and I got second money. I sure ragged the boys that time. I remember Dad was there and he was tickled as could be. But the cayuse had only crowhopped and I could have ridden a tougher one.

Dad had a little sorrel mare that Art and I had more or less spoilt trying to break her. She got to be a pretty bad one to ride. Art and Pierre Burnstad added her to their rough string and, at the Charlie Wilson stampede where Art broke his leg, she threw her rider, then the saddle and flank rope; everything but the halter. Which reminds me of a yarn a feller used to tell about his Paw and a horse. He told it with quite a drawl and very seriously thus: "She bucked the saddle and bridle off and damn nigh bucked Paw off." This sorrel mare was well bred and, as she wasn't a consistent enough bucker, she got broken to harness and put in a chuckwagon team and did pretty well at that.

"Hicks" Burnstad and Buster Johnson, two neighbour boys, and I figured we'd take in the Calgary Stampede one year and we put in every opportunity we had to practice out on the range: riding steers, roping and tying calves, and wild cow milking. The steers all had horns in those days. We roped our steers and I did nearly all the bulldogging to hold them. The other boys were younger and never tackled holding two- and three-year-old steers by the horns except while I was loading on. Then we rode them out to a finish on the wide-open range and, if possible, pulled our loose rope off (so we wouldn't have to rope them again) and jumped off. The other boys brought the rider's saddle horse up, and away we went again for another steer, a calf, or to milk a wild cow, whichever came handiest. The neighbours never caught us at it or we'd likely have been hung.

I was over-age for the amateur class in Calgary so didn't go to the stampede. The other boys were young enough and they both took money there. Hicks went right on up in the calf roping and got in the top money several years at Calgary and smaller shows.

Around that time Pierre and old J. M. Johnson got hold of a real bucking horse. He had been an orphan colt raised on a bottle and was quite gentle to handle, but when he came of age for breaking, the story was different. He bucked everyone off and was soon up for sale. Stampedes were a going concern in those days and every little town had an annual stampede. Any picnic or celebration or get-together of any kind usually had some exhibition riding and roping, whether planned or spontaneous. When they bought this grey gelding for a stampede bucker, believe me, they had the genuine article. The local boys all tried him time and again but he was too tough for them. So they named him "Grey Dynamite" and started taking him to all the stampedes within reach and finally to Calgary. He won them quite a lot of money as top bucking horse, and nearly unloaded the famous Pete Knight, world champion saddle rider, at a stampede in Stettler.

But the old pony had one failing. If it was wet weather and the ground was slippery he wouldn't do his fancy stuff. The year they took him to Calgary the weather was bad and he didn't do his stuff. Then Art bought out J.M.'s share and he and Pierre decided to break him for a saddle horse. They rode him in relays one after the other without trying to make him buck. He piled them time and again but gradually they won the battle and from then on when he bucked, as a rule, he didn't really turn everything loose. They changed his name to "Smokey" and from there he started his career as a useful horse instead of an outlaw. Even I got brave and rode him out twice after he was semi-broke. Both times he went after me but although he kept it up quite a spell for me, he didn't throw the crooked stuff in and I stayed put. But he wasn't a kid's pony to the day he died. Anything a little haywire to his way of thinking was apt to uncork him and get action aplenty for anybody who wasn't a pretty forked hand.

I was breaking a little mare of Dad's, Fanny by name. She was part standard-bred and part thoroughbred. I got the bright idea of riding her bareback on the race track at the first of July doings in Big Valley. I only took time to take her round the track about three times. She didn't really let herself out too much but her ancestors were pretty fast horses so I figured she might be. I never had monkeyed around with race horses and didn't know anything about training them, so she went into the race untrained. She got scared at the take-off and fell in behind and stayed there. She had the speed to overtake quite a few but I couldn't persuade her to pass anything and I was taking dust all the way. Then we came to the gate we had come in at. Without a warning she shot off out of the gate. I left her and sailed into the gatepost, hitting the post with my back. I saw stars of every colour and then a lovely blackness enveloped me. I seemed to be falling for a long, long time before consciousness left me. I woke up about four hours later under Burnstad's wagon in the shade. They had had a doctor look me over and jerk me around some to see if I had any broken bones, and poured water over me to bring me to. There didn't seem to be any damage done and I took in the dance that night. Was this one of my nine lives shot?

I rode Fanny about twelve miles to a dance up past Burnstad's one night. That, after working all day and dancing most of the night, was all I needed to put me to sleep as soon as I got aboard and started back for Adshead's after the dance. She could have taken me any direction but when she stopped, and I came awake with a start, she was standing at the barn door. It was time then to go to work so I made a fast change, hit the Chinese cook up for mush and hotcakes, and went to work. It was pretty hard to keep awake on the job all day but I made it some way. No rat hunting that night!

Finally, the old Model-T Ford came along to our part of the range. It belonged to a huge cattle buyer, Ted Gardner. Ted must have been six-foot-six and big every way, but all solid. He was a redhead and kept his hair cut short, sticking straight up like porky quills. His whiskers were never shaved close any time I saw him. Just picture this huge man with a big Stetson on, tobacco juice running out of both corners of his mouth, rattling over the prairie road, or no road, in a little old Model T. He seemed to dwarf the outfit and it sure looked like he could pick it up, roll it over or shove it out of a boghole.

CHAPTER III

Drugstore Cowboy — Starvation Trip

During high school I had taken a liking to chemistry and made pretty fair marks in the final exams, so the folks planned that I was to be a chemist or druggist. They were quite friendly with the lady who owned and operated the Big Valley Drug Store and talked her into taking me on as an apprentice. She had studied to be a doctor but the messiness of that was too much for her, so she switched to the medicine end of it. I was to be a clerk and study drug dispensing under her tutorship. I would probably have had to take a course at the university later to be a qualified druggist. To say the least, I was out of my element. Mathematics had always been a tough one for me and I had some great times figuring out change. I guess some customers got gypped and some got the best of the deal. I played no favourites but likely a good-looking woman would get me flustered and I'd be sure to make wrong change one way or another.

We sold records in the store and the hits and new records were played over and over again till I would like to have heaved the records, gramaphone and all, at the persistent customers. I could eat all the candy and chocolates I wanted and promptly lost my taste for them. Any time I could get off, I either got out home or to some of the neighbours where I could ride with the boys. That was where I got my nickname "Dude." The boys called me the "dude cowboy" while I was working in the drug store. After I left the store the "Dude" stuck but they left off the "cowboy," and I've been called "Dude" more or less ever since.

I used to get in quite a little boxing and wrestling in the evenings. I had always been pretty handy at wrestling but had not taken to boxing much, but now I had a chance with a gym in town and decided I should learn the art of self-defence. There were three Flannagan boys (Irish, as the name implies), all good boxers, and I had them for sparring partners. The oldest, John, was a little too hefty for me. The youngest was really skilled and later went right up close to the top in Chicago. Piius was his name, and I learned more from him than anyone. We liked each other and got along fine.

Mike was the one who went for my blood every time. He was a good boxer, but had been drinking and smoking too much to keep in condition. He called me a damn Englishman and our matches were never friendly. At first he could whip hell out of me. But I had far better wind and found that if I could keep from getting battered up for four or five rounds, I was well on the way to winning. He'd draw plenty of blood in the first few rounds and then I'd gradually take over as he got winded; from there I'd draw the blood and take him to the cleaners. That gave me a lot of satisfaction, he got to respect me a little more, and we got to be right good friends.

My health didn't stand up to the indoor life and being on my feet all day; after about eight months I quit the drug store.

I went to working on farms and ranches around the neighbourhood, on a power line construction project, and for cattle buyers. I worked for cousin Ralph part of three years, and helped Dad out now and again between jobs. I broke some horses for both of them. When I was working for Ralph he sent me out to buy a bull for him once and to buy a work horse another time. That really made me feel like I was a pretty good hand.

At Dad's I went into the waterworks pretty thoroughly. He had several springs for winter water supply for stock but they had to be pumped into tanks and troughs. I dug out the spring heads and curbed two of them and then laid pipe with enough fall so they would run continually into troughs and never need any further attention. The other two I fixed up were different. When all the stock was home there was little surplus water to run over, so I dug out two big reservoirs and curbed each of them. Then I laid pipe to the big watering tanks below so that, as the curbs filled up, the tanks did also. When all the stock came in to water they lowered the water in the curbs as well as the tanks, since the water level was the same. The extra reservoirs kept enough water available to water the whole works. We had to use tank heaters in cold weather but there was no more pumping. Coal was very cheap and plentiful there (we could mine it on the place if we wanted to) and the tank heaters had to be tended only once a day.

Cattle buyers working in the Big Valley district got the idea it was cheaper and better to drive cattle to Stettler than to ship by rail. I got work bunching cattle from the sellers' places till I got enough to take to Stettler. The big bunches or anything over ten were easy to handle as a rule, but getting one or two head at a place, and taking them a mile or so to gather three or four more, was a pretty tough assignment at times. I had a couple of top saddle horses, both well trained on the rope, and if a critter had too much of a homing instinct I'd have to rope it and bust it. That generally took the orneryness out of them so they'd travel any direction to get away from me and all I had to do was head them.

The worst trouble I had on the whole deal was at a place where the buyer had bought two big four-year-old steers. There was a lake with mud springs around the edge near the layout, and before I could get them lined out they got in next to the shore and had me stymied pretty badly, as I was afraid of running into a quicksand hole if I did any fast work trying to head them. I worked the devil out of my horse heading the steers this way and that but could never get both of them away from the lakeshore at the same time. So when I got one out I roped him and busted him and hogtied him. Then I went to work on the other. He was just about to take after my horse by then but decided against that and, seeing that he was alone, he struck out into the lake. I just reached him before he swam out of range, and got my rope on him. I was plenty mad by then and I snaked him through mud and water till he pretty near drowned. Then I let him up and chased him ahead on the rope to the other one. He was plenty willing to stop when I got them together and I tied the rope onto the other one's horns as close as I could get them and turned the other steer loose. They went round and round for awhile but all the fight was gone out of them, and by the time I got them to where I was headed they were paired up travelling like a team of oxen.

When we took the main drives into Stettler I had a big half-breed cowboy, Jack Robinson, to help me. One night we were pretty late getting into town with about five hundred head and, just as we were in sight of the stockyards, a train came along and tooted the whistle a few times. That sure played hell with our plans. The herd scattered like birdshot from a shotgun. The big trouble was that everything so close to town was fenced with barbed wire. These cattle had mostly come from open range and didn't savvy fences. So we had one hell of a time getting them back through the holes they made in the fences while stampeding from the train. It got dark but we had to keep right on trying to gather them. It seemed like we had more than we could hold so I worked the herd on into the stockyards, and then went back to help Jack. He only had one but that had been a tough one, and he had had to bust him and then he hung onto him and broke him to lead ahead and was chasing him in that way. I circled every which way and couldn't locate any more so we called it a night and hit for the livery barn to take care of our horses.

In the morning we found we had all our bunch and a few extras. The odd farmer was around to see who had got his milk cows and ruined his fences. We left the cattle buyer to straighten that mess out and lit out for Big Valley and another drive.

One of the cattle buyers, Mike Kennedy, was real nice to work for. He paid good prices for the cattle, paid Jack and me well, and was always around to welcome us in off the drive with a bottle and all arrangements made for the night. He even rode with us a time or so. He was a big strapping Irishman around six-foot-four-inches, right good looking and, I would guess, a real lady killer. Well, this feller bought cattle regularly for three years and was cutting the other buyers right out by paying a little extra. Then the fourth year he didn't show up. But his name sure showed up plenty in the headlines. He had got all the cash in advance he figured he could get away with and, instead of buying cattle as he was supposed to for the company, he absconded and lit out for Ireland. As far as I know, he got away with it. He had taken just under the limit and couldn't be extradited so I guess he got an Irish Colleen and they lived happily ever after. I'm afraid the ranchers weren't too much concerned that justice was not carried out. They liked Mike Kennedy and the prices he paid.

Art had finished school at the coast and worked for about four years in the woods. Then he went out to Saskatchewan for awhile one fall and late that fall came back to Big Valley.

We had had a bad autumn and farmers were very late with their threshing. There was good money in those days following the threshing rigs. I was running a bundle team on a steam outfit. Art and a tillicum of his got work on the rig and we were together again. It turned way cold and snowed quite a lot. All of us were rigged out with leather boots, gloves and hats and had no chance to get warmer rigging. Leather boots and gloves are no outfit for 20 below zero in the early morning, and there were a lot of frozen toes and fingers.

Some of the folks around had a real winter sport. They would chase coyotes with hounds, trailing behind a saddle horse, cooped in a covered sleigh or, still better, with a car on ice. The latter is about as thrilling a sport as I know. Some French neighbours of ours had the perfect setup and we got in on a chase once. Their place was right on the shore of a fairly large lake and they had killed an old horse half a mile or so out on the ice for bait. They kept the old Model-T Ford spotted on the steep bank, so taking the brake off was all that was needed for a quick getaway.

We were visiting them one Sunday and spotted a coyote out at the bait. Several of us piled into the car and away we went. The wind-swept ice was slick as could be, just right for skating. They didn't get too much speed up till they could see which way the coyote was going

39

to head. Then they turned the old Ford loose. We caught up to the coyote in no time but he turned off at right angles. We tried to turn too, but went round and round like a brace and bit, only faster — much faster. We still had the momentum to get speed up quickly, as soon as we got lined out in the right direction. The coyote almost went flat when he turned and then he had to scratch and slip a lot before he got speed up. By the time we got out of our tailspin, he was well on his way in another direction and away we all went hollering like wild Indians till we caught up and about the same thing happened again. One of the boys in the back seat had a rifle but spinning in circles doesn't make for good shooting at a runaway coyote, and it seemed as though the coyote had about as good a chance as we did. The boys said lots of coyotes made it to shore and occasionally they had upset the car when it had hit the bank sideways too fast. I think about the sixth time we caught up, the sharpshooters connected with the coyote and our chase was over.

We used to play crack the whip on ice with a string of skaters holding to each other and the leader holding to a tow rope on the car. The tail-enders needed to be pretty good skaters to avoid a crack-up when the car switched directions at full speed. Try it some time, it's real fun!

There were a lot of small grassy sloughs and lakes in our neighbourhood that were ideal for muskrats. For a long time their pelts had been practically worthless but they went up in the late 20's from $1.50 to $3.00 for extra good ones, and everyone was after them.

Art and I used to hunt a lot with the Burnstad boys and stayed at their place quite a bit. Art and Pierre used mostly shotguns but Hicks and his Dad and I used .22's. A box of 50 shells was only about 50¢ and less when bought by the case. So we shot lots of shells and got to be pretty good sharpshooters. The most sporting time was late in the fall when ice was slick and clear and not too deep. We would tap on a run or house till we saw a muskrat stir up a cloud of mud in the run and then follow up on skates. We could see them and they us. They would zig-zag this way and that, swimming very fast and sometimes they would go down out of sight and be lost. But they swam up close to the ice a lot and if we could follow them, sooner or later we got a shot with a .22 rifle. If the shot was almost directly over them, it would penetrate the ice and we could chop the rat out with a belt axe. But being on skates, it was mighty hard to get directly over them and have time to get sighted for a shot, before the rat turned and headed lickety split another way. You'd likely shoot a couple of feet behind him, or shoot too glancing a shot which would richochet.

Occasionally Art and I shacked up for rat hunting at a cabin that had been our Uncle Bill's. The walls were papered over logs and the tacks struck us as being wonderful targets for indoor target practice. We both had .22 repeaters that held seventeen shorts and we could unload them like machine guns and drive tacks across the room like mad.

We did a little poaching too. Some folks didn't hunt rats themselves and tried to stop anyone else hunting on their places. So we would highgrade the odd rat to keep them from getting too thick. One place in particular was ideal for rat hunting but had "no trespassing" signs. This was Ed Adshead's. He only let anyone working for him shoot rats on his layout and so I went to work for him. After hours or Sundays, I got the cream of the rat population and made a whole lot more on the side than on the job. I got so I could shoot a rat swimming in the moonlight almost as fast as I could see him.

Art had itchy feet. He'd got the notion he wanted to locate a ranch and around that time there was a lot of talk about Grande Prairie and Peace River country in the north. Art hadn't piled up any capital working in the coast logging camps. He did what most of the boys did: pile up a stake, hit for Vancouver and blow it, and back to the woods when it was gone. The summer after he came back from the coast he and a feller by the name of Jack Spence gathered up a little outfit and headed north. They had a saddle horse apiece and a pack horse with darn little to put on it. They rustled up an old pack saddle and had a henskin blanket or so apiece and an old canvas horse blanket for a ground sheet, bed canvas, tent or pack cover. It was very inadequate to say the least. A lard bucket to boil coffee in, a fry pan, a few eating tools, and a Boy Scout axe about made up the damn outfit. Jack had a .32 six-shooter and was fairly handy with it. They figured that it and a fishing outfit would allow them to live off the country. They rode through to Edmonton, picked up a very ancient .22 single-shot rifle and replenished their grub supply. They then headed west-northwest aiming to shortcut through a large forest reserve with practically no trails in it. They aimed for Whitecourt hoping to go straight through to Grande Prairie.

June was a rainy month and one creek after another got too high to find safe crossings. The trip should only have taken around a week, but they waited for the water to go down to find a creek crossing and lost several days. They had to build a sort of pole corduroy and put spruce boughs on top to get up out of the creekbank. Water was lying everywhere in the flat muskeg country. They were flooded out a couple of times at night and had to sit it out all night to keep their

41

riggin' from being washed away. Their grub was running short and all the game in evidence seemed to be moose, bear and squirrels. Moose and bear were too big for either gun they had. Jack tried to get a moose with the six-gun but it only shook its head as though the flies were bad. He ran out of ammunition and threw the gun at the moose.

Then they got their pack horse stuck in a muddy crossing. They worked all day getting him out but he had been in the cold water too long and he died that night. There they made their biggest mistake. They left their pack behind instead of tying it on a riding saddle and taking turns walking and riding. They figured they'd be able to travel faster and would be out in a few days travelling light. They ran into the East Prairie River cutting across their line of travel and had not a hope of crossing it in such high water. Up to then they had been following an old and little used forestry pack trail. Now they decided they had to cut back and head for Slave Lake, without benefit of any trail. Much of the country was swamp of a kind that horses couldn't traverse. Detouring took days and days. Their grub ran out. For their last meal they had six spoonfuls of baking powder to three tablespoons of flour and half a squirrel between them. Then the old leaded-up .22 plugged and they were without weapons.

They were good hefty men when they started, around 180 pounds each and in good, hard-working shape. They were too young and impatient to take time to snare squirrels or rabbits, figuring if they hurried they'd soon be out to a settlement. But time marched on and they lost weight and strength daily. By the time they got out to the Swan Lake settlement, some twenty miles south of Kinuso on Lesser Slave Lake, it took the two of them to hoist a saddle on a horse and Art was down to 120 pounds. Could be one of their nine lives shot!

The first place they came to, when they got out of the swamp and muskeg country to open grass flats on the Swan River, was a bachelor's cabin with nobody home. They later found out the cabin belonged to Mike McNamara. They went right in and made up a feed, their first decent meal for over a month. Then they rode on up to another settler's cabin and there again found nobody home, but fresh-picked strawberries in a bowl and pans of milk and cream. They ate again. The folks caught them at it and the ladies really went all out to fill up the boys. For months they said that they could eat a whale of a feed and in an hour or so be hungry again. They both got work there in the valley and stayed the summer. Jack left in the fall and we never heard of him again.

CHAPTER IV

Gambling Cowboys at Slave Lake

That fall I went up to Kinuso near Lesser Slave Lake, and Art and I located on an abandoned homestead and shacked up for the winter. The owner of the layout, Rice by name, had a store in Kinuso. We had quite a time that winter. We only had about four horses of our own to look after so had time for most anything that came up. Every little while, a settler would want to go out to Edmonton for a week or so and would get Art or me to run his layout. I even looked after a bunch of sheep for a week for one outfit!

We got quite a few horses to break for Kline Bros. in Kinuso and nice horses they were too. Nobody seemed to have much money but there were community doings every week and we didn't miss anything. I did more dancing that winter than I've done ever since. There were a lot of half-breeds around and they made some pretty potent moon-shine that livened up a lot of the parties. Then there was a poker game going pretty regularly and our shack was headquarters for it. That was where I learned there was a whole lot about poker I never would know. I was playing quite awhile one evening and then got a straight flush, queen high; right next to the best hand you can get. I got buck-fever right bad; I bet and raised and one feller kept coming back for more. I went up and up till I had no more cash and called. The other guy had a royal flush. I've always been convinced that that was more than coincidence and since then I have shied away from anything but a little penny-ante game to pass the time.

I shot my first moose that winter. Art and I were riding home from town a few days before the season closed and I saw a moose across the river. We were just going by an ex-policeman's place at the time and we had no gun. So we went in, borrowed a gun from the policeman, went back and stalked the moose and I shot it. It dropped right away; we found a crossing on the river and when we went up to it we saw it was a cow and we'd sure be in trouble. So we figured best we hurry back, return the rifle and tell the owner we'd missed. Then we went down to Cornell's place where Art had worked all summer and knew the folks wouldn't be against getting a little cow meat. We figured all

43

we needed was a hunting knife to butcher and didn't get a gun. When we got back, our moose had come alive. It was paralyzed but could raise its head and thresh it around. So we had to bulldog it and kill it with a knife. Then we found it was an old skinny bull that had shed its horns, and had huge rose warts all over it. I had pretty much drawn a blank on that deal.

It was a great country for chinooks. The snow would get to be about two feet deep and temperatures as low as 70 below, and then the temperature would go way up to 50 above for a few days and the whole country would be a sheet of ice for awhile.

I'll never forget Tom Grono's driving team. He used to come to the poker sessions at our layout and had a right fancy black driving team and cutter. We saw him coming like the very devil, splitting the wind, on a glassy ice road one afternoon. Of course we were sure the team was sharp shod all round. We could hardly believe our eyes when we found they were barefooted. He claimed that as long as he didn't try to start or stop or turn quickly they could do as well barefooted as sharp shod. The ice never lasted more than a few days, hardly worth shoeing for, and then there would be snow trails again.

I went hunting in the early stages of one of those chinooks. Snow was deeper than usual, quite a bit above my knees. I started before daylight in the morning with a couple of hotcakes in my pocket for a lunch. It was quite cold when I started; the snow was dry and powdery, and easy to wade through. But the chinook wind started and in no time the snow was wet and soggy and travelling conditions got worse by the minute. Around noon I saw a moose get up about two hundred and fifty yards away through the timber. He stopped with only a small portion visible between trees. I took a shot but apparently hit a tree. That was about noon. I tracked him for just over four hours and was going to give up and head back, but thought I would go to the crest of one more ridge first. There he was broadside, about three hundred yards away in the valley below me and this time I didn't miss. He dropped like stone dead. I waded over to him and was just about to cut his throat when he came to life and reared his head up. I had stood my rifle against a tree several yards away and was down on the moose's neck. I wasn't going to let him get away after all that chase, so I grabbed his horns and threw him back down and hung on to one horn with all my weight and strength till I could cut his throat. He had been shot a little too high in the shoulder and the bullet had gone through the backbone where it dips down in the hump and that had paralyzed him for awhile. He couldn't have got up but had regained control of his head and forequarters. By the time I had him

44

butchered out it was dark, and this was all new country to me. I should have built a fire, barbecued some meat and stayed the night. But I was soaking wet and hungry so I cut a chunk of meat off and headed for McNamara's, where I had come from.

There was a hazy moon and I have always had a wonderful sense of direction. I had never seen this patch of territory before, but seemed to be plumb sure which way to go and headed straight across country. I dipped my chunk of meat in the snow every little bit to blaze my trail, and waded on mile after mile, getting hungrier by the minute. Around ten o'clock I weakened. Instead of stepping over a windfall I sat down on it and started eating on the chunk of meat I was carrying. Everything was dripping wet and I was so tired. I despaired of building a fire. I had to eat something so I ate about a pound of raw meat and I liked it. The meat gave me renewed strength and I waded on till I finally got into camp about two in the morning. My sense of direction had brought me right in like a searchlight beam.

Later in the winter we went to work in a short logging camp and, after that shut down, across Lesser Slave Lake building a camp for an oil prospecting outfit. We had quite a cook on the outfit. He was a hard-bitten, tobacco-chewing, old battle axe who should never have been inside a cookhouse. The tobacco juice dripping off his chin into the mulligan pot didn't look good to us at all. But we were over thirty miles across the lake from Slave Lake town and if anybody quit they had to walk out and pack their riggin'. But if anyone was fired the outfit was obliged to take a rig out to haul them back to the nearest town.

We had to figure a way to get someone fired. The boys picked on me. I guess likely because I was youngest and greenest. I was to be just as ornery as I could be and do such poor work, or so little, that they couldn't help but fire me. I was notching logs on a cabin wall we were building. I worked so slowly that my partner on the other end of the log was continually waiting for me. Then I would notch logs so deeply that when we dropped one on top, it would break the end off the one below and we would have to take logs off to replace it. I broke the odd axe handle. The contractor knew I had been doing better, and it was only a little while till he got mad and fired me. The next morning a sleigh was readied to go out to Slave Lake and all but two of the boys quit and loaded their riggin' on and we got our ride out.

Art and I wanted to get back to Kinuso which was another thirty-five or forty miles up the lake. There were quite a few outfits fishing on the lake and we got a sleigh ride for our packs with one that was

45

going out thirty miles or so our way. But the outfit was heavily laden with horse feed, camp and fishing gear, so we had to walk. The ice was terribly rough. It must have frozen together in a big wind and there were jagged peaks twenty to thirty feet high with long ridges of ice piled on edge running long distances each way from the peaks. They had had to cut trails over the top of a low spot on the ridge. It was close to 30 below and the ice was "booming" steadily. These booms on a lake of that size could be heard for miles and, not being used to it, Art and I were pretty jumpy.

The old team wasn't too enthusiastic heading that way to camp out for a couple of weeks in anything from 20 to 70 below weather. They were too slow for us anyway and, after the boys made a noon camp, we shouldered our packs and struck out over to the railroad track along the lake shore and walked the cinders and ties about twenty miles. I just had moccasins on and my feet were blistered for a month afterwards. But we made it in to Kinuso that night.

We both hit for Big Valley that spring and worked here, there and yonder. We got into the odd stampede and did our stuff and we worked on threshing rigs. That was pretty tough going in those days. I was about fourteen when I saw the first threshing outfit working. There wasn't much farming done in the neighbourhood before, being mostly ranching country. But there got to be more farming done as the country got more settled. The first fall after I was done with school, Dad staked me to a team and bundle wagon and I got on a threshing outfit. The novelty sure didn't take long to wear off. The darn outfit started poofing at six in the morning in the dark and went on poofing till nine at night! This meant getting up before five to feed, water and harness the team and have them ready to work at six. We had breakfast, then six hours' work pitching bundles on and off without a break, then one hour for dinner and then an eight-hour shift with only a fifteen-minute break with a light lunch. Then we had a team to feed and look after, supper and bed, and we even had bedbugs to fight at night.

It was certainly no wonder that working men started striking for shorter hours, more pay, and better working and living conditions. I started the ball rolling on that particular outfit and we got the operator to shut down an hour and a half earlier at night, which seemed to be a mighty big concession. The threshing machine owner was being paid by the number of bushels threshed. Mostly he was threshing for small farming outfits and they would follow him through for the season to pay for their own threshing bill. Also, the sooner he finished other places the sooner they got their own threshing done, which all added up to highballing through when weather permitted. But it was only a very few years till practically all the threshing outfits were down to starting at seven and quitting at six, and wages went way up. Also, the afternoon lunch was a sure thing at all places, and most places you could figure on a morning coffee break and a lunch. The ladies seemed to try to outdo each other sending out lunches with three or four kinds of cakes, cookies or even pies, as well as apples and coffee. At some places the dinners were like Christmas dinners, only better in that you would be really hungry and so enjoy them more. However, the grain prices went down to rock bottom, till farmers could hardly sell their grain and just before we left for B.C. the wages had dropped from around twenty dollars a day for man, team and bundle wagon to around two dollars, all you could eat, and shorter hours.

I nearly always took at least one unbroken horse on my team and often a team that had only been hooked up a few times. Many of the other boys did the same and there were some great goings-on the first day or so. The threshing machine would be running empty pretty regularly while a skinner was getting his bundle rack close enough to heave bundles into the feeder. You'd just get started to pitch bundles in and away the team would go. You'd have to circle and try to get in close again.

One morning I spotted a big bunch of mallards on a slough and I got hold of a shotgun and shot several before breakfast. They dropped in the slough so after breakfast I rode my bundle team into the slough to retrieve them. I got two in between the horses and reached down to grab them. But one horse shied out from under me, dropped me flat on my face in the muddy, ice-cold water and pulled the other horse over top of me. Talk of looking like a drowned rat! I was the genuine article and a shivering, muddy mess to boot, but I did get the ducks before I waddled out.

One Chinese cook used to serve the mulligan and he always piled more on my plate than I could eat. I had been taught "waste not, want not," and trained not to take more than I could eat. I kept complaining to him. But he would counter with, "eat lots, Boss Man say 'more eat, more steam,' so eat lots," and he would pile some more on my plate.

I went back up to Kinuso one fall to try to get in on another moose hunt. I sure got in. The Kline boys had a couple of brothers up from the prairie and they made up a party of six with three Klines, Fred Arnold (an old-timer of the district who was around seventy-five), the postmaster, and me. I was the baby of the party, being around twenty and fit as a fiddle.

47

Charlie Kline was the best hunter and knew all the country around, so he was automatically boss man. Fred took a team and wagon with camp outfit ahead. We first took the postmaster's car about thirty miles from Kinuso and set up camp on the Assinau River. In the morning Charlie, his two brothers, Fred Arnold and the postmaster went in one direction, and I struck out on my own in completely strange country. About 10 a.m. I got two nice little deer, one for me and one for camp meat. The day was young yet so I went on and got in a long running shot at a moose, but missed. I packed a chunk of deer back to camp and was pretty tickled to find that I was the only one who had connected.

The next day Charlie's brothers wanted to go with me. They figured I was the lucky hunter and would be sure to show them game. I told them they would be crazy to follow me as I was a complete stranger in this part of the country and just happened to hit a bit of luck. Also, being younger, I'd covered a whole lot more country than the other boys. Charlie figured I had gone close to thirty miles that day. However, the boys wanted to go with me anyway and they tramped behind me all day without seeing a thing. That day Fred Arnold and the postmaster had shot a deer but found it had a huge rotten abscess on it and was no good.

We hunted a couple more days without seeing game so Charlie decided the game was in another area. It had snowed heavily one day and I was a little afraid of not being able to find the deer I had shot on the first day's hunt. So I went to it and blazed a trail down a coulee to the river. There was a big bend in the river and I didn't want to follow the trail along it so I headed straight for camp in a blinding snowstorm. I should have got lost but I came out on the road only fifty yards from camp.

We packed the meat in, moved back to Kinuso, then on down the Swan Valley to McNamara's and went in five miles from there. We set up camp in an old cabin. It turned cold and we had quite a bit of snow by then. First morning out we were all walking together before separating to hunt. Less than a quarter of a mile from the cabin a huge buck and four does crossed about twenty-five yards in front of us. There were thick little jack pines and spruce in an old burn and the deer all hopped over a big windfall one after another. We were all a bit chilly, beating our hands and blowing our noses and such like, and not one of us could get in a shot before it was too late. So we separated to comb the brush and try to find them again. We had no luck that way but a big bull moose got up about two hundred and fifty yards in front of me. I lowered the boom on him with my old

48

30-30. It held eight shells and I shot them all, then poked one more in and shot that before he moved a muscle. Then he piled up in a heap and when we butchered him we found that you could cover all the bullet holes with one hand. He must have died on his feet and just didn't fall. I have never seen anything like it since.

I had a full house now but none of the others had any game and I told them they could take mine if they didn't connect so I could go on hunting. That was still early in the morning so we went right on. We didn't go far before we ran into all kinds of game and Charlie got one. Then two more jumped and Charlie told the postmaster to take one. One was a grey moose, a yearling, and looked about the colour of a blue persian cat; it was already as tall as a full grown black moose. He started shooting at it running. He must have had a little buck fever as it was quite close and he only wounded it. So I figured I should get into the act and help out all I could. The moose was running in thick little poplar and between us we mowed off a whole lot of the sidehill and finally bedded it down. I got the fever so badly I was pumping a good shell out and poking a new shell directly into the barrel out of my pocket. I didn't have the faintest idea how many shots I took. We had quite a little butchering to do, then ate lunch and started for camp, but not by the way we came.

Just before dusk we came to a steep canyon and a great big bull got up on the far side of it, probably three hundred and fifty yards away. Charlie lined the boys up on the brink of the canyon. Three of them hadn't got any meat yet so they were to shoot first, then on down to the tail end of the line. The bull stood broadside up on the skyline, a perfect target but a long shot and apparently too long for most of us. They all missed before it came Charlie's turn with his .30 U.S., a much more powerful gun than my old 30-30. He shot and still nothing happened, then I shot right away and the moose flopped. I will always believe that Charlie hit it and the moose just dropped when I shot, but nobody ever found out. I was the youngest and so they let me hightail it down the canyon and up the other side and I was almost over to the moose when it started to weave around trying to get up.

I tried to shoot but "click," nothing happened. My gun was empty and, worse, my pockets too. I went right up alongside the old boy and sized him up for bulldogging. But this was no moose for a little guy like me to try that on. He was mad as a wet hen and had a neck on him like an elephant, only bigger, and that huge rack of horns waving around scared me off. So I backed off and lay down flat. The boys were just coming up over the edge of the canyon about a hundred

49

yards away and I hollered, "Shoot, shoot, I'm out of shells." The moose got up on his front legs and then gradually onto his hind legs but with his feet bent back from the ankles. Finally the boys guessed what was wrong and started to shoot over me. But I think they were a little scared and thought they best shoot high or they might hit me. Anyway, they did no damage and the old bull got right up and slowly made his way across and down over another ridge out of sight. I ran back and got one of their cannons, ran as fast as I could the hundred and fifty yards or so to the edge of the hill, and there was the moose going across an open burn at a good walk down below the hill. I was puffing like a steam engine but got in two shots at him and that gun was empty and still no damage done.

All the other boys but Charlie had quit the chase and headed in on the trail. I ran back to Charlie, got his gun and ran the moose down again. But this time I had to go nearly half a mile before I caught up to him and it was almost dark. He was right on the edge of a thick patch of spruce. If he got into it I wouldn't be able to see to follow. I was completely winded and knew I'd have to be right up to him to have any chance of hitting. So I got right up alongside, not more than fifteen yards away, before trying to shoot. "Click." Charlie hadn't ejected the last empty shell and I never had time to throw another shell in before the moose got into the trees, and I had to give up and go back to Charlie. By then I hadn't the least idea which way camp was. Had I been alone I would have been completely lost after all that excitement; being in country I had never seen before and not knowing anything of the drainage system, and black dark besides.

Charlie led us back to the trail and we headed for camp. But the trail crossed a creek and apparently went up or down in the creek channel before going out on the other side. With no flashlight we couldn't seem to locate the trail on the far side of the creek. We separated and circled this way and that. We both located it at the same time, only I was across the creek. We hollered to each other. I started on a trot to catch up to Charlie and went quite a distance and still no Charlie. So I hollered again. Charlie was away off in the opposite direction from where I had been travelling. So I hollered: "You're lost, Charlie. You're travelling the wrong way." "No, this is the right way," says Charlie. So I took my compass out and looked and sure enough I was going backwards. That was about the biggest hunting day I ever had and I had had plenty of buck fever. I likely ran a few moose down in my sleep that night.

We tracked that moose most of the next day before his tracks mixed in with too many other moose tracks. He had bedded down two or three times and it looked as though he had been shot high through the withers. It likely hit a hump bone and knocked him down and partially paralyzed the hindquarters for awhile but all bleeding stopped. He was stretching right out at a good long stepping trot before we lost his tracks.

We wound up the hunt and hauled the meat out and split it up, and I headed back to Big Valley and helped Dad through the winter.

Art and I worked on a power line project quite a lot of one summer. We worked from the ground up, literally. We started digging holes; then soon we were promoted to "grunts." That meant either sitting or lying on your back and watching the man up the pole. Mostly you could guess what he needed next and sent it up on a handline. That, I think, was the easiest job I ever had. But we aspired to greater heights and borrowed the climber's spurs every chance we got and shinnied up the pole. We got to know what was to be done and, had we stayed with the job and taken a short course and exam, we could have got on as climbers.

The boys really had a party one night. It went on till time to go to work next morning and then a lot of them didn't show up for work. It was a Sunday and the linemen were to change over the system from the old to the new powerhouse. There was no truck driver available and the boss hit me up to tackle the job. They had an old wreck that had an extra set of gears put in. It was the only one with a key in it so they loaded their riggin' into it and told me where to drive. I found out mighty quick why the key was left in it. The driver likely figured no one without knowing it would get far without piling up. You had to whirl the steering wheel about three times around before it took hold. I got across town in about super low, I guess, but just before driving off the bridge across the Red Deer River, I had to cut it down off the grade and make a U-turn and another U right back. I got down off the grade okay but I was only on the second turn back on the wheel when I slammed into a power line pole. The truck was tight against the pole and against the crank, the only means of starting it, so I had to holler for help to get it out. The boss came a-running. He wasn't concerned at all about damage done. All he wanted was to get the blasted thing on the job with the tools so the crew could get going. So we heaved it back away from the pole and straightened the crank with a sledge hammer. He got behind the wheel and went to whirling. He rammed into the next pole, trying to make the sharp turn. I didn't feel near so bad then and when he said, "Seems like the steering is pretty loose on this damn thing," I agreed readily. It had no brakes either. I didn't tell him I'd hardly ever driven any kind of car before and had hollered "Whoa Babe" just before I hit the pole.

During my last summer in Alberta, I got a haying contract on Usher's Lawton Lease working for Dan Colvin. I got a team and mower from Dad, went about seventy-five miles to Dan Colvin's, and then on to the lease with the rest of the haying outfit. Bill Johnson, one of our old tillicums from west of the valley, hired out as cook. Mrs. Johnson, his mother, primed him up on how to build biscuits, high toned bannocks, pies and such like, and turned him loose on us. He had had practically no experience but this seemed like the opportunity of a lifetime to practice the culinary arts. Cowboys are supposed to eat beans and sowbelly three times a day and like it, so he didn't figure he'd need to go into much fancy cooking. One of his first mix-ups was with biscuits. He loaded them heavy with soda instead of baking powder. We lined into the cookshack for the noon feed and big Ole Larsen, six-foot-six in his stocking feet and an axe handle across the chest, grabbed a biscuit as he straddled the bench and poked it into his mouth and got a taste of it. Everything seemed to get awful quiet and then big Ole grabbed a handful of biscuits and young Bill hit for the door instanteously, with a shower of biscuits flying at him like buckshot.

There was another haying contractor, Herb Church and his crew, about eight miles away working on the same lease and whenever we didn't work we would swap visits. They had a mule over at Herb's camp that would always do a pretty fair little buck jump. Some of us would take turns riding the mule, either saddle or bareback. Ole was the best rider and I don't remember seeing him get piled, but the mule unloaded some of the boys pretty regularly. I could navigate him bareback but bit the dust when I tried with a saddle. We would try about every kind of acrobatic stunt any of us could think of. There was always a competition going throwing half-hitches with a lass rope on a wagon tongue. Most any time you moved, somebody was apt to rope you and throw a few half hitches till you were pretty well hog-tied.

We had pretty hefty acreages to work on. We'd mark out a half section (three hundred and twenty acres) to cut, rake and stack at one time. It was very dry and dusty and the prairie wool grass was tough as wire to cut. We would need anywhere from four to six sickles a day and have to put in a set of ledger plates every two or three days. This meant having a full-time handyman and blacksmith to keep all the mowers running. Milt Gould was the man for that job. He and his brother, Mert, were both working on the job. They were twin brothers and both very heavy set but had exceptionally short arms and legs. Milt weighed two hundred and fifty pounds, the same as Ole Larsen, but he only came up to Ole's chest. Either Milt or Mert could sit on an ordinary chair and have any average man stand on their feet and raise their legs straight out. None of the rest of us could lift our legs that way with a man on them. Try it some time!

Milt had an old rattletrap Model-T Ford and every two hours he'd make a rush trip out to the field with sharp sickles and hunt the mower outfits up and swap sickles, give us a drink of water or part of a can of tomatoes, then on to the next and back to camp to sharpen more sickles.

One afternoon we could see an awful-looking storm coming up. We high-tailed in to camp and were unhooking our teams when the storm came over us. It was dead calm on the ground up to about seven feet high for quite awhile. But seven feet above ground the air was loaded with fine dust travelling probably seventy miles an hour or more. It seemed as though it would cut your hand off if you held it up in the path of the dust. It was black as night and gradually the air current got down to the ground. Our camp was blown to pieces and we had quite a time hanging onto our hats and riggin' and keeping from getting swept away ourselves. Everything was filled with sand, including our mouths, nose and eyes, and we were chewing grit for days afterwards. One half section of hay was in the swath and every straw of it was blown away, a complete loss. What was in raked bunches was almost as bad, but what was in windrows just rolled over and over and we rescued quite a lot of that after the storm.

The Hand Hills Stampede was on and, as it was too windy to do any haying for a couple of days, we went over and took that in for a day. A lot of the riders practicing for the Calgary Stampede were there so we really got our money's worth. I think it was a three-day show. It was the first stampede I had taken in as a spectator.

It was on this haying job that I first got to know Slim Montgomery. He was working at Herb's camp and was only about fifteen years old then. His folks lived right alongside the lease and had a little horse ranch. One of Slim's brothers was a circus rider and a sister of his was pretty handy at roping and riding. I made the odd visit to Slim's folks and then, after the haying job was done in the fall, Slim came up to Big Valley. He wintered at Watson's mostly, and came out to B.C. with us in the spring.

I believe each contractor put up about seven hundred tons of hay. Dan Colvin had a wonderful buckpole outfit. The buckpole is worked with a team on each end and is about the simplest and least expensive stacking outfit there is. It has to be dry and fairly smooth ground to work well. The lease was ideal for it. Dan's buckpole teams were all well matched black Percherons about thirteen hundred pounds and high spirited. He would gather up a load of bunches that would be ten feet high and about eighteen feet each way wide and long, and trot the outfit into the stack. I think Mert took over the cooking and Bill Johnson helped stacking part of the time and they sure piled up hay in a hurry. Both camps got in a supply of liquor and we had a bang-up farewell party with quite a few neighbours present, song and dance, midnight supper and dawn breakfast. Then we broke camp, piled all manner of haying equipment into hayracks and headed north.

Art and I had partly broken Smokey to harness so now we had a rough-broke team. Art had already gone out to B.C. and sent word back that he had spotted the makings of a ranch. We gathered up a lot more riggin' of one kind and another that winter. Some of it was pretty haywire but it served the purpose to get us started. We had roamed around quite a little but none of us had gathered much moss. Now we all aimed to change our range.

CHAPTER V

The Move to Quesnel, British Columbia

With Art and I having been raised on a ranch amongst ranchers, it seemed natural — almost imperative — to go into ranching on our own. We had therefore been looking for a ranching setup that didn't need capital to develop.

In 1930, Art, Pierre and Tom Watson went out in Tom's old car to Williams Lake, B.C., in the central Cariboo country. Art and Pierre stayed and got work at the Gang Ranch, in the lower Chilcotin, and made a few dimes in the wild horse races and wild cow milking at Williams Lake Stampede. Tom returned home in the fall. Burnstad returned in the fall also, but Art went further west, out into the Chilcotin country and got work at Duke Martin's ranch at Alexis Creek. Then he got a feeding job at the old Martin meadow, forty miles away by wagon road, working for "Butch" Helwig who had rented the four-hundred-ton meadow from Duke for five years. Butch got his monniker butchering for Pat Burns in the construction camps on the old P.G.E., in the Hazelton and Barkerville areas.

While working at Butch's, Art got pretty well acquainted with Lexie Long Johnnie, a Chilcotin Indian, who offered to show him a string of meadows in the spring for ten dollars. He couldn't lose, he figured, and went on the trip. He wrote to Burnstad and me right after the trip and said he liked what he saw and best we all gather his and our own riggin' and what cayuses and haying equipment we could scratch up, and ship the works out to Prince George in a settler's car.

In the spring of 1931, Pierre and I gathered up Slim Montgomery and Walter "Shorty" Watson (Tom's brother), and we all rode the "Sidedoor Pullman," as it was called in those days, clean through from Big Valley to Prince George with six head of horses, two wagons, three mowers, a hayrake, an eight-hundred-pound stove, saws, axes, blankets and even a bedspring piled high on top of everything else. This was the deluxe part of the trip! We spent our three days travelling time, and one day sidetracked, on top of this bedspring and mattress where we could easily duck down out of sight into the maze of junk underneath when trainmen came around. There was only

55

supposed to be one person ride the car. We brought a lot of grub out with us but very, very little cash. I believe we had three hundred pounds of flour and about two hundred of coarse ground wheat mush, some canned meat, three buckets full of hard-boiled eggs and some canned fruit the neighbours and folks had kindly supplied us with. So, although we didn't have too much variety, we sure had plenty to eat.

They never unloaded the horses after we passed Edmonton and we were sidetracked for a full day at McBride. We got out of our boxcar nest and camped outside while at McBride. While there we saw a grizzly bear swim the Fraser River; we also caught a ling, a snakey-looking fish. Pierre had heard this critter was good eating and, being all hungry youngsters, we decided to tackle it and found it pretty tasty, although repulsive to look at in the raw state. One old mare we had in the outfit, Kate by name, got pretty cranky on the trip and she chewed on the division rail every time there was a bump. So for something to do, Burnstad put some snoose on the rail and she took to that like a pup to a root. Before we got to Quesnel she liked snoose so well she would come up and bum for a chew, nuzzling his hip pocket where he kept the can.

We landed in Prince George about the sixth of June. Art met us with a saddle horse and a pack horse. We unloaded our junk and set up a camp in what is now the middle of the city. After travelling in restricted quarters for several days, the first necessity was to clean up and do a washing. We had no tub of any kind and the best we could do was to find a secluded spot and set up a sentry while each one took a bath in the Nechako River. We got away with that okay as that part of town wasn't very active in those days. Not having anything big enough to heat water in, the next best bet was to wash clothes right in the river. That wasn't so bad in the more or less clear water of the Nechako but later in Quesnel we decided to do a washing in the Fraser River. It should have been named the "Big Muddy" like the nickname for the Mississippi. There is always sand in it, so much that you can even hear it. We hung our clothes in it to soak them a while before getting into the serious scrubbing business. Something came up and we forgot a batch and left them in the river overnight. Next morning they were just loaded with silt. We got that worked out more or less and the clothes were the cleanest they'd been since we left Big Valley, but we had to dry them out and then shake the sand out. By the time we got through the whole process, it was mighty nigh time to do another washing.

Left to right. Back row, Burt Adshead, Harrington, Ed Lavington, Seaward, Ed Adshead. Front row, Harry Kolterman, unknown, Jack Adshead and Woodward.

Taken at Ed Adshead's during the 1904 or 1905 round-up. Note mosquito nets on some hats. Those were the days when ranchers had to build smudge pens for their stock.

The old pony "Babe" they rode to school, the author is the one standing.

Left, Art Lavington ready to leave for the Peace River
Country. A farewell photo with brother "Dude" right.

Lavington Brothers putting L^C brand on
calves for Lavington Co.

The author at Ramsay Creek barn.

Art standing on the eight-horse brush
breaker plough.

Cattle in the corrals for de-horning.

Swimming the outfit across Baker
Creek in high water.

Cattle cautiously approaching a creek crossing.

A new crop of horses coming up.

Roping a mare with foal to take them away from a wolf area.

The author breaking "Tony" in the corral.

Loading machinery for moving.

Moving haymaking machinery to a new meadow.

Mowing hay.

Raking hay.

Stack built with mast and boom stacker.

Loading stooked green oat hay.

Haymaking

Stacking with gin poles and horse sweep.

Unstacked hay fed on top of snow.

Ron Kolterman hauling a load of firewood in the iron tired wagon.

Wrong mama, wrong end.

The covered wagon outfit bringing in a load of grub.

The winter sleigh outfit, the white horse is "Smoky."

Moose in the stackyard.

Cache for storage of grub, most important from November to May til after high water and breakup. The cache was, however, used all year long.

*Grub
and Freight*

The tandem-hitch freight outfit above Stanley, B.C., this outfit could pass most narrow pack horse trails.

Building furniture with split poles and moose rawhide lacing.

Art's wife Emma churning butter while he is doing carpentry work. Art did most of the woodwork with axe, saw and jack-knife and the author did the moose rawhide lacings.

Inside Ramsay Creek cabin at Christmas.

Part of the winter fur catch, note scoop roof construction to help the rain and snow drain off.

Ron Kolterman at Long John meadow.

Cutting winter fuel supply with a steel wheeled tractor and "buzz saw."

Baker Meadow cabin.

Cabins
and Building

The author notching the corner logs on a barn, the helper is peeling logs.

*Home Ranch
and the
Finished Buildings*

Sign on road to Lavington's ranch.

Ramsay Creek, ten-horse barn.

The outdoor facilities at Baker meadow.

L^C Home Ranch Buildings.

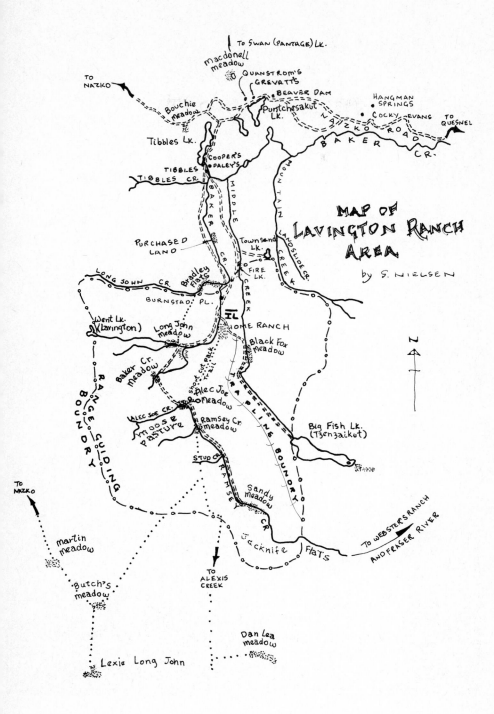

MAP OF
LAVINGTON RANCH
AREA

by S. NIELSEN

Surveyors at Long John or Cooper meadow cabin.

The stove and homemade furniture, Baker meadow cabin.

We figured to set wagons together, load up and head for Quesnel pronto. But when we tied our cayuses onto the load, we changed our minds fast. We had one small but good team, old "Shorty" and "Kate." Then we had a horse, "Pete," that had been spoiled badly and was so balky that Burnstad had picked him up for next to nothing. Also we had a saddle mare, a kind of dumb critter, not broke to harness. Art and I had Jean and Smokey, but they had only been hooked up together the two or three times to take a sleighing party to a dance, and were really only saddle horses. None of these horses weighed over thirteen hundred and two of them only eleven hundred pounds, hardly a first-class freighting outfit which was what we needed when we got our junk all loaded. We hitched four onto the heaviest load and two onto the other — mixed up the good with the bad and hoped for the best. Nothing good happened. One in the team balked and the leaders in the four-up didn't savvy any whistling or hollering and just stood pat. So we decided Prince George was as good a place as any to break horses and went to skidding logs or anything else that would educate them to the rigging and the signals.

Then came an incident that will always stick in my memory. Art decided we had to shoe all our horses. Shoes were plentiful, all we had to do was to dig around in old construction camps to find kegs of them, but Art also decided a wagon wheel wasn't good enough to shape thirty-two shoes and we had to buy an anvil. We blew ten dollars and eighty cents on the darn thing and that left us with around thirteen dollars between five of us. That anvil didn't look like much for eating purposes. Slim also had been downtown to buy some dishes for us. He bought two little cups that took three dippings to fill an ordinary coffee cup, two great big deep enamel plates and a baby fork. That was supposed to fill out our pressing needs in the way of jewellery and eating tools. Some day when I can spare the time and expense I aim to mount that little old anvil and Slim's eating tools in a glass case.

Altogether we put in better than a week camped in the forks of the Nechako and Fraser rivers at Prince George, breaking and training our horses. We hoped all was in readiness to proceed and headed out for Quesnel. Every steep hill we had to juggle horses to get a four-up that would pull true enough to get the wagons to the top. Then we were on our way. Smokey and Pete balked every morning for the first week but they got to be true pulling horses before we got to Quesnel. It took us a whole day to pull the mile-long Cottonwood Hill. We would go ten steps and stop for a breather, then ten steps more and so on to the top. When we got to the top with one wagon, back we

57

went for another, and then took all the horses back down to the flat to camp for the night.

Art had met R. L. Marsh in Quesnel at the livery barn he ran, I believe the only one there at the time, and had made a deal with him to rent a small meadow to put up hay on shares for our stock. Ruric Leon Marsh, "R.L." or "Marsh" as he was familiarly called, was raised in Rochester, Vermont. He had arrived in Quesnel in 1909, having walked a lot of the way from Vancouver, and took up a homestead twelve miles south of Quesnel on the west side of the Fraser River. The house he built on the original homestead in 1911 is still standing. He acquired a meadow several miles up from the valley and across Deserter Creek. This became known as Ruric Meadow, and was our destination for that trip; the little creek and lake on it are still known as Ruric Lake and Ruric Creek. The Marshes had seven children, Florence, Leonard, John, Richard, Gordon, Leona and Lillian, and had thus found it necessary to move to town to get the youngsters closer to school. Whenever we put our horses up at the livery barn, Mrs. Marsh figured it was her duty to look after us and feed us. They didn't make any money out of us as we never had any. I don't think anyone west of the Rockies can make Huckleberry pie as good as Mrs. Marsh.

Marsh built and operated the first store in West Quesnel. Then he saw a need for accommodation for travellers and started building the Log Cabin Auto Court; likely the first motel or auto court in Quesnel. The cabins were built of picked logs in a beautiful setting between the old Fraser River Bridge and the confluence of Baker Creek with the Fraser River. The log work was of the very best, all neatly dove-tailed corners. The cabins were all sizes, from one room for a single bachelor to the large family type with several rooms. I guess beef drive time gave them their most use and, possibly at times, abuse. They sure filled a pressing need for us folk from away out in the sticks.

They are all gone now, victims of progress to make way for the new "Moffat Bridge."

From the auto court venture Marsh went on to his masterpiece. Built in 1934, the landmark of Quesnel (particularly West Quesnel), on top of the hill west of Moffat Bridge and straight up from the old Fraser Bridge, stands the "Big Log House" overlooking all of Quesnel. This is a most fitting monument to the skill of a master of the art of log building.

When we sized up our outfit in Quesnel, we decided a few things were absolutely necessary to our equipment. We made out a small list and went into C. D. Hoy's store for the supplies. We read it off to Hoy, and Art was adding up the total as Hoy priced the items. Midway through the list we decided we would need at least ten dollars credit. Hoy came through. Needless to say, strawberry jam, pickles and such like were omitted from the list. Most of our grub list was for flour, sugar, salt, beans, rice and baking powder with a little dried fruit for special occasions. We loaded the wagons a little heavier and headed down the west side of the river for ten miles, then west ten miles straight up to Marsh's meadow. When we started up the hill out of the Fraser Valley, we had to unload part of the load. This was something brand new to Pierre, Slim and me. That wagon track going straight up the hill didn't even look like a saddle horse trail to us prairie chickens.

We unloaded the eight-hundred-pound stove and a whole lot of other stuff that we didn't require immediately and started up. Art and Pierre were skinning the outfits and the rest of us followed. I was sure the horses were going to fall right over backwards onto the wagons. We even had to rest our saddle horses. However, with many rests, the outfit wound its way up and up out of the valley and from there, although rough and winding, it wasn't so bad.

Then we hit Deserter Creek and the road dived down into it. We had brakes on the wagons and sure needed them. Even with them on full, the wagons pushed the ponies into high gear and they crashed down on the rocks into the creek crossing below, then straight up again. The first time I was driving over that crossing I was thrown clean out over the horses into the creek. The old freight wagons had boxed-in seats that you could tie yourself into. For some of the stick roads you sure needed all of that and some glue too.

On our arrival at the meadow we found a two-windowed, one-room, sod-roofed log cabin, somewhat dilapidated. But after camping for a month, it certainly looked good to have a roof we could throw our junk under. We went to work right away getting ready to put up hay. Art, Slim and I were to go out to haying jobs in the Chilcotin country by August 1st so we had to highball to get our own hay up. We got everything into the meadow except the big stove, then set the haying machinery together and started haying the meadow. That big eight-hundred-pound stove stayed on the trail at the foot of the hill for nine months until we moved out to the makings of our ranch in the spring. We figured the Marsh meadow was too small to supply our needs so we went out and looked up a meadow on Deserter Creek further up. We cut six to eight miles of road into that so we could put that hay up later.

One of the first things we had to do was to get meat. I was elected for the first hunt and took my old 30-30 and headed out bright and early on foot with a couple of hotcakes in my pocket. I figured out quite a plan of action. It was to be more of an exploratory tour than a hunt, I guess. I figured I would make a big circle. It was bright and clear and thus easy to tell directions. All I knew of the country was the road in. I headed about straight northeast for an hour or so to get to the outside circumference of my circle and then started bending right, just enough to keep from getting no further from home. According to my figuring, at about the time I wanted to head home, I should hit somewhere up on little Ruric Creek. Then I would follow the creek into the cabin. What I didn't know was that this was just a little short creek and I had gone right around it without crossing it. So all I could do was to keep on and on. I stopped bending and headed straight about northeast by east, figuring if I didn't strike anything between, I was bound to strike the Fraser River and settlement sooner or later. I kept going after dark for about two hours and then hit a creek too big for Ruric Creek, but running in the same direction as it would be if I had struck it. I was plumb befogged by then and got down in the sand and mapped my course with a stick and figured that I just made too big a circle. But this wasn't the nicest time to find all that out. I looked up a good spruce tree and lay down on a bed of needles with a small fire in front of me, ate my hotcakes and slept till daylight, except for replenishing the fire a time or so to keep warm. I only had summer clothes on.

In the morning there were no chores to do, and no breakfast to get. I just grabbed a burning stick or two and threw them in the water without first looking up. Imagine my surprise when I saw a nice big fat buck jump away from the pool, nearly scared out of his hide when I threw the burning sticks in the water. I couldn't reach the rifle fast enough to get a shot. Not knowing where I was, I probably wouldn't have shot anyway. I headed off down the creek at a fast clip, getting hungrier and hungrier by the minute, and wondering how far to the Fraser River or settlement and grub. About five miles from my night camp I struck the wagon crossing on Deserter Creek. It was only five or six miles into camp from there and I got in before the boys finished breakfast. I sure helped them out plenty. Up to this time, Art had been doing most of the cooking. He and I had batched quite a lot before, and I had done most of the cooking, but that was inside and on stoves. Art had the better of me in camp cooking, having had more practice. Butch Helwig had instructed him in the art of running sourdough for making hotcakes, biscuits and bread. Wherever he went from there on he packed a little sourdough kettle in his pack outfit. That was his baby! His secret, too. Us apes didn't know all the intricacies of running this critter!

I aim to tell you we were a hungry bunch of youngsters to feed. We were working from daylight to dark in July, fourteen to sixteen hours quite often. Slim, Walter and I were still either growing or filling out some and took on a lot of nourishment. What I am driving at is that this little sourdough pot of Art's seemed to remind me of the Lord feeding the multitude. Art would make hotcakes and more hotcakes and more and still more. Right to now, I can't figure out where they came from. I watched him, fascinated, hoping and wondering if there could possibly be enough. Before we got meat, hotcakes and mush were breakfast. Afterwards when just Art and I were together we had a bigger sourdough kettle and I was running it myself. I couldn't begin to make as many as he did even with a bigger kettle that held more.

We hunted in relays and one morning before breakfast I got a little buck. We were so meat hungry by then, we ate a hindquarter for breakfast. That little deer was gone in two days and we were hunting again. This time Art got an old moose. It fell in the creek and he had to butcher it in the water. Whether that made the difference or not, the meat was so tough you could chew on a chunk all day like spruce pitch and never get it down to swallowing size. Likely it was one of the moose that came to the Cariboo at the time of the Gold Rush! But it was meat and we enjoyed trying to chew it up anyway.

We got the hay up on the home meadow all in good weather and then moved up to the new meadow to which we had cut a road. We were getting a little short of time so this was to be a highball job and didn't give us time to build a bridge across the creek. Instead we crossed on a gravel crossing higher up and made our camp on a point overlooking the meadow. There we set up our machinery but had to tow it across the creek. We crossed a team above the meadow and wended our way through the willows into the meadow. Part of the crew stayed on one side of the creek and I was the go-between in the creek. I stripped off everything but my hat to do my job, ferrying the machinery across. In the middle of taking the rake across, Pierre saw a deer fighting flies and coming straight towards us. By this time we'd pretty well got the best of the tough old moose and needed fresh meat. So Pierre raced back to camp and got the rifle. But the deer was out of sight when he returned and he was too out of wind to shoot anyway, so gave the rifle to me. I waded across the creek and took out after the deer through willows, brush, rose bushes and tall grass, still with nothing on but my hat, and lots of flies and mosquitoes. I didn't get the deer but I bet it would have made quite a picture.

The weather turned bad and our hay got quite a soaking, so we didn't get it up in very good shape. It came in pretty handy even at that.

Back at the home place we cut a set of logs and threw up a cabin in a hurry. Just the walls and a split timber roof, for the time being, with sod on it. That was to be for Slim and me for the winter, and was my first log cabin building in B.C., and Slim's first anywhere. Then we packed our outfit and headed first for town, twenty miles, and then Nazko, sixty-eight miles, and up the Nazko River thirty-five miles and then six miles across to Duke Martin's big meadow where Art and I were to go haying for Butch Helwig. Pierre and Walter had gone back to Alberta. Pierre was to get Jessie, his wife, and their new baby boy, Bud. Walter Watson had had enough sourdough hotcakes before then, and had left us at Quesnel.

Going up the Nazko we met some of the characters of the Nazko Valley. Art had been through that way and had met them and others before. I say characters meaningly. At one time I hoped and planned to write a book on the Nazko characters. I don't think one could run across so many folks who seemed to be so different from the average run of folks living in civilization. One of the characters, a female, claimed she had gone to sleep on a sunny sidehill one spring. According to her story, when she woke up, she saw a cowboy riding away — and she was to become a mother! Only in the Nazko could this happen!

I figure the hardships they had endured while pioneering the country, living so long alone, seeing practically no one, completely dependent on their own resources to bring them through all those things, would have contributed to stressing their individual characteristics.

Paul Krestenuk, a shrewd Russian, was one of the rugged individuals of the Nazko. He ran trading posts at Nazko, Kluskus and Ulgatcho. The one at Nazko, over seventy miles from Quesnel, was more or less headquarters, with Kluskus next on the line, another sixty miles or so out, and Ulgatcho away further on into the wilderness some seventy-five miles. Paul seemed to spend all winter on the road freighting supplies in and fur out, and he must have had many a tough trip. He used a four-horse team a lot of the time and often had one or two Indians with two- or four-horse teams freighting for him.

I was riding late at night on the Nazko road one trip and caught up to Paul's outfit. He had his sleigh box covered over with canvas and a kerosene lantern lighted inside. He was headed for town with practically an empty sleigh. I didn't see any sign of a skinner and wondered if anything was wrong so I hollered, "Hello, the house. Anybody live here?" Paul came back, "Who's that?" I told him and he uncovered and there he was patching his underwear down in the bottom of the sleigh, by the dim light of the old kerosene lantern in the middle of the night, around 20 below and a good many miles from any habitation. No time wasted and, I noticed later, no clothes wasted. Paul had an old blue sweater that looked like he'd used up many a roll of yarn darning it. I believe he'd been wearing it for twenty years or more.

It was really something to see Paul undress his feet in cold weather. He needed plenty of room around the stove. First he had a pair of moose rawhide mukluk sort of rig. I don't know if he had made them or if Indians made them for him, but he had them about six sizes bigger than his feet and they were stuffed with a whole lot of coarse swamp hay. So when he got them off he proceeded to pull the hay out and scatter that around the stove to dry and air out. That took up all the room around one side of the stove and then he shed a few pair of socks till he got down to a pair of buckskin moccasins with still another pair of socks under that. By the time that outfit was well spread out to dry you had to look for a spot around another stove to dry your own and the atmosphere got a bit high all around. Something tells me Paul didn't do his laundry very regularly in the winter, when freighting. Maybe around Christmas and again after break-up in the spring.

When Paul got caught with a heavy load and bare ground in many places, after a thaw or too late in the spring, he would "put de brush" as he said. He would cut saplings, pine or poplar, and lay them about three feet apart all across the road. Everybody cussed him plenty as he never picked up the brush and the first wagon outfits had to move them all. Paul could speak several languages, probably Siwash best. From listening to him and old Cocky Evans giving the political situation the once over, he must have kept pretty fair track of what went on in the world. He had probably camped out in the winter about as much as anyone in B.C. by the end of his time.

Joe Spehar lived differently from most folks. He believed in getting really hungry and cooked up a great big feed and ate it all at one sitting. Then if there were oranges or peanuts around he kept right on eating. His big feeds didn't run to anything fancy or any great variety.

The spring Art was riding to meet us in Prince George, he stayed a few days with Joe and broke a horse for him. One of Joe's big feeds was a great big bucketful of dandelion greens, another was sucker fish.

63

Joe cooked a whole sucker for himself, about two and a half feet long, and ate the whole thing — head, guts, tail and all. Art, kidding him, said, "You must have been hungry, Joe." "Huh," Joe said, "if I be hongry, I eat an odder one lak dat!" Art only got a feed of dandelion greens.

On the trip we first touched down at Shorty Harrington's. Fred Norberg was there and to listen to the two of them talk and rave at each other made me wonder what manner of men they were. Shorty was a little sawed-off Virginian and Fred was a Swede. They made quite a pair. Shorty's was the meeting place and jumping off place for the Nazko Valley folks.

You didn't have to stay there long before you'd see everybody from the Nazko Valley. Shorty's hospitality was a legend. Everybody stayed at least overnight and likely longer before going on out to civilization or into their Nazko homes. The coffee pot was never cold and Shorty's biscuits were something to write home and tell the folks about. Shorty was the model host. He had a great big chair and he would curl his legs up under him and start telling jokes. He seemed to be able to estimate his company right well and just what type of jokes and stories would go over best. Then he was off for hours. He had had many experiences and a joke would remind him of a story and a story of a joke and so on, ad infinitum.

Come bedding down time, if there weren't enough bunks, there was plenty of floor space in the old shanty. I've seen a lot of it used and used it myself a number of times. Speaking of the shanty, whoever built it must have done so without benefit of plumb bob, level or square. Nothing was straight up, level, or square. But it was really homelike for all that, with the genuine old Southern hospitality you read about.

From there up the river to the next habitation it was about thirty-two miles. Al Loomis, mostly known as "Muskrat Loomis," lived there. When we arrived he was just going to clean out his well and got us to help him. According to my guess he had lived alone a bit too long and, being of a nervous type, it wasn't too good for him. He would be plumb nervous and laugh and talk in a high-pitched voice for quite awhile. But, as he got used to being in company, he calmed down. He lived on the shore of a lake, deep between high hills with the river running through it. He had a plan to raise rats and beavers. He would grow lots of turnips, carrots and cabbage and build a chute to take the vegetables into the lake out of the root cellar under his house. That would entice all the rats and beavers swimming up and down the river to stay and call 'er home. Most folks figured it was a crazy notion

64

but it worked mighty well. Clarence Fuller, a fur buyer in this part, showed me some of his rats once. Clarence said he had bought lots of rats here and there, yet Loomis' rats were one-third larger and several shades darker than any he had bought anywhere else.

Next step, only three miles up to Big Jim Blaine's. Now if any Western story writer had ever got a hold of old Jim, he'd have had his fortune made. Jim really filled the title "big." If he straightened up he would have been over six-foot-six and wide to fit the height, with a big booming voice, and could he ever tell *big* yarns. He was a broken down cowboy from Montana and you only had to look at his legs to see that he really had been "broken." They were all knots, twisted and bent and scarred. Jim used to tell about the time he brought the herd in out of a mountain blizzard. The other cowboys either quit and went home or froze to death. But Jim was too tough for that and stayed with the herd through all the worst and brought them into the ranch. When he got there he was frozen solid in the saddle and he had to be pried out and thawed out in kerosene.

That experience and too many broncs too tough on him had really wrecked a magnificent specimen of manhood. But it sure hadn't hurt his spirit and humour any.

About that time, he was hatching up quite an idea. What he aimed to do was start a kind of guest or dude ranch, strictly for female teachers and nurses. Actually the place was an ideal spot for any such venture: a beautiful valley, river running thirty or forty yards below the house, good fishing, bunch grass sidehills either side, little poplar, willow, pine, spruce and fir trees all up the benches, a cold spring with a lovely little waterfall quite close to the house, and lots of game in all directions. Truly a beauty spot out of a dream. Then with Big Jim Blaine as host, chief guide and entertainer, what more could the ladies want?

Everything had to be packed into Loomis' and Big Jim's, there being no wagon road. The Indians did have a sleigh trail up the valley in wintertime but it took an Indian to find and follow it. Jim and Loomis went out to town only about once every two or three years. They both got groceries at Shorty's little store or occasionally out the other way to Chilcotin at Tom Lee's little store in Alexis Creek. They used to tell a yarn on Jim about his 4x beaver felt Stetson hat. Claimed he was down to the store in Chilcotin and wanted a hat. "But you ain't got anything good enough here for me," says Jim. "Just what specifications do you have in mind, Jim?" says Tom Lee. Jim grumbled some and says, "Nothin' like you see around here. I want a real hat, big enough to look good too." A few more hints and

Tom marked it all down and said, "I'll send it out to you in a couple of weeks or so." They say Jim was bluffing and thought Tom was bluffing too, but when he got the forty-dollar Stetson he had to peddle a steer to pay for it!

That reminds me of another yarn about Jim. He always claimed to have a big bunch of cattle. On one occasion he was kidding a group about his large herd and there happened to be a range inspector in the group. He at once jumped Jim for range fees that had never been collected and Jim kicked through for two hundred head! He didn't have more than a couple of old broken down saddle ponies at the time, so the story goes.

Jim was a good bachelor, everything neat and tidy and clean, and he was a good cook too. Folks claimed his pies were most delectable but I never happened to catch up to one. I never did see any female guest ranch, either. Too bad, but we had to leave Jim with his dreams and wend our way on up the Nazko and across to the Martin meadow.

Haying at Butch's

We got into the meadow July 31st. Butch was supposed to be there to start haying August 1st and we had just barely enough grub to see us through, making the most of Jim's and Shorty's hospitality on the way. Our packs were empty of grub on arrival, other than a feed of rice for the first night, so in the morning we went to raid the kitchen in the old cabin. Well, it seems that Butch had been out on the summer roundup branding and had been delayed and thus used up practically everything left in the cabin from the spring. All we could find was some farina (wheat mush). We boiled up a good, big potful, as this was to be breakfast for three hungry men; no sugar, milk or any decorations. We all started to eat the stuff, but not too many mouthfuls before Slim got up to see if he could find anything among the spices that would help it down a little. He did. He found some red peppers, and said he'd eat one if I would. Never tried that before and I don't aim to again. But we got the peppers down and ate mush and drank water, more mush, more water and then some, till we cleaned the mush pot. If your appetite ever fails you any, try a red pepper. You may not get an appetite but I guarantee you'll keep eating to get the fire out of your mouth and gullet.

We shot the odd duck and chicken and got a few berries, and got hungrier and hungrier. We built about half a mile of Russell fence for something to do besides hunt. I think it was four days before Butch rolled in with a four-horse team and freight wagon and another team load following, all loaded down with grub for haying. Sho' nuff we were plumb tickled to see the big California cowboy and hear his booming voice. When he called "muck-a-muck" you could hear it for three miles against the wind, and the first "muck-a-muck" holler sounded awful good to us. Butch figured if we kept eating like we did for the first week, he'd have to send out for another load of grub right quick and lose money fast on us.

Art hadn't known that Slim was going to be with us, and Butch had a full crew without him, so Slim was told to head into Alexis Creek and he'd get work for sure around there. Slim got in nearly three months' haying for Jack Maindley, a bachelor living out of Alexis Creek.

Butch had brought in an old Englishman, Harris by name; a Finlander, Einer Nordberg; and Lexie, as his stackerman. Art and I made up the rest of the crew. Butch was married and had two boys and two girls all under six. So there was quite a gathering of us there away out in the sticks.

Art and I set up our tent, Lexie had his tent, and the other boys used the bunkhouse. Seemed like everybody came out and sat around our campfire in the evenings and yarned for a spell before rolling in. Every third morning it came our turn to wrangle. Art or Lexie or I had to roll out about four-thirty and go wrangle horses out of the big meadow. The meadow being probably between thirty-five hundred and four thousand feet altitude, it was plenty chilly and frosty at that time of the day. Butch had an idea I wasn't too well climatized and wanted to know if I had any wool underwear. I didn't. That was only for winter, according to my notion, and this was August. But Butch told me he had an extra suit which I could use if I needed it. I didn't wrangle many mornings till I weakened and got into Butch's long woollies — Stanfield's Red Label. I had had a cold streak down my back every morning, and all over most mornings, but when I got into that underwear I was snug as a bug in a rug. I have worn wool underwear in this high country summer and winter ever since.

Butch, being a sourdough expert, nearly always made the hotcakes in the morning as his wife Aggie had quite a little to do getting the youngsters all underway. One or other of us milked a cow, and breakfast was mush, hotcakes and steak and lots of all of it. After we'd all tucked in a real good feed, Butch would say, "Well, we might die, but it sure won't be from starvation." Another of Butch's yarns or sayings came from the type of help he had at one time. Duke had sent out a couple of green Englishmen to help him with the winter feeding. Everything they did — or didn't do that needed to be done — Butch had to check over and either do it himself or undo it and do it over right. First chance he got, he sent word to Duke to come and get his green Englishmen. Butch wrote, "I can look after the four hundred head of cattle okay, but I can't look after four hundred cattle and two green Englishmen!"

I never had a boss I liked better to work with. It was really something to watch him butcher out a cow critter. Art and I figured we were pretty handy around butchering but found out about all we could do was get in the way. We'd stand back and in just a little while Butch would have the critter all trimmed up neat as a pin.

68

I learned quite a little about stick ranching working there too. There is quite a difference from ranching back in Alberta where we had come from. The old prairie wool grass in Alberta would slide along in front of a buckpole away out past the teams on either side and pile up ten feet or more high at the back. Here, these high meadows are all damp morning and evening, and hay just doesn't slide so well. In those days everybody used sleds and pitched the hay onto them out of little haycocks which were all raked and bunched, then cocked by hand. This entailed a lot of hand work and thus needed a big crew. Since then, we have found we could use sweeps, cut out most of the hand work, save a lot of time and cut the crew in half. Butch's outfit used a mast and boom stacker with swinging arm. Nice rig to build a stack with, but the moving and setting up took a lot of work and time and too much rigging for anything but a big meadow where a lot of hay went into each stack.

We swung into the haying right away, then in wet weather did a little fencing, repaired buildings and barnyards, etc., built gates and dams, and did some ditching. Meat was a necessity and we mixed beef and moosemeat. Lexie got a huge moose away back in the sticks. He and Art went to pack it out and Art took Pierre's old Shorty horse for one of the three pack horses. Quite a storm came up and they got caught in the dark still a long way out with the three heavy meat packs. Shorty strayed off into a pothole meadow and they couldn't locate him in the black dark, so had to leave him all night with the heavy pack on. When they found him next morning, he didn't seem to be any the worse for wear and was eating away quite contented, although ten miles from the other horses with a three-hundred-pound load on and saddle cinched tight all night.

The next fall, Butch let me do the meat packing. Harris, who had taken root out in the Chilcotin and got a haying job every year to finance buying grub and gear for the winter, came with me partly to help and partly for a change of scenery. We got caught in a storm. We were in a patch of burnt timber and a howling wind came up as we finished packing. Trees started blowing down all around us and a whole lot too close for comfort. Harris would have left everything and got out in a big hurry. I would have too, but we were practically finished packing so I finished and lined the pack outfit out before leaving. One big tree crashed down just ahead of us and the horses froze with fright and started pulling back. Then another tree crashed behind us and that jarred the horses loose. We got out of there in high gear. Harris figured we'd had the course before we got out of there. I think he sweated a little blood and would have drunk a bottle of rum alone if he'd had it. He also claimed there was colour in his underwear!

Later in the fall, Butch took Art and me off the haying crew to go rounding up beef on the Nazko for a week or so. I hadn't ridden much in rough country like the Nazko sidehills before but I know cow critters. It didn't take me long getting to know you had to look for tracks first instead of cows. Some of those old dogies away up in their high hill paradise sure didn't aim to come down, and you really had to ride to keep them from going higher instead of heading down into the gather at the bottom.

We saw salmon in a lot of the riffles in the river and it looked like a sure thing we could get us one. Butch spotted one by a rock and he tied his jackknife on a stick for a spear, got on the rock and made a stab for it. He slipped and lost his balance, and fell down into the pool. Art saw the fish going through a deep pool and jumped his horse off a twelve-foot bank into the water. All we could see was a great spray in every direction and we never did see any more of that fish. We never tried roping them!

I was riding a big brown gelding Art had broken for Butch the year before. One time I got into camp and was just going to grab a snack and hit right out again, and left big Brownie trailing his reins. Something must have goosed him. He lit into bucking, and man, did he go high! He threw my old cannon about twenty feet in the air and it came down barrel first and drove two feet into the ground. Duke Marten had come down to see how we were making out and says, "That's the kinda horse I like — does his buckin' after you get off."

We camped at Al Loomis' one night while driving the river. Sure tickled him to have company and, after talking pretty late, we bedded down. Loomis very hospitably donated his only bed to Butch and Loomis slept on the floor. Loomis also ran a sourdough and he mixed up some extra at night to have enough to feed us hungry cowboys in the morning, and then hung the kettle up on a post. It just happened when he bedded down, the sourdough pot was right above his head. The extra mixing was all the combination needed to boil the mixture up over the top where it dripped all over Loomis' head and on the top of his blanket roll. When he got up he sure was one comical-looking critter. While we were all laughing at him he was telling us he dreamed he was camped out and it was raining on him but he couldn't wake up enough to cover his head!

We rounded up and cut out about two carloads of beef and started back for the ranch, then on out to Alexis Creek. I was promoted or demoted to chuckwagon boss from the ranch in to Alexis Creek. Got my start cookin' the old sourdough hotcakes on a campfire as Butch just had to have them every morning. By then I was getting pretty handy, cooking over the campfire. I had a saddle horse tied on behind, and any time the boys needed help I'd tie the team up and take the old pony and go to hollerin'.

We all put up at Duke Marten's in Alexis Creek where Butch's drive mixed in with Duke's and went on the ninety-five miles to Williams Lake stockyards. I had to wrangle horses out of Duke's horse pasture right early one morning. Art tipped me off it might take half a day and if there was a fog it might be more. He told me best I hit the Chinese cook up for some raisins as that would be quite awhile to wait for breakfast. I did and soon found out the wherefore. You go straight up, and I mean straight, for quite a spell into rimrock bluffs. The trails wander here and there all over till you gradually work out to more open country and good feed in the big pasture on top. Well, after you find the cayuses it's anybody's guess which way to head 'em to hit the track that may take you out and down again. If you can head the ponies right they'll lead you out. In a fog though, I guess a man could really have his troubles to find the snake track through that rimrock.

One morning we loaded the old freight wagon up again and headed back for the ranch. When we got there the haying was about wound up on the Marten meadow and the outfit ready to move on to what they called "Butch's meadow," some five miles away, to put up eighty or ninety tons more. There was just a one room, one window, dirt floor cabin there. Art had helped build it the winter before. Talk about rough! That was the roughest meadow I ever worked on. I was mostly on a mower or rake and sure had to put some padding under me and then needed to be cinched down to hold on. A mower got broken and I had to take a pack horse and make a rush trip in to Alexis Creek for a welding repair job.

While we were working on Butch's meadow, the Indians got a parcel for me from Alexis Creek and one evening I went over to their camp to get it. I still hadn't too much experience in swamp country and our prairie horses hadn't either. Lexie went with me and headed right across a neck of swamp on his "swamp cayuse" (web-footed). I had my doubts but followed rather than have him laugh at me. Just a little ways out my horse bogged down. We finally got her out but I had to go away out around the swamp both ways. The parcel was a wonderful surprise: a .32 Remington rifle for a birthday present from my cousin Ralph in Alberta. When in Alexis Creek for the

71

mower repairs I got two boxes of ammunition for it at Tom Lee's store. Those two boxes looked like they'd been in stock for forty years or better and apparently they were well past their prime. We did some target practice and found that only about one in three would go off.

The Indians brought out a telegram to us from Pierre, saying that he would be bringing cattle out to Prince George, and wanting one of us to meet him with saddle horses and pack horses to bring the cattle down to Quesnel and over to Marsh's meadow. Art and I could have got in another week's haying, but Butch told us we'd better go. Slim had come back over from Maindley's, so we shod our horses and started out right away, as I was the only one to meet him and only just had time to make the date. We gathered our riggin' and headed across country on the trail Lexie had shown to Art.

An empire of hay and grass awaited us. Grass that had grown and rotted down year after year since time immemorial, had fertilized these meadows and creek flats, and in some there was a growth of wild hay well over six feet high. This looked to be the makin's of a good-sized ranch for the four of us. Our second night's camp was at what we called the "Long John" meadow, as Lexie and his Dad, Old Long Johnnie, had trapped there for years. This was the meadow that Lexie figured was the ace in the hole. To us it wasn't the best, with such coarse rip-gut hay; the finer grass on the other meadows and creek flats was more to our liking, but the total was impressive.

It was around October 10th and the moose were still running in high gear. An hour or so before daylight, a big bull came right close to camp and scared old Kate into trying to drag the big root she was staked to right into camp. I heard the commotion, jerked my pants on and grabbed my rifle, then went out to see what was going on before we got set afoot. The bull had got up to within a few feet of old Kate who, finding her root too hard to drag any further, just stood frozen. I didn't want to shoot the moose, as we had all our packs loaded and it was too far to take the meat. So I just watched awhile and finally the moose decided to investigate some of the other horses and started grunting his way up the meadow. I got the bridle on Kate and climbed on to follow up and try to stop the bunch from being stampeded.

There were two horses tangled up with stake ropes on the trail and the moose went right through between them, sedate and majestic as could be. They stood frozen like scared rabbits. Twenty feet from a mad bull was a lot closer than they cared to be. The other horses were still further up, some hobbled and some loose. The bull headed on towards them but stopped when I got even with him about twenty yards from the edge of the meadow. Suddenly he swung towards me.

72

It was still dark enough for the flash of the rifle to show and I had hopes the noise and the flash would scare him away, so I shot in the air. He stopped and I shot again but he paid no attention. I tried to shoot again but the cartridge wouldn't go off, even after several tries, and the next one was the same. Made me some nervous and I wondered just what would be the best procedure if he came right after me. But he stayed put and I oozed away towards the horse bunch, aiming to get hold of as many as I could. However, as soon as I started to move, the horses came out of the freeze and stampeded every which way into the timber, as much towards me as away. I got ahead of a few and started catching them and tying them up, just as Art came up on foot to help. We left the moose to his own devices. He was still standing there right where the horses had stampeded from, when we were ready to leave a couple of hours later.

On the fourth day from Butch's we passed through Tibbles' and Paley's. All the kids ran in and nobody came out so we rode on to set up camp at Beaver Dam. That was about the only time we never stopped to say "howdy" or throw our feet under the table for a meal or stay overnight. But I'll bet there was plenty of curiosity over our outfit of three men and eight horses. While we were camped that night Jim Tibbles came along in what everyone called his "Old Yeller Knight," a one-ton truck considerably the worse for wear. Alec Paley was with him. They stopped and we all got acquainted.

In view of these folks being our nearest neighbours by road for forty-odd years, I will introduce them here with a few highlights of their pioneering.

Jim Tibbles was raised in Washington and Nebraska, and worked in construction camps in Idaho and Montana. Sarah, his wife, was raised a Mormon in Utah. Her folks migrated to Montana and I can remember her telling us that they circled their wagons at night and set up a guard in case of Indian attacks. In 1912 when Jim and Sarah decided to move up to Canada they gathered their riggin' into an immigrant car and brought Joe Spehar, an Austrian boy who could hardly speak or understand English. By then they had three children, Thelma, Lizzie and Helen. They landed in Ashcroft and started from there in a covered wagon, with five horses, a burro and a big St. Bernard dog. They made it to Quesnel in early August and moved on up to Six Mile on the Nazko road. Most of the Nazko road from there on was nonexistent at that time. They rode around scouting for land and gathered up some help to cut the road to Nazko Valley.

Jim pre-empted land on the Nazko River two miles from where it ran into the Blackwater River. This later become Joe Spehar's home ranch. Jim built a small cabin there but then decided to move back thirty miles to Udy Creek. In April of 1913 he decided he was too far from town and so moved his family back to Charlie Bouchie's place, a few miles west of Puntataenkut Lake, familiarly known as Tibbles Lake. During the summer, he found a flat along Baker Creek, homesteaded it and cut over four miles of road to it. As soon as the road was cut, the family moved to within half a mile of the homestead and lived in a tent, while they put up some hay and built a log house. Here they had four more children, Fred, Jack, Elsie and a little boy they later lost. The children were all born at home without benefit of doctor. Jim was midwife for the little boy they lost. Mrs. Julius Quanstrom was midwife for Elsie. The Quanstroms were new neighbours about eight miles away, not long out from Sweden. Lizzie tells of how shy Emma Quanstrom was at first. She saw somebody coming when she was out helping Julius in the hayfield and hid behind a haycock till they left. She was wearing a pair of Julius' overalls, something that was unheard of back in Sweden, and she sure didn't aim to let anyone see her in pants!

Another time she was out fishing and saw somebody wearing a red coat. She figured it was a Mountie and wasn't sure if she was obeying the laws of Canada, so she crawled out of sight till she could get up and run home! Still another yarn about Mrs. Quanstrom concerns Old Jerry Boyd stopping at Quanstrom's. Julius and the boys were away. Jerry says, "My horse sick." Mrs. Quanstrom says, "What kind sick?" Jerry says, "Bad sick." Mrs. Quanstrom: "What trouble?" Jerry: "My horse can't pish." Mrs. Quanstrom hunted up a bottle of sweet nitre and showed Jerry how much to give. Despite the broken English on both sides the message got across and the horse was shortly relieved of his suffering.

From 1915 on, Julius Quanstrom, Fred Norberg, Jim Tibbles, Kluskus Mac, Old Michelle and Billy Townsend trapped all over the Baker Creek and Nazko areas and way up into the Itcha Mountains. On these longer trips they used dog teams and snowshoes. On shorter routes where feed was available they used saddle horses and pack horses.

Alec Paley migrated from Iowa and Montana to Canada in 1920. Alec was a man of many parts. He had been a professional baseball player, had served in the U.S. Marines, was a professional gambler, a prospector in Montana and later in the Barkerville area, a fur trader and from there to a cattle rancher. He started a trading post in Kluskus in 1925 and in June of 1926 he and Lizzie Tibbles were married.

Alec and Lizzie lived in Kluskus for four years, although Lizzie came home to the Baker Creek place for her children to be born. They had six boys and one girl; Wallace, Bob, Harold, Wayne and Mary were born at home, and Ken and Fred in hospital. When they were living at Kluskus they were approximately one hundred and thirty miles from town and doctors, all of this wagon or saddle horse road at that time; being so rough a road it took two long days with a team from Kluskus to Nazko, and nothing but an Indian rancheree and Paul Krestenuk's store there. It was close to seventy miles, another long two days' travel, to Quesnel. Lizzie tells of one trip she made, riding out on a saddle horse packing Wallace in front of her on the saddle, to get medicine for sick Indians. She made another trip in the wagon from the Nazko with two babies. The mosquitoes were so thick at the Summit meadow where she noon camped, that she just fed the babies cold milk and kept coming to keep herself, the babies and horses from being eaten alive.

Thelma Tibbles married Joe Cooper and they had seven children, Emma, George, Tom, May, Bertha, Fay and Flora, before Joe passed away. All her children were born without benefit of doctor. In the spring of '25 Themla and Joe were finishing up feeding at the Townsend meadow, twelve miles from home. Thelma found a colt bogged down in the meadow. Lifting it brought on the signs that indicated Tom was about to be born. Joe was out beaver trapping or riding range. She knew also that Lizzie and her Dad were in the general area trapping beaver, so she shot a rifle off a few times hoping someone might be near enough to hear and come in to help her. Apparently no one was near enough to hear the distress signals; no help arrived so Thelma went about the business of having her baby alone. Tom had only his mother, four-year-old Emma and two-year-old George to greet him when he arrived on the scene.

Tibbles ran some sheep and cattle, and trapped and hunted, and worked on road construction. Deer, fish, and garden produce were the mainstays of life. There were no moose in the country when they first came in and it was not till about four years later that they saw their first moose track. Apparently moose migrated in from northwestern Alberta, attaining a peak population in the late thirties and early forties. Then timber wolves also reached a peak population and decimated the moose herds, probably reducing their numbers by more than two-thirds before being controlled somewhat by predator hunters. Jim and Fred Tibbles and Julius Quantrom and his boys, Harry, Willie and Carl, started guiding moose hunters, and Fred and Carl are the oldest original guides in the whole area still in the business.

Tibbles Sr., the Coopers and the Paleys, and later Fred and his wife Elsie, all lived for years within a half mile of each other and the

Tibbles' homestead, thirty-five miles from Quesnel. R. L. Marsh used to tell of one time Jim and Sarah were in town in the winter. Snow was fairly deep and trails were bad. As they were leaving town with their sleigh load of groceries, Sarah reminded Jim that Grevatts had asked them to bring out a twenty-pound bucket of lard. Jim figured they had all the load the team could handle and he hollered out for everyone to hear, "To hell with Grevatts and his lard. Let him spit in the fry pan." Jim then whipped up the team and away they went for home.

From Beaver Dam, where we got acquainted with Jim and Alec, we went on to Quesnel. The first and most important thing to do was to file pre-emptions on strategic meadows in the area we had seen. Art filed on what we called the Ramsay Creek meadow, Slim on the Long John meadow, and I on a meadow at the far end of Big Fish Lake that none of us had seen but Marsh had recommended as a possibility. Burnstad filed on a creek flat on Baker Creek that was supposed to become the home ranch for all of us. This cost us two dollars each. The homestead laws require a man to live on his pre-emption six months of the year and to do fifteen hundred dollars' worth of improvements in five years. Paley used to say, "You bet the government two dollars you can make it and they take your money in advance, knowing you'll lose and owe it to them anyway."

Slim was to go out to Marsh's meadow, fix things up ready for winter there, and then bring the wagon to town to meet Pierre and me with the cattle from Prince George. Art had to go back over to feed for Butch now that he had successfully guided us through the trail Lexie had shown him.

I left the boys in town and hit right out for Prince George as I only had two days to make the trip by the date Pierre was supposed to arrive with the cattle. Since it was a distance of eighty-three miles, I rode fairly late the first night and then headed into a place which seemed to be a farmhouse to see if I could get horse feed and put up for the night. Apparently I had struck either a widow's place or the old man was away and just the lady of the house and her two daughters were home. The elder daughter came to the door and I spoke my piece. She looked goggled-eyed at me and said, "Mother, there's a real cow-boy here and he wants to stay overnight." That likely brought a blush to me and brought mother on the run with the younger daughter trailing close. Apparently the lady wasn't sure that this would be according to Hoyle, there being no menfolks around, but the gals kept whispering, "Oh, can't he stay, Mother?" and she allowed as maybe I could if I'd look after my horses myself, which I fully intended to do.

They produced a lantern and pointed to the barn. I looked after my cayuses and went back in for the question period. I was hungry as a bear but didn't mention it. However, finally they had a light lunch before bedding down and I made the most of it, trying not to let them notice I could have eaten the whole works and a full course dinner on top of it. No, I didn't get to sleep with the baby, as the saying goes. Had to roll my blankets out on the kitchen floor. Sure did plenty of justice to breakfast, too, but not very early, so it was quite late when I arrived in Prince George. I had quite a time locating a livery barn to put my horses up. Then I took on an outsize feed myself to make up for all I had missed.

Next day I started making enquiries at the railway station, post office and telegraph office, but no word from Pierre. I moved my horses out of the barn and set up at our old camp by the forks of the Fraser and Nechako rivers, and still no word from Pierre. At the end of a week I said "to hell with him" and went back to Quesnel. Slim was in and had just got a letter from Pierre to say he hadn't got the cattle; the letter had been sent after he was supposed to meet me in Prince George. I was some little peeved.

CHAPTER VII

First Winter

By now it was time to get ready for winter. Art and I had each bought us a new Stetson hat over at Alexis Creek, and had sent to Eaton's for a Hudson's Bay blanket apiece so we wouldn't have to camp in henskin saddle blankets any more. Slim saved all his wages for grub. He figured it was apt to be a long winter and he'd need it all. He knew he was a good feeder and had a lot of room to put it in. He was only about eighteen then but the makings of a big man. So we bought a load of grub and some winter underwear and other rigging we figured we had to have. Then we invested in a jug of wine and a small bottle of rum, mixed them, and proceeded to tie one on. During the evening we got mixed up with R. L. Marsh, Henry Perry, John Carlson and Cope, some of the old-timers around. In the morning we had some extra livestock. Perry had given us an Airedale dog, Marsh had given us two cats and two old hens. Well, we named the dog "Joker" and the cats "Black Jack" and "Calamity Jane," loaded cats and hens in the wagon, tied the dog behind and headed out to the meadow.

Slim and I went to work getting things ready at the meadow for winter. We chinked the new cabin up, peeled the bark off the logs, put a window and door in, then repaired the other cabin. Then we built a toilet; for the seat we split and hewed a big green jack pine. The Marshes came out to visit us a time or two and Mrs. Marsh called it "the refrigerator."

After Pierre and family came he decided to buy a few heifers from Websters down the Fraser below Quesnel. We made a trip down there to pick them out and bring them home. We were lucky and ran into a dance where we got acquainted with quite a lot of folks. During the winter we got to several dances up at Six Mile Hall on the Nazko road and got to know folks up in that neighbourhood. There didn't seem to be much to do though, with Slim and Pierre and I to look after about eight head of heifers and six horses, so I headed over to the Martin meadow to visit Art for his birthday, February 1st, and to make plans for the coming summer.

Before setting out for the Martin meadow I was enquiring about stopping places on the road as I had forgotten mileages, and summer and winter travel are quite different. Someone told me "Frenchy" was in town from the Nazko and I ran into him and asked his opinion. In his broken English he said, "Don't stop at Cocky Evans, he will sharge you. You stay with Wally Gravett, he will sharge you nutting." I'm afraid I didn't put too much stock in this advice and first night from town I stopped at Cocky's and, then as always, I was welcome whether or not I paid. Frenchy had done something not quite according to Hoyle that put old Cocky on the fight, and had lost his welcome. Cocky was tickled to see me and we chattered away into the night, at least he did, with plenty of hand-waving like a Frenchman to dramatize his yarns. He was a little withered-up Cockney right out of London and that night I sized him up as not being long for this world. He was a veteran of World War I. That, and all the benders he'd been on for a week or so at a time, had been pretty tough on him. I heard his old tummy gurgling away and wondered if he'd make it to green grass.

About fifteen years later I packed a moose in for him off Milburn Lake Mountain on my way through with a horse outfit. I told Cocky to climb on one of the cayuses. "Oh no, you don't get me on none of yer bloody broncs," says Cocky, and hits out on foot leading a pack horse. Believe me, that cayuse was winded going up the mountain empty before Cocky drew a deep breath, and him around sixty-five then. He was another old-timer who helped build the Nazko road and he told me the yarn about how Hangman Springs got its name. I guess the road camp cook's lady friend had jilted him; anyway, when the boys rolled out for breakfast one day, there was the cook hung between the cook tent and bunk tent. A real appetizer for breakfast. The story goes that Cocky went to town to get the police. By the time he got to town he had worked up a hefty thirst and one drink led to another telling the gory details. The upshot was Cocky was away on a week's drunk, before telling the police. When he finally went broke and sobered up enough to hunt the police up and escort them out, they met Jim Tibbles bringing the corpse in. Of course by this time it was getting pretty high smelling. Probably saved the taxpayers a few dimes.

The night after Cocky's I was just going to make camp in the old Bouchie meadow cabin some twenty miles further on and planned to make it to Shorty Harrington's the next night. The old shack was a pretty dingy-looking rat hole and I didn't have much of a camp outfit or grub. However, it was too far to go on over the mountain and so this was to be home for the night. Just then Harry Quanstrom and Fred Tibbles came riding up. We introduced ourselves and Fred talked me into going back and over to their place with them. That night I met the whole Tibbles and Paley families. Fred had a set of boxing gloves and he and Jack, Harry and I, all did a little sparring and some wrestling and did most of the stunts we could think of. They even put the big gloves on little Bob and Wallace who were about four and five years old at the time. Then they talked me into staying the next day to go fishing. They would have kept me around for a month, I think, if I hadn't had other plans.

After I got to Shorty's it turned cold and went down to 58 below. I sure didn't need any coaxing to stay with Shorty. I stayed a whole week before it let up enough so I could wend my way up the river. Shorty and I went down to the Rancheree one morning and every klooch in the Rancheree was out bucking wood, either with a crosscut or swede saw. A lot of them had buckskin coats on with long fringes and they really looked picturesque with all the fringes swinging back and forth to the sawing rhythm. Flem, Shorty's oldest brother, was running in partnership with him at this time. He was feeding the big stock at MacFarlane meadow, twelve miles up off the Nazko, and Shorty just had calves and bulls to feed. Mostly there was the same routine of work every day: a few chores feeding horses before breakfast, etc., calves and bulls to feed after breakfast, then up the Pennington Mountain to First Creek meadow six miles away for a load of hay, feed that out and feed up in the barn, get wood in and by that time it was about four-thirty or five. Then we would cook dinner and supper in one, and take on a big fill. After supper Shorty would curl up in the old chair and tell jokes and yarns for four or five hours till bedtime. Not till I'd stayed a week did Shorty repeat a joke and when that happened I figured best I be a movin' on.

Next day I hit the saddle and headed up the river to Big Jim Blaine's for the night. Saw thirty-seven moose on the day's ride and lots of them close enough so that I could have tossed a rope on. Jim wasn't too flush for blankets and I had a brand new experience. Jim had a moosehide stretched in a bed frame and tight as a drum, hard as flint, dried rawhide. With the hair side up it looked as though it would be warm. I've slept on lots of corduroy floors, bare ground, rock even, but there was something different about that tight-stretched moosehide. I just couldn't get comfortable enough to sleep. Probably I was a wee bit chilly as I was only packing a light henskin blanket behind the saddle, and Jim hadn't much to add to it. The tag end of the cold snap was still around 30 below at night. If I'd been warm enough I think I could have slept on a tack!

Jim wanted me to stay longer but I could still make it for Art's birthday and headed on up to the Martin meadow next day. Butch and family were all there but Art was still feeding over at Butch's new meadow. I took another day getting over there as we all had to swap news at Butch's, and nobody in the sticks forty or fifty miles from civilization will let you get away without staying at least one night. I got over to where Art was feeding next day and we were sure tickled to get together again and had plenty big pow wow to make. Art had nearly finished the hay at Butch's meadow and I came in right handy helping to move the cattle and outfit back over to the Martin meadow. I stayed a few more days before heading back.

We made some of our plans for the spring operation. Slim and I were to load up a load of hay, good camp outfit and grub, move out five miles past Tibbles to the end of the wagon road, make camp and start cutting road, around March 15th. Art would come over and meet us as soon as he was done feeding.

Shorty had talked of letting me take some horses to break and I had spotted a couple of Indian horses I could buy cheap. Art figured that was all to the good and I took Smokey from him as I would need him to make a four-up on the load. That left him with "Sis" and "Blackie," two mares that he had bought the year before.

After a few days' stay at Butch's I headed back down the Nazko. Big Jim talked me into staying over a day to go hunting. He wanted to get up in a big open burn and demonstrate that he could easily shoot a moose anywhere from one thousand to two thousand yards away. But as soon as we got away from the river we ran out of tracks and so I just had to believe without seeing. Down at Shorty's again I told Shorty I would take one or two horses to break. He said he had a couple of old mares that were well bred and would make us good brood mares. He said he would give them to us for breaking the others if I wanted to take them. Also, he had a six-year-old bay gelding which an Indian had tackled breaking but found there was too much horse, so Shorty told me I could take him to break.

Little Jimmie Lick from the Rancheree came up and said he'd sell me a couple for thirty-five dollars so it looked like I was really going to get into horses right quick. Jimmie and I rode up to First Creek and Shorty took the hayrack and we rounded up the horse bunch. We found all we needed, corralled them and cut out the ones I wanted. I went right to work breaking the bay gelding to lead so I could take him home, along with one of the mares I bought from Jimmie and one Shorty gave me. We left them in the corral there that night; next day we went up and I tied the saddle on the bay. Shorty said I wasn't to call him "Red." He was a very reddish bay. I would likely have thought of some other name but from there on Red stuck!

I found I had quite a piece of horseflesh to rassle. I was in too much of a hurry to take it slow and easy, and loaded onto the red pony right quick and got unloaded almost as quickly. Twice more he throwed me way off into a snowbank. The next time I made it stick but was too played out to work him out enough to lead horses on him, so I went back to Shorty's for the night again. I got Jimmie to help me next day and tailed all the gentle horses together, and one that I had broken to lead, and let him take that string. Then I took two half broken ones to lead on my saddle horn and headed over to Joe Spehar's meadow, some four miles, so as to be as far on the way as I could for taking the outfit over the mountain next day. I sure had quite a pair to lead. One would run ahead and one pull back and it's a wonder I didn't get hung up in the middle. But I made the grade and the ponies learned quite a little more about leading.

Jimmie and his family were staying at Joe's, helping him when he needed it and trapping between whiles. So I got Jimmie to help me again in the morning. Once we got the horses turned onto the Nazko road in the right direction, I figured I could handle them okay. I would like to have taken a lunch but nobody suggested it and I didn't either. Breakfast was at six and we got away at seven. Jimmie left me to it after we got about a mile on the Nazko road. There was nothing to it from there till I got to where I wanted to turn off. The deep snow hemmed the horses in but made it practically impossible for me to head them off. I knew I had to be on the Nazko side of them or they would break back and I'd sure lose them.

I wanted to turn in on a shortcut to the Tibbles as they told me to be sure to come in on my way back. I was riding Smokey, the strongest saddle horse in the outfit. I swung out to try to head them but found the snow nearly four-feet deep. The gentle horses made the turn okay but the three unbroken ones kept right on. That was the worst that could happen as there were Nazko horses in both bunches and I didn't know what to do. I chased the gentle horses in some distance and then tried for a mile to make the others break off the trail before I finally made it, but when I got them to the gentle bunch, one of them had gone back. I had just about played out myself and Smokey trying to head the other bunch but hated to lose that one, so I took my rope down and started after her. She was paddling along in no hurry, taking careful steps to keep from breaking off the sleigh trail.

I knew if I tried to run her she'd perk right up and make better time than I could, so I just spurred Smokey into walking as fast as he could to catch up on her easy without scaring her any till I could get in roping distance. I figured one try would be it, as it would take half the night to catch up again, and it was already about ten p.m. I never made a luckier shot and I had the rope tied hard and fast so I wouldn't lose both horse and rope on a long shot like that.

This horse was "Klooch," one I had bought from Jimmie, and I swapped riggin' onto her right there and headed back. By this time the whole bunch had come back onto the Nazko road and I figured I would have to make it clean to Quesnel before I could take a chance on turning them again. But most of the bunch turned into the old Bouchie meadow when they came to that trail and it was no trick to turn the others in this time. I wasn't too enthusiastic about going in there with no corral and a cold old rat-nest cabin. It was about 20 below zero and nearly midnight. Man, was I tickled when I saw a light in the cabin. Fred Tibbles and Fred Norberg had been moose hunting and had wounded one with a six-gun the day before. They had had to hunt it up and butcher it, so they had camped there and had a big stew pot of this moose cooking.

I was as near to played out as I ever got, and also badly shaken up from bucking that deep snow, with my saddle horse breaking off the trail every which way and throwing me back and forth every jump and pounding hell outa me. Also, I was hungry as a she wolf with ten pups. I waded right into that mulligan pot. Well, the darn stuff wasn't so good. The moose had died overnight without being bled and that bloodshot meat made me sick. So altogether I don't have any pleasant memories of that night.

I didn't have any more trouble on the trip. The working over that night and the big day's travel made the ponies bunch-broke and all I had to do was to head one and they all turned. It was nice getting back to the meadow with all those horses. We had always been used to good horseflesh and plenty of it. It was plumb agin our religion to put a collar on a saddle horse or ride anything that had ever packed a collar. At least we would have cayuses to ride now although we still had a nondescript outfit for freighting or even haying. So we set about breaking out the broomtails. Despite Slim's having been raised on a horse ranch he was a little young to know much about breaking horses. Well, I figured one of the mares Shorty had given us would be a good one for him to practice on. I was mistaken. We called the mare Flossie and the more we saw of her the more we liked her. She must have been really well bred as she had perfect action for a saddle horse but was very high-strung and would get panicky and tremble all over if handled too roughly. Had she been broken carefully and gently she would never have bucked and, although middle-aged, she was very easily trained.

Anything for fun and excitement in those days. We helped Slim get his riggin' on her and get aboard, then turned him loose and told him to throw the steel to her. Flossie uncoiled and lit into bucking and unloaded Slim pretty fast, but he was game to get on again and go for more. He pulled leather a little till we hollered like hell and told him that wasn't according to Hoyle. The old gal kept right on bucking, seemed like for twenty minutes. It probably wasn't that long. Then she quit and just stood her ground, balked and wouldn't move a muscle and Slim couldn't make her move. I had brains enough then to realize we weren't working with any cold-blooded cayuse, so I told Slim we best let her go for the day. Later I took her over and petted her a lot, then gradually worked onto her bareback and guided her this way and that with my hand on her neck. In just a little while she seemed to know what I wanted her to do and was plumb willing, so no more rough stuff for her.

I took a different tack on Red. I tied up a hind foot, then saddled him and got on and off either side time and time again; petted and slapped him all over and slapped my chaps, coiled my rope, threw it and repeated this over and over till he paid no attention. Then the boys turned his foot loose and I jarred him loose. He went after me but I stayed glued down that time and rode him out. Then he bolted through thick willows and into the timber. He nearly got rid of me in the willows but once clear of them I was okay, and gradually headed him back into the open meadow and got a quirt working on his neck to break him to neckrein. By the time I got him back to the buildings he was handling pretty well. I was mighty weary and some gaunt.

The other mare I bought from Jimmie was an easy one to break. She was as gentle as a kitten. Pierre was leading her out to water and wondered if it wouldn't be as easy to ride as walk, so climbed aboard bareback and she packed him right down to the water hole and back to the barn without seeming to notice the difference. Before we finished properly breaking her I sold her for forty dollars. So we made a few dimes on her.

CHAPTER VIII

The Move to Baker Creek — Cutting Lavington Road

Our next move was for Slim and me to shoe our four-up, pack our junk and hit for town. There we bought what riggin' we needed to head out to cut our highway. We had hauled Marsh's share of the hay we put up on his meadow into town and we hauled in some extra to pay our barn bill. By this time Slim and Florence (Marsh's oldest daughter) were commencing to pay quite a little attention to each other. Marsh gave us a few tips on what we would need and said he figured we might be a little early, as the snow was pretty deep yet and might stay quite awhile. But we were too young and impatient to be starting something on our own to pay much attention.

Before we left town we'd got down to about three dollars. We thought that would buy us a going-away mickey of rum. But Slim remembered he needed a pair of moccasin rubbers. I told him the rubbers would be more necessary than the rum, but that he had to figure it out. We started out with the load and Slim rode back to get either the rum or the rubbers. He caught up to me on the Six Mile Hill, riding like a wild Indian, a hootin' and a hollerin'. I guessed right away he'd gone for the rum. He had, but what really tickled him was he'd got as cheap a pair of rubbers as he could find for one dollar and still had enough for a small bottle of rum. Then he was afraid the bottle would wear a hole in his pocket so he packed it in his hand and temptation got the better of him. The bottle had a cork and Slim had no corkscrew, so he hit the bottom of the bottle with the palm of his hand and popped the neck right off the bottle. He had to start lapping up the rum as fast as he could to keep from wasting it. Then he tied his bandana over the jagged end — all this on a saddle horse. He found it was still spilling out some so had to take a few more guzzles before he caught up to me. Being too difficult to pack like that we just had to kill the works and before we got to Six Mile we had a high old glow on for a send off. This seemed to be the ideal place to dump about three ovens off the 800-pound stove. As far as I know, they're still there.

We landed at the end of the road and set up camp ready to start road cutting on the 18th of March. We had had to break trail through over three feet of snow for the last few miles and things didn't look too prosperous for horse feed for awhile. The first night we tied the horses to the hay load and rolled our bedrolls out on top. Those hungry cayuses ate and ate their way in under us till we had to hang onto each other's hair by morning to keep from rolling off the load. After that we portioned hay out to them pretty carefully to spin it out till grass showed up.

It was uphill work cutting road in that much snow. We had no experience but from all the crooked roads we had seen we decided we'd make this one straight and be different. Also, high stumps didn't appeal to us any and we had all decided to cut them right down to the ground. Every tree had to have the snow tramped down or kicked away from round it so we could cut low. We went dead straight for two hundred yards. You could see from one end to the other and, man, we were proud of it. But if we kept on straight we had to go across a creek canyon. That didn't look good at all. The next best bet was to make a gradual curve around a sidehill where we would have to make a grade later when the ground thawed out. From there on we rode ahead and figured out the best grades and the lay of the country, and blazed ahead a long distance to avoid running into insurmountable objects. But we found we had to do as others did and make bends every little bit.

Some days we hit thick timber and would slow right down. Then we'd hit open timber and the snow would be shallower and bare around the base of trees and we would go like a house afire. Other than time for cooking we worked from daylight to dark. We had so much energy and ambition we'd even rassle and twist wrists after supper at night. Slim was bigger than me by then but, being older, I could still hold my own but not for long.

One night we decided we had to have a bath. So we built two campfires far enough apart as we figured to have a bath in between and be warm both sides thataway. Slim tried first. It was just right while he was dry but as soon as he got wet he came a-whooping out of there. The steam almost scalded him to death. So it was a case of kick out one fire and do a kind of revolving dance to keep warm on both sides. Had anyone been around with a modern movie camera they could have taken some comical pictures.

We got up to where a swamp blocked us off on one side of the creek. That meant crossing the creek to continue up the other side so Slim and I decided a bridge had to be built. This also was new

86

doings for us. We picked our bridge site some seventy feet from bank to bank. We couldn't figure any way to get stringers across other than falling them straight across the creek, so the site had to be where we could fall at least three stringers across. That was the most we could find in any one place, two on one side and one on the other. They were great big spruce that we figured would hold anything. I had enough experience falling to get them all to go right where we wanted them and then we got them set.

We moved the camp up to this site and found the flats up there had bare patches on them so we turned all but the wrangle horse loose. We cut the covering for the bridge, got a team in and hauled it in, covered our bridge and then did a step dance across it. Slim said, "That'll hold the biggest freight train in the world." I jumped up and down on it and he wasn't so sure then. So we decided to put piers under the stringers and that did make it quite solid. It was our first bridge anywhere and the first bridge on Upper Baker Creek. We learned quite a bit building that one and by midsummer had built sixteen more, some large and some small.

By the 4th of April we had cut our way up to Burnstad's pre-emption and had cut a few cabin logs when we heard a holler that sounded right good to me. Art had broken trail through to join us and he had a can of strawberry jam in his pack. It was unopened. We opened it and cleaned it up at one sitting! Four pounds of it!

We had run out of meat and had eaten a long way into our beans and rice sacks. We still had to wait for high water to come and go before we could go out for more grub, so meat was a must and I went hunting. It was all new country to all of us. At that time of year there were no deer, and moose had left the valleys and headed for the hills. I followed one moose all day and it never fed or even bedded down so no meat that day. Two days more and still no luck. Then I saw one the next morning before I got far from camp. It was over six hundred yards away and I was sure I'd never get closer, so I opened fire and connected on the second shot. But I couldn't connect again and ran out of ammunition before it got out of sight. I had to light out for camp to get ammo and then tried to circle the moose and come in from the other way. There was still good tracking snow in the timber although the meadows were bare. I was lucky and got right up close and got in a good shot. We had meat for quite a spell.

So we went to building the cabin. This was to be headquarters for all of us so we built a pretty good-sized cabin about twenty-four feet by thirty feet. We used the saddle notch in all our buildings. It is a good strong notch if cut right and needs no nails or pegs to hold the logs. We split timber to put on the roof, put moss in the cracks of the split timber and then put about a foot of dirt on top of that. This type of roof loses no heat and will hold quite a shower. But it does leak in a heavy storm (and quite a while after). The 800-pound stove had its final resting place.

Then we back-tracked down the road to where we had to put in grades. We had an old walking plow and we built a little V grader. We had no powder so if we ran into stumps or rocks too big for the plow, we just had to get down and dig like badgers till we could get a chain on them and pull them out with a team.

High water had started by then. The neighbours from the settlement, Tibbles and Coopers, had started out on their beaver trapping and we had visitors quite regularly. We thought we were getting pretty popular with the neighbours and then one day Fred told us the wherefore. We were camped right close to a beaver dam and this dam was practically on the dividing line between Tibbles' and Cooper's trapline. There was considerable friction and dispute between them over who was to get the beaver. They both figured we were camped there to beat them out altogether. But they had been watching from the hills around and saw we were plumb wrapped up in our own business and, although they could hardly believe it, we didn't even know the beaver were there till Fred told us.

Fred camped with us one night and helped build grade all day. We had three quite long grades to build and had to widen out the odd place. Then the road was ready to bring wagons and the rest of the outfit as far as the new cabin on Burnstad's flat. As soon as high water started to go down a bit we headed to town to get grub, and on down to get Pierre and family and his cattle. This was around the 10th of May, I believe. But on the way down we found out that the old bridge on Tibbles' West Creek had been too much shaken up with high water and so we had to stop and build another bridge. Jim Tibbles helped us and we stayed at his place. Slim and I got our first feed of vegetables in nearly two months. Mrs. Tibbles had a big feed of turnips cooked up when we got there and, although I never liked turnips before, they tasted real good that time. The bridge only took us a little more than a day and then we were on our way again.

On this trip to town Art decided to tackle the lion in his den. He went to the government agent and explained that we were cutting nearly thirty miles of road into a prospective ranch site. Could we get any government help? It paid off. They supplied us with two shovels, two grubhoes, two old dull axes and a very precious box of stumping powder. We found Burnstad had moved all the outfit down from the meadow to Marsh's homestead near the Fraser River, only twelve miles from town. Three of the Nazko horses had headed across country for home. As Baker Creek was still high we figured they might have bottled up in a bend of the creek somewhere so Pierre and I went after them, and the rest started out for town and on to our new home. Pierre and I rode up through Higdon's and on through Baker's meadow over to Baker Creek. We struck horse tracks on the bench above the creek and they were easy to follow. It was pretty cold the first night out with nothing but wet saddle blankets for bedding and a kettle of rice for supper. I was used to camping out and slept fine but Pierre didn't do so well.

Next day we found where the horses had run into a little creek that just fell over the edge down into Baker Creek in a series of picturesque little waterfalls. The horses hadn't been able to find a crossing on this little creek so they dived down over the edge and over to Baker Creek where they made a crossing and were well on their way to the Nazko. We were too far behind them for further tracking to be of any use. So we went up to the Nazko road and towards Quesnel till we met the wagons and outfit camped at a place near Walter Merz's, eight miles from town. They had lost some of the cattle the night they camped below Six Mile and had to go hunting. Most of the heifers had calves and we could hold them easily by roping the calves and tying them up at night. But the dry heifers had mixed with other stock. Slim and Jessie had moved the wagons on up and Art had gone back for the other cows. He found them that night with the help of several of the young ladies around Six Mile. From all the female help that seemed to be around, Slim and I were sure wishing the cows would get lost again but it didn't work out that way.

On the way through Quesnel they had bought a case of eggs (thirty-six dozen) and the night they camped by Merz's, Art and Slim had an egg-eating contest. Slim quit at eighteen but Art went on to twenty-two and said he could have easily eaten more if they had been fried softer. Art's willing female helpers were there in full force to see us on our way next day and some kept us company nearly to Cocky Evans' before turning back.

We made it the rest of the way with no setbacks. When we got to Tibbles' they had a big three-year-old steer out in the yard. I told them we could have some fun if it was okay for me to rope him and ride him. They were all for it so we dabbed a rope on him and I tied a loose rope surcingle on him, climbed aboard and they turned him loose. He bucked all over the place, then headed down into the creek

89

and stood pat. I had to pull the rope off and whip him out of it to get back to high ground.

Our big job, as soon as we got the outfit into Pierre's homestead, was to get organized to cut the rest of the road to Ramsay Creek meadow. We figured if we surveyed and blazed the few miles closest to Pierre's, he could cut that by himself whenever he got time and still look after things at home. So Art and I went to surveying the six miles up to the first meadow, Long John meadow. It was cloudy, stormy weather and we had all kinds of trouble getting this patch of road located. There are blazes all over the sticks where we headed out and we ran into one thing after another, and had to back-track and detour. Finally we went up to the meadow, worked back to join up, and made the connection. I believe that was the toughest patch of road we had to locate. Had we known the country better, it would have been much easier. First there was a long, steep hill up out of the Baker Creek valley. It was tough to find a decent grade on that hill. Then there were interlapping coulees coming up from both sides with steep banks. It wound up with our road being half-moon shaped. But we did get good grades on all the hills.

This first meadow up the road we also called the Cooper meadow. We found out after Slim filed on it that Joe Cooper had filed on it about six years before. Cooper had done nothing, so eventually the homestead inspector had to inspect it and Cooper's and Slim's claims were both disallowed. The government thus made the decision that the lot could only be purchased. But at the time we didn't know this and carried on figuring Slim would get it.

Slim, Art and I moved up there, started cutting road from that end and started building another cabin there. We got the cabin about six rounds high and had put a corduroy floor on it when we decided we might not have time to finish it and the road too. So we left the cabin and concentrated on the road on up to the Ramsay Creek meadow. This was to be our meadow headquarters, a distance of some thirteen miles on up. There was an old Indian trapline trail through this country and we followed it quite closely a lot of the way. Of course, where it went straight up or down hill, or across too wet or wide a swamp, we had to make detours and would be off it some distance at times. We never cut right straight through from anywhere but cut some from either end and joined up in the middle. We even went right up to Ramsay Creek meadow and cut from that end for awhile. I guess we figured a change was as good as a rest every so often. But we camped as close to the cutting as possible and worked hard from daylight to dark. At that time of year, that is a long, long day. I remember at one camp we had run out of nearly everything except meat. The cooking was very simple; we just kept a big mulligan pot of meat on the campfire and whenever we got hungry we would gobble up a plateful and hit back to work again. But the straight meat diet wasn't too good. We got hungry too quickly and gradually weakened. We ate seven times one day.

We finally got the road connected up to Long John or Cooper meadow and Pierre and Jessie moved up with us, having got things organized well enough to leave. We made a camp by the first creek over from Cooper meadow, about five miles further up. Our one little tent, seven feet by eight feet with two-foot walls, was the cook tent and the family bedroom for Pierre and Jessie. The night we camped there, we didn't get in till late and it was pouring rain, black dark, and we hadn't even a lantern for light. It was raining so hard we had our troubles getting a campfire going and no lights till we could get it roaring. After we had a much-delayed supper, Slim, Art and I grabbed our blanket rolls and went hunting a spruce tree we hoped wouldn't leak too much. We were all dead tired and soaked already. One of us thought of a big tree out in the middle of a little swampy meadow just back of camp, so headed for it. It looked good enough in the dark and we rolled in under it. We found it was pouring worse under the tree than outside and soon figured out the reason why. The tree had one stump but split into about six little ones and each funnelled rain onto the other and on down onto us. Slim stayed with it and almost drowned, but Art and I rolled our turkeys and went looking for another tree. We stumbled and wandered up the edge of the meadow till we finally found a really good tree and got a whale of a fire going. We dried out a lot and then called it a day around three a.m.

Another camp Art, Slim and I made in the dark was on a steep sidehill, all rocks. Art must have got propped against a rock or tied up to a tree and slept right through. But Slim and I kept falling downhill, sliding out of our blankets till we'd get on too wet or rocky ground, and have to move back up hill and try again.

Some nights it stayed warm pretty late and the mosquitoes in that high meadow and swamp country just swarmed in on us. You could reach out slowly and grab a handful. Most of them were full of blood. We had to keep smudges going till it got colder. They would leave us till sunup and then back to the attack. We were building what we called the "Kitty Corner Bridge" in the bottom of a steep little coulee where no wind could help keep the pests moving and they nearly ate us alive. That night our horses stampeded. We had some staked, some hobbled and some loose in a little meadow nearly half a mile from camp. We were just going to bed when the bells stopped ringing, then suddenly broke loose jangling to beat everything and away they went.

We all lined out after them in the dark. I got a head start in the trail. Somewhere we had picked up a black collie dog with a white tip on his tail. He was generally hunting rabbits and pretty much useless, but this time that white tip on his tail came in right handy. He trotted ahead of me on the trail and I could see that white tip. Knowing right where to go, I trotted right along behind. But even with Whiskers' white tail the horses got about five miles up the trail to Ramsay Creek before I caught up.

When I did, old Smokey was still hobbled and trailing behind. I started whistling and talking to him as soon as I could hear him so he wouldn't be scared, and finally he stopped. I was a little leery about riding the old bucking horse bareback in the dark, after he had just been spooked. All I had was a hackamore which was the first thing I picked up before starting out. However, I needn't have been scared. He was all stock horse and went right to work trying to stop the bunch for me. But they wouldn't stop. A big limb nearly took me right off and I lost my hat. I would get ahead and hold them for a few minutes and then they would pass me on both sides. So I tried a new wrinkle. I'd get ahead of one and jump down quick and catch it, take whatever rigging it had on its feet and tie it up; then catch up again and repeat till I got enough tied that they all stopped. I had horses tied up for three-quarters of a mile. Then the other boys caught up and we started back for camp and got there in nice daylight, in time to start work. Before I went to work, I went back and hunted up my hat.

Soon after that we had a long holdup. We found there was no way around one swamp where the headwaters of Baker Creek and Ramsay Creek intertwine. On two different swamps, the north end runs into Baker Creek and the south end into Ramsay Creek. So we had to find the narrowest crossing and build more than a hundred yards of corduroy and a small bridge as well. Here again the mosquitoes took their toll. It was scrubby timber with huge butts, spindly tops and long limbs. We had to use these or haul timber a considerable distance. We hadn't connected the road up to here yet, so had to skid all timber for bridges and corduroys. At one place along what we call the Baker Creek meadow we found a hogs-back for nearly a mile, just like a big railroad grade. This was formed by glacial action, I believe. There was very little timber on it and it was very conveniently going our way so was incorporated into our highway. Another place we went through a desolate patch of fresh burn, burned the year before we came in.

This was the genuine "sticks"; black sticks devoid of green or limbs. The stuff was hard and tough. We found we could almost push some of them over. So we tied a rope on and jerked them over with saddle horses, using team and chains on bigger ones. There were no stumps on this patch of road but lots of rocks.

One mountain had quite big timber on it so we used most of our stumping powder there. Art had had quite a little experience with powder working on the B.C. coast, so he was the powderman. I'm sure a lot of powder monkeys on present-day construction could learn plenty on the economical use of powder from Art. He sure spread one box of powder a long way.

Finally there came a day around the middle of July when there was only a short length to cut to join up the whole road. Pierre and Jessie were moving up from the lower end with wagon and camp outfit, and Slim and I came down from Ramsay Creek way to finish up. We had no dignitaries to cut ribbons or drive golden spikes, and not even a bottle of whiskey to celebrate the occasion. Slim and I cut the last trees, one on each side. This would have been dangerous at any time. Slim had been raised on the bald prairie and was no axeman. By this time he had whittled his boots down to a point. Unbelievably, he hadn't drawn any blood. Also, when trimming limbs, he had missed the limbs with the bit of the axe and broken them off with the axe handle about half the time. I hadn't realized how badly his axe handle had suffered from this treatment. On the final swipe at that last tree Slim took a mighty wind-up about three times around his head and drove her for that last cut. The axe head flew off with all of us right there and we never did find it again. Whether it flew off in mid-swing far enough or buried itself deep in the ground at the foot of the tree we never knew. We dug around but could find no evidence whatever. It was as though, since we were finished with the axe, it was spirited away. My cut felled the tree and we let a mighty whoop out of us, and started up the highway for Ramsay Creek.

Our next project was to build a cabin. We all cut logs for awhile, then Art and Pierre laid out the first round and squared them up. Slim cut more logs and I skidded them in till night.

Slim had been complaining of a pain in his right side and, fearing appendicitis, Pierre and Jessie started down the road next morning with Slim in the wagon. They took him right to town in the iron-tired wagon. He had to have an appendix operation. Slim never came back. After coming out of hospital, he started working for Marsh. The public works department allowed us a little money for the building of the road; with this we paid all Slim's expenses. Later he got work driving a ten-wheel truck up at Wingdam, then a job so far up in the north it took ten dollars to send a letter to him, as the saying goes.

Art and I highballed on the Ramsay Creek cabin. It was getting close to the time we'd have to get our hay up as we had a date to be back to Butch's for August 1st again. We rolled logs up and notched them down in less time than it takes to tell about it. Some didn't fit too well but we needed the practice and figured some time when we weren't in so much hurry we'd do a better job.

The whole project took us eight days exactly, from the ground up; a twenty-four by thirty-foot cabin, floored, roofed and hewed walls inside, not a spike in it except in the door and window jambs which we hewed out of straight-grained timber. At that time lamp gas and kerosene were sold in square five-gallon cans, two to the case. We only needed kerosene as we didn't use gas lamps for the first few years. But once we got one of those five-gallon cans empty we had the makings of a wash tub. We cut a side out and rolled back the sharp edges and crimped them with pliers. Then we had dish pan, wash boiler, wash tub and bath tub. You could only get one foot in at a time but if you stayed with it long enough you could make a pretty fair job of cleaning up. The boxes were well made — quite good lumber with dove-tailed corners — and were promptly made into shelves, cupboards or packboxes.

We had no lumber for windows as yet but bought enough lumber for a table, three long shelves and two windows on our next trip to town. This cabin and meadow are about seventy miles from town and, believe me, some of those miles, with team and iron-tired wagon or sleigh in deep snow, seem to be damn long ones. To this time we had cut nearly twenty-five miles of road, built two cabins and had nearly half built another cabin, built seventeen bridges, a one-hundred-yard corduroy and several shorter ones, and six grades of varying lengths, the longest about a quarter of a mile. All this was done from March 18th to some time before July 15th.

If we had to do it now, forty-five years later with our present infirmities, all with double-bitted axes and no machinery, I think it would take us seven years or better.

CHAPTER IX

A Hundred Head Rustled

Pierre was expecting his Dad and three sisters in to visit us all, so Art and I went right down to the settlement to meet them coming in. The folks — John Burnstad and Dorothy, Hattie and Jean — came all right, but we sure didn't have much of an outfit to meet them with. The wagon was pretty well loaded with groceries, camp outfit and everybody's warbag or suitcase. We had no extra saddle horses with us, so we took turns riding, and strung out a lass rope for anyone walking to hang onto. I'll bet the neighbours got quite a laugh out of all of us "prairie chickens."

From Pierre's we picked up another wagon and loaded on mowers and rake. Art, Pierre and I headed right on up to the Ramsay Creek meadow to start haying. John wouldn't stay down at the Burnstad place, so he walked up a day or so later. He met Pierre on the way back and asked him how far it was. Pierre told him about four miles. Then he met Art a couple of miles further up and asked Art how far. Art told him about four miles. "By God," he said, "I'm holding my own anyway."

While he was up at Ramsay meadow, John cut a wide swath of timber down to the meadow from the cabin so we could see out and up the meadow. This improved our view a hundred per cent.

The Ramsay Creek cabin got quite a warming when we all got in later with nine of us in that tally. Then Florence Marsh and Hazel Rawling rode up later to bring the tally to eleven.

I took the three Burnstad girls out one evening to the lakes about two miles from the cabin to see if we could see any moose. We sneaked up to the edge of the timber and there were seven moose out in the lake at varying distances from us. There were three little calves just a little way out in the water and later we found there was another on shore right close to us. I carefully hung onto old Whiskers for a long time, then forgot him for a moment and he got away and went after the little calf on shore. That really brought action and in a hurry. I had never guessed moose could swim so fast — almost as fast as they trot. The old cows came a-snorting to get their calves. The ones which

95

had their calves in the water took them out to other points on the lakeshore. But the one with the baby calf on shore near us came out and fought the dog off, then took her baby into the lake a ways and started feeding again alongside her little one. We watched till dark and the moose never did know we were there. We had quite a thrill.

Before starting haying operations we decided to take John and the girls over to Fish Lake and up the lake about six miles to see what kind of a place I had homesteaded. According to the map it was about fifteen miles but I think it seemed like fifty to some of us, not being too well mounted and not a bit sure of where we were going. There was an old survey trail across to Merston Creek which drains out of the lake. But the trail hadn't been used since the survey was made, and some had been burnt out. So what with flies, windfalls, mud and uncertainty we didn't enjoy the travelling too much. But the sight of Fish Lake cheered everybody up. It is a beautiful sight with a lovely campsite at the end where we first struck it. We made noon camp there and then pushed on up the lake and fought our way through windfalls at the far end till we came to my pre-emption.

It was most disappointing; not worth cutting road to. It was just a little boggy meadow around a very boggy pothole, mud lake or slough. There was no amount of feed around it and it was a real boghole trap for stock. We wanted no part of it, so I gave up the pre-emption; but we camped there overnight. In the morning there were three moose in the lake and one of them got stuck trying to get out on the shore across from us. It was almost out of sight in mud, but before we got breakfast ready it had wallowed its way through and on out. It was a lovely morning and we gave John and the girls coffee in bed so they could drink coffee and see some wildlife. Then we cooked a good old campfire breakfast with lots of sourdough hotcakes for all.

This was to be our last trip together and these were the folks we had been raised with. We had all enjoyed many good times together. Art was more or less going steady with the eldest girl, Dorothy, before he left for B.C. and I thought maybe he would talk her into staying in B.C. and building a ranch with him. But either he didn't talk enough or she didn't listen well enough 'cause they all got away on us. I could never make up my mind which one I liked best. I loved them all, Maw and Paw included.

I'm afraid our last evening together wasn't altogether a happy one. We had at least two campfires outside. Art and Dorothy had one and talked long and seriously, far into the night. Jean, Hattie and I had another one and we tried to be cheerful, but I just couldn't be. I hated to think of them leaving. I hadn't got to like the country yet although

I really got a thrill out of the road building and cabin building; with no womenfolk I could see a lonely life ahead. But it was a pretty tough set-up to ask anyone to share. We were thirty-three miles to nearest neighbours over a rough old wagon road in summer and snowbound in winter. We only had a bunch of nondescript horses and no marketable stock. Wages were then at their lowest ebb and work was scarce as hen's teeth. Then we were so mixed up in partnership and had enough friction already that none of us knew what the outcome would be. The only thing we were sure of was that we had enough ambition, guts and physical fitness to whip most any obstacles.

I'll never forget the next morning when the folks all pulled out. From all the noise and chatter of eleven people to just Art and me and the flies was quite a change. The silence just about beat me. But we gathered up a few tools as soon as the folks left, walked up the meadow, cut timber and built hay sleds until dark without stopping for dinner and hardly talking to each other all day. Being tired and damn hungry when we got back, the cabin didn't seem so empty.

From then we started turning moose pasture into hayfield, working early and late to be sure to get enough hay piled up to take care of any stock we had or might acquire. Pierre was aiming to put up what he could with Jessie's help down at his place and we were to help him stack it before going over to Butch's.

We got the walls up on an eight-horse barn during wet spells when we couldn't hay. There was so much old dead grass from years and years back that it had to be pretty dry to mow. So we got in a little time on the barn most mornings. The first haycrop on meadows is very poor in quality consisting of so much old bottom grass and moss. So we had to put up extra to make up the difference. The quality improves a lot for three or four years, and on a fairly high ground meadow the hay is nearly as heavy and as good as tame hay after two or three cuttings. It turned wet before we finished and we had to leave some in windrows and some in little haycocks. We hung our grub up from the ridge logs of the cabin hoping mice and rats wouldn't be too tough on it before we got back. But the roof leaking was something we never calculated on. When we returned from Butch's, our hundred-pound sugar sack was solid as a rock and dripping syrup. The flour was caked solid on the outside but still okay on the inside.

It was only twelve miles across to Butch's on the old Indian pack trail and we made it through in a day, although swamps and windfalls made it very slow travelling. We found on arrival that things were quite a little upset over at Butch's. When he made his summer roundup to brand, he found nearly a hundred head of cows and calves missing.

Somebody had gone to rustling with more than just a long rope and a running iron. They must have known Butch's schedule fairly well and run this bunch off the range soon after the cattle were turned out, when there was no one in that whole country for a couple of months. Lots of rain had washed tracks out completely and, since it was done in the height of the growing season, the places they had held the stock didn't show much sign. Butch took two Indians — Johnny Sam, the best trapper and tracker in the country, and Lexie, who knew the whole country. They travelled for about three months trying to locate the bunch. They found two or three holding places, enough to establish the direction the cattle were being taken, but then the rustlers crossed through range that had lots of stock on it. Tracking from there on was useless.

A lot of the cows came back home fairly early in the fall, but some not till after Christmas. However, the cows were all dry. Their un-branded calves had been weaned off them and mixed into someone else's herd. We tried back-tracking the cows that came in after there was snow, but they had invariably stopped at meadows any place there was feed enough to hold them awhile. The closer they got to home the longer they were apt to stay, and tracks back from there were unreadable. Also, they came in from different directions as though they had been held and probably turned loose in small bunches from different localities at differing times, so there wouldn't be any well-defined trail of a herd to follow.

Whoever did the rustling planned well and never slipped up on even the smallest detail and must have had a lot of cow-savvy. Poor old Butch was out two-thirds of his calf crop and several cows, also his time and wages for two men for three months, and all to no avail. Someone asked the inevitable question, "Did you look up that new outfit of cowboys who moved into the country north of you last year?"

"Oh yes," says Butch, "I got the missus keepin' track of them and I been all over their layout too and not a cow manure or track on any of it." So that let us out.

Butch put Art in charge of the haying outfit and we worked to beat the devil to make a good showing to help Butch out. This was his last year on the Martin meadow as his five-year contract with Duke ran out that year and he was not renewing it. He had to turn over one hundred head of cows to Duke, and horses and machinery, as he had taken it over five years before. With his loss, and the beef going out to pay wages and grub bills, he was pretty badly set back. We sure liked old Butch. He was always so cheerful, and a darned good all-round cowman and so good to work for.

98

Pierre had left Butch's before we finished haying there, to try to put up more hay at the Cooper meadow. He had quite an experience with a big bull moose the night he stayed at the Ramsay Creek cabin. He had his old Shorty and Kate staked out on the edge of the meadow some hundred and fifty yards from the house. This huge old bull took after Kate and made her break loose and run for the house. Pierre saw it happen and grabbed his rifle. He didn't want to shoot the moose but when he lowered his head to lift the mare up on that big rack of horns of his, Pierre opened fire only twenty-five yards from the house. He slowed the moose up but he kept on coming and Pierre didn't get him down till he was practically on the doorstep. Pierre butchered him out and stood the quarters up on the shady side of the house. Those were the heaviest moose quarters I have ever seen either here or up at Lesser Slave Lake where I saw a grey moose dressed out that weighed close to a thousand pounds. We kept the set of horns at one of our cabins. That was pretty late in October and after freeze-up. The meat froze solid and kept all right.

Before leaving Butch's we had ordered a cook stove for Ramsay Creek. We had had only a light tin campstove there before. Since we would have to pack it across country, we knew we'd need to have enough weight on the other side of our pack to balance the stripped stove. So we bought a hundred-pound sack of oats, twenty pounds of beans and twenty pounds of rice, and figured that this and all the stove lids and removable parts would make up enough ballast. Our camp outfit and bedrolls were too light and bulky to work for this as we only had a narrow Indian trail to pack on.

Old Klooch was a good solid-built pack horse and nice and low to the ground so she was chosen to pack our precious stove. When we loaded it on we found it was so much wider than the other compact load for the other side that it took more weight to balance the stove. Klooch really had a load on before we got it balanced; close to four-hundred pounds. She was agin it and ducked her head and went to hoggin' right away. But she had so much weight she couldn't jar it too much. We figured she'd be more careful loose (not led) and do a better job of wiggling through. We thought we would have to cut quite a lot of timber to get through but Klooch wiggled so well we only had to cut two trees to get the load in to Ramsay Creek cabin.

When we got to the Cooper meadow, Pierre had started a stack. The hay there was very coarse rip gut and still quite green. It had been up to our hats in June and I don't know how much taller it grew but it was terrible stuff to handle. Pierre had piled one load on top of another with the derrick, without pulling the loads apart and stacking them properly. I took over the stacking and got about three loads higher, trying to put a top on it when, "whoosh," the whole works went over and I sure went flying through the air, landing spread-eagled some thirty feet out from the furthest hay. That was sure a mess to do anything with.

Later in the fall Art and I were stacking up some more hay that was cocked. We were camped on the edge of the meadow as there was no liveable cabin yet. One night it snowed quite heavily and, not having bothered to set up a tent, we just pulled our blankets and canvas up over our heads. We had an extra quilt over us in the morning, beautifully white, about four inches deep and quite warm. But that wasn't our only surprise when we got up. A huge timber wolf had come up and apparently sniffed the blanket roll. The tracks were so big you couldn't cover the full width of them with the palm of your hand and the closest track crossed a corner of our blankets. (Wolf at the door — if we'd had a door!)

Also during that winter we would see a smaller wolf track, likely a bitch, down in the meadow where we had an old roan wild mare rustling. This wolf apparently was trying to work up courage enough to tackle the old mare but she made it keep its distance. This was the first sign we saw of wolves in the country but it sure wasn't the last.

After finishing haying, Art and I went back to Ramsay Creek to put scoops on the cabin roof and finish the barn as we had to go back to work for Butch for two or three months. These scoops were made by splitting big logs, and then cutting the centre out with axes, leaving them looking like troughs or scoops. This was a scoop roof to catch all the rain and snow water and drain it off. It is a pretty hefty day's work to make twenty of these. But when that roof was in place there were no worries about a leaking roof for twenty to thirty years. The dirt and moss was the absolute in insulation. When the walls were chinked these cabins were about as weather-proof as can be made; cool in the summer and easy to heat and keep warm in winter. We made them all pretty much the same.

We went back over to Butch's about the end of November to start the fall roundup on the Nazko and anywhere else we could find those scattered cows. They had to be taken out to their fall rustling north of Butch's meadow towards our Ramsay Creek meadow. As the stock needed feeding we picked them up and took them to Butch's meadow where we were feeding what calves there had been to wean. Old Einer Nordberg was living there running a little trapline. He ran into some ptarmigan before Christmas and shot a brace to have for Christmas dinner. When the day came he pot roasted them in butter on top of the stove. He had also made a homebrew of potato whiskey for the occasion. The old boy was quite a cook and we really had a bang-up Christmas dinner. Those ptarmigan were the "piece de resistance" and were really delicious.

But Art and I couldn't let our hair down and absorb too much of the alky. We had nearly run out of feed and had to make all the preparations for moving the five miles over to Martin meadow the next day. We had over three-hundred head of cattle, a sleigh load of riggin' and quite a string of horses to move. So we were working late Christmas Day and up at four-thirty next morning to get the outfit on the trail by daylight as we had trail to break all the way. Then we would have to separate stock and feed everything on arrival at the Martin meadow. Butch had an awfully good dog he had let Art use. They called him "Skokum." Art had started training him the year before when he was just a little puppy — so small in fact that as the snow got deep he played himself out working on stock. Then Art would have to pick him up and pack him on the saddle horse. By this time he was almost better than another cowboy. Art would take a bunch of thirty or forty cows in the lead and Skookum would head the rest into the trail and follow the last ones, sometimes two or three miles behind, when the whole works was strung out on a deep snow trail. He never got too rough but insisted that they keep moving and never lost one.

Butch had moved back to the meadow but had left the family in at Alexis Creek as two of the youngsters, Hazel and Norman, were old enough to start school. We helped get everything organized at the meadow and stayed on for New Year's Day. Einer Nordberg came over; he brought his gallon of spud whiskey along and we had a New Year's farewell party together. Einer saw Art and I weren't taking to the spud whiskey very much and asked us if we were scared of it. We proceeded to show him we weren't and took on quite a load. I got an idea Art was going to get sick so I shoved him out the door and gave him a push with my foot as he went out that upended him into the snow. I went back in and shut the door on him. Butch almost died laughing. He figured that was pretty rough treatment for a man to give his brother.

The next day we packed our riggin' and headed over to Butch's cabin, and the following day on over to Ramsay Creek, breaking close to three feet of snow in places. We figured we would need a little more grub to see us through the winter and till after high water and break-up. We rigged up a box on the front end of the sleigh and I headed out for town. Breaking trail I could only make about seven miles a day so had to camp out twice before I got to Pierre's. The trail was broken from their place so I made better time. Every place I got to along the road we would sit up till close to three in the morning telling all our past history and future hopes, and then up again around five in the morning to feed the team and get ready to hit the trail again. The whole trip both ways was one big prolonged visiting of the neighbours. A man sure did consume plenty of coffee on that kind of a trip. It's a wonder I didn't float before I got home.

The trip back from Pierre's on up was pretty tough. I left the sleigh four miles out and rode the team in to break the trail. When we came out to get the sleigh with a four-horse team and a couple of saddle horses to tramp the trail down, we found marten tracks all around the sleigh. So I took a few traps out and set them. Art and I had applied for a trapline when we pre-empted and we were given a block about seventy-five miles long and twenty to twenty-five miles wide in places. All we had to do was learn to trap. Pierre came up soon after I did and got a marten out of my trap at the corduroy where I had left the sleigh. It was our first marten. We had never seen one before and didn't know what it was!

Around this time, by mutual consent, we dropped out of the informal partnership with Pierre. It hadn't worked well from the start and friction was increasing steadily. Pierre and family kept the place and stayed on it at times, but finally returned to Alberta. The place is still referred to as the Burnstad place. Art and I were now on our own — without the proposed home ranch headquarters.

CHAPTER X

Bucking Hell and High Water —
Prospecting and Packing

Our first winter alone at Ramsay Creek was considerably taken up preparing to hold and handle horses. For this we needed a barn, barnyard and small pasture. For going anywhere where there would be no fences, we needed stake ropes and hobbles; and for handling the horses we needed lass ropes, hackamores and lead ropes. Moose rawhide was our main asset. We made a handy rig to soak hides in for making rawhide. We found out that the hair plucked off very easily for about half an hour after the animal was killed. This was a big step in getting it ready to make strings. Cowhide had to be soaked several days in fairly warm water and then the hair scraped off with a fairly blunt tool. This was a hell of a lot of hard work. Once the hair was off the hide, it had to be stretched wet and then dried until it would hold its shape. We rigged up a cutting gauge with a very well-sharpened section out of a mower sickle secured onto a piece of hardwood. For lass ropes that we wanted to be really good we had to rig up a similar tool called an "edger" to slope the edges of the strings. Then we also had to make a tool to split the flesh side off so as to have nothing left but the top grain side and no extra.

For beds, chairs, stake ropes and such like, we weren't so fussy about splitting and edging. The strings had to be pretty well soaked and then they were ready to lace chairs or beds, or braid rope. We made some very comfortable chairs and beds for each cabin and quite a few general purpose ropes, all out of moosehide. We also made a lot of hackamores, mostly cowhide. Art made a pretty fancy thirty-two string hackamore bozelle. Later bushtail rats got into a lot of our rawhide work and chewed the strings up, and the rats got that fancy hackamore. That one winter, we braided ropes and hackamores, made five pack saddles complete with rawhide breeching and breast straps, and moosehair-and-gunny-sack pack blankets. This was to be an outfit for a pack train, so we could get work in the spring.

We had to have grease for boots, ropes, cooking and, at times when the kerosene ran out, to make what were rightly called "tallow bitches." Nobody ever used one by preference. Any piece of rag in a can, saucer, or whatever was handy, with one end in the grease and the other hanging over the edge made the "bitch." When you first lit it you got the foul smell of burning cloth and from there on an equally foul smell of burning cloth and grease mixed. It was always smoking and flickering but was light enough to see to do odd jobs. No hell to read or knit by in case you think of trying it! We used rendered moose or bear grease mostly for this. For all cooking, bear grease rated pretty high, even with the womenfolk for making pastry. It is quite a bit the same consistency as lard but slightly softer and more oily. Sour- dough hotcakes, steak and coffee was pretty regular fare for breakfast. Dinner and supper were mostly boiled or roasted meat with beans, rice or macaroni for vegetables. We made bread at times but very often bannock and occasionally sourdough biscuits. As long as we had meat we did pretty well but when the meat ran out, the beans, rice and macaroni sure got powerful monotonous. We tried to have some dried fruit on hand especially in winter as we'd heard and seen enough of scurvy to be pretty leery of it. The fruit was mostly "C.P.R. straw- berries," the high-toned name for dried prunes.

Right now I don't care if I never see rice, beans or macaroni again, but I still like prunes. I guess we never got enough of them. They can be spruced up so much with cream or ice cream that you'd never know it was the same dish. After about the second winter without any green vegetables I decided the next winter we would have spuds any- way. I broke a horse for the Higdon boys down by Quesnel and took vegetables for the job; we lived pretty high on the hog after that. It was so damn hard to make a dollar more than you needed for absolute necessities in the thirties. Nobody seemed to have any money. So we didn't buy any butter or canned milk to amount to anything, and eggs were only dreamed of most of the time. We could have had mush right along if we'd had milk. Fur prices had gone down to rock bottom and all we could catch in a winter's trapping would bring in so little cash that it hardly seemed worthwhile. Even when we did make a few bucks there were so many things needed it was quite a job to figure what to spend it on. Somehow we seemed to figure coffee and tobacco were very important to keep the morale up, as actually they were the least necessary otherwise. But we practically never ran out of those two items and yet we did run out of everything else at times. I always seemed to need quite a bit of sugar and I think I missed it about as much as anything when we ran out of it. Everything which needed sugar seemed so tasteless without it. We always tried to save enough, before we ran out, to keep the sourdough running as it wouldn't per- form well without sugar.

We built a barnyard, made a start on a pasture and did some clearing for a set of corrals that winter, as well as running what few traps and snares we had. We didn't catch much fur as we had very little trapping experience and hadn't bought enough traps to practice much. The snow was awfully deep to break trail to go anywhere by saddle horse, so we stayed put most of the time. We were to get a couple of horses for the last work we had done for Butch. He figured he would have them over at the Martin meadow towards the latter part of the winter. Art tried to break trail over there one day in March. He ran into drifts he figured were twelve-feet deep along a lake that wasn't safe to cross and so he had to turn back. We therefore made another sashay over there in April. It was very warm but the snow was still deep.

Art was going to ride Red and would not ride a bronc without putting on his riding boots. Red still wasn't reliable, unless you could call reliability being able to rely on him to give you a buck jump occasionally. The riding boots were fine as long as Art was riding. But it got dark before we finished breaking the fifteen miles of trail and cold enough to put a crust-like glass on the wet snow. The horses went through it fairly well in the timber but when we had to cross open swamp or meadow they just wouldn't. We had only two miles to go and we didn't want to turn back. Being so close to Butch's meadow we hated to camp so I got down and started to break trail on foot. The snow was too deep for me to keep it up far enough, so Art got down to spell me off. We made it to the timber before Art said anything but then something had to be done. His boots had filled up with snow. The warmth and motion of his feet had settled snow right down tight as it could go around his ankles and shut off circulation completely. I tried the old boot jack stunt — turn about-face, straddle his leg, take the boot between my legs and, with Art's other foot pressing on my rear end for support and extra push, pull; but she just wouldn't wiggle at all. So I built a fire right quick and Art mighty nigh burned the boots off him before we could get them off. Lucky he had brought an extra pair of socks on the pack horse so we were all set again, and we worked our way on through and got to Butch's meadow cabin about two in the morning. They had left plenty of hay at the barn so the ponies were rewarded some for the tough break through. It was better than pawing deep-crusted snow for old junk grass as they would have had to do if we had camped.

We made it to the Martin meadow early next morning and had a little visit before gathering our knotheads and heading home again. Butch was aiming to turn the cattle out down the Nazko River in a

105

week or so and hit for Alexis Creek where the family had wintered. That was the last we saw of Butch. The family moved to California soon after and Butch died within a year or so.

We got a very early spring in 1933 and, thinking it would be still earlier in Quesnel, we started out for town by saddle horse and with pack horses. On our way in, we made a noon camp at Cocky Evans'. I had a little black dog I called Shorty. Don't ask me what breed he was 'cause I don't know and I doubt if anybody could guess very accurately, but Shorty had learned to heel horses like a cow dog. He was heeling the pack horses to get them started on the road again. He got a little too ambitious and I called him off. He had just heeled a little mare in the string when he turned to look at me, and she clipped him on the end of the nose and broke about seven teeth out, all in one chunk. It was still attached at both ends and I jumped off and set them back in place, thinking they might knit in again. But the second I turned him loose, Shorty scratched them out with a hind foot and as soon as we hollered at the horses he was all set to heel them again to get his revenge. But I held him back, figuring that was enough punishment for one day.

The closer we got to town, the worse the feed situation was. There was absolutely no green grass in Quesnel so we about-faced and went back to Pierre's place, as they weren't living in it then. On our way past Tibbles' we had dealt Jim out of a green bullhide. We went to rawhiding for a month. We turned our horses out and set ourselves on foot. After preparing the hides, we went to cutting strings with a more efficient pistol-grip leather cutting gauge we had bought. We must have cut over five hundred feet of string, without using any of the back strip or too low in the flank, or shoulder, and no neck hide. These parts are either too thick or too thin. Next we soaked the strings and coiled them and were ready to start braiding us a rawhide lass rope each. We braided morning, noon and night till we had a rope each and this was something to be pretty proud of. They were good ropes and mine lasted twelve years before I broke it. It would have lasted longer had I not had to use it for staking my saddle horse too often. Sometimes I neglected to grease it often enough. A good rawhide rope doesn't get stiff and hard when it gets wet, is always in shape to use, and is so much better than ordinary ropes that there is no comparison. But they take a lot of time and work to make and require precision work to make them smooth and uniformly strong. They are very expensive to buy.

That spring Jack and Fred Tibbles came up on their beaver trapping. They wanted me to go up to Fish Lake with them. This sounded good to me and they rounded up a saddle horse for me. I asked them what groceries I best take along. They said they had lots of grub — I didn't need to take anything. But I put a little flour and some baking powder into the pack along with my blanket roll. We had had quite a bit of cold weather and a few late but heavy snows so there was still plenty of snow in shady timber, higher up towards the lake. They set some traps on the way up and I watched carefully to learn the technique. By the time we got to Fish Lake it was dark and I at least had worked up a right hearty appetite and was sure hoping the boys had the makings. I was to be quite a little disappointed when all they produced for grub was some bannock and a fry pan. Then they told me the master plan. We were to live on fish; all we had to do was catch them. So we ate undecorated bannock that night. Jack and Fred just had two Hudson's Bay blankets and a canvas. They put one blanket under them and one over and went to bed with all their clothes on. In the morning they were about twenty feet apart with just a blanket apiece and the canvas stretched out between them.

Next morning I dug out my flour and baking powder and built some hotcakes so we'd have a little foundation to go fishing on. The fishing didn't work out. We found there was a light skim of ice, then about four inches of water, and then ice an axe handle deep underneath. So we couldn't get down to the fish; we had to get by on hotcakes that day. We tried one creek coming into the lake and the one emptying out of it. Next day we headed down the creek. We got one chicken (grouse) on the way down, made camp right away, fried that chicken and ate it in a hurry. We saw two moose up on a sidehill about five hundred yards across a little neck of spruce swamp, just about two and a half miles before we got to Pierre's. Everybody was out of meat and we felt as though we could eat a quarter for supper. Fred said, "Can you connect with one that far away?" "Well," I said, "I'd never be sure without trying and I sure am hungry for meat."

While we were making a decision it was getting pretty close to dark. Then one moose walked up directly below the other one so that there was actually the full depth of two moose to shoot at. The decision was made. I held for the top of the high one, figuring the drop would likely bring it down to the middle of the lower one. It did and the moose went down. That gave me quite a little confidence in my new .32 Remington.

Later that spring Art and I started trying to catch a few beavers and rats on our trapline. I took a pack horse and saddle horse to make my first trip up our road, bucking "hell and high water." To a lot of folks this expression doesn't mean much, but after living in mountain country for a few years it gets to be plumb full of meaning.

High water is an annual event that you have to figure on and it can't be ignored. When we first came into the Cariboo, we didn't know anything more about it than as a good expression. In the hot summer the creek that ran through the barnyard was sometimes reduced to a mere trickle, and we paid very little attention to it more than to catch the odd fish, dip our water for the house and water our stock. But the first high water changed our attitude toward the little stream to one of concern, fascination and considerable respect and awe. As the snows melted the creek opened up and, in late April, the creek rose daily till we started taking notice and putting markers on the banks. Quite often the markers were under water or washed away before we looked again as the creek grew into a raging torrent of muddy waters, leaving its banks, flooding all the creek flats and valleys, and washing everything moveable away with it on its rush to the mighty Fraser. All our crossings were swimming deep to a fairly tall horse and many of them looked too tough to tackle. Klooch, the cayuse I was riding, had legs so short they hardly reached the ground so, although she was a good swimmer, you were plumb sure to get into more water than if you had a tall horse. The first creek crossing was above an old beaver dam, ordinarily about eight inches deep and twenty feet across. Klooch stumbled off into it and right up over the saddle horn before she levelled off and went to swimming with darn little but her head out of water. The water is plumb chilly that time of year. Running fast, I think it can stay quite a little below freezing; sure felt like it to me. I gasped and grabbed for holds in case I had to go swimming on my own hook. Also, my camp outfit on the pack horse got a good wetting.

I aimed to make seventeen miles before stopping so didn't take time to dry out, but started wondering just how tough the next creeks would be. The next two creeks were smaller, much narrower and swifter, but we navigated them okay. However, I had to build a bridge on the next one as the regular bridge was now out in the middle of a lake. I knew nothing of floating bridges and, after wading out to it, let my horses go right on. They just got full length onto the bridge when their feet started going through, and down they went. I had brains enough to jump clear and jumped onto a rider log supposed to hold the covering in place. But my end was loose and swung out into mid-stream. I lost my hold and out I went into the icy current and had to wade ashore. The first time I only got wet to the shirt pockets. This time I had the upper half of my head dry, but I was getting closer to my objective and kept thinking, "One more river to cross!" I had an idea I was really in for it as I could see the creek was fairly deep and plenty swift. So I gave the pack horse the full length of my lass rope to work on and headed old Klooch in. It came about halfway up on her ribs, not quite swimming deep but almost enough to take her legs out from under her. Klooch made it but the pack horse didn't. She rolled and went hell for leather downstream till my lass rope tightened and I yanked her out. By this time the expression "bucking hell and high water" had a meaning for me.

That summer, 1933, and also '34, '35, '36 and '37, we headed up east of Quesnel to try to get work enough to make a winter grubstake. Each spring, as soon as we figured there would be feed in that high country, we would make the migration. One or two summers we had to make an extra trip back and forth for something or other. Most years I made an earlier migration home to put up hay for our horses, and several times went back up after haying. Other times Art stayed later to get more work and then migrated home in late November. In '33 we went up the Quesnel River and did quite a bit of prospecting. Towards fall Art took pack horses over to Barkerville country and got some work after I went home. The other summers we headed first for Beaver Pass, some twenty miles on the Quesnel side of Barkerville, which we made our headquarters quite a lot. Later we moved up to Stanley and worked from there. The winter of 1936-37, Art got work freighting for McKinnons with a team and stayed in Barkerville all winter.

We camped out in West Quesnel. Very few buildings were there then and I think where we camped on Baker Creek there was only one building, Happy Norman's. Now there isn't room to camp with a jack rabbit.

While we were camped in West Quesnel an old Scotsman came around one morning and asked us if we'd care to dip into the placer mining business. We told him if it didn't require any capital to get going we might. He claimed that he and three boys he had with him had dug a test hole down and found quite a patch of ground that ran heavy to pay dirt. The main trouble was that the pay dirt was from six to ten feet down underneath the overburden. His idea was that with our horse outfit we could plough the surface and scrape it off, then scrapers would work without ploughing. While some of us were thus engaged taking off the overburden, the others would build a hopper and dump, sluice boxes and a water wheel in the river. When we got down to pay dirt we would dump it in the hopper. The water wheel would pick up water from the river and dump it in the sluice box, wash the gravel off and leave the gold and, presto, we'd have 'er made!

There were three boys from Princeton, Floyd and Roy Shook and another youngster (I forget his name). They had an outfit of horses and rigging quite a bit like ours, and we were all in the same boat — making next to nothing, no work in sight and horse feed running short in town. We had been tightening our belts a little every day so we figured we didn't have anything but our time to lose. We all threw in together and bought screens, a little lumber, flour, rice, beans, salt, baking powder and sugar. We rustled round and got hold of an old walking plough and a couple of old quarter-yard scrapers, loaded our wagons and headed up the Quesnel River to "French Flats," some twenty-five miles east of Quesnel.

Mac had the claim staked and showed us the set-up and turned us loose. Talk about activity! We really went to work on that deal and it was no time till we had a pit probably seventy-five feet square and six feet deep. Old Mac had showed us how to pan gravel to test when we got through the overburden. He came around once or twice a day and tested the bottom himself and I guess about the fourth day he started getting colours. They were very fine and so thin that you couldn't see them turned on edge. The sluice box, water wheel, dump platform and hopper were well underway and pretty soon we started the whole plant operating. We were making one big mistake; we didn't realize it but Mac should have. When we dumped a scraper of gravel into the hopper, it would run right through in a heap into the sluice box and plug it. This would dam the water up till the dam would burst and take everything in a mad rush down the boxes and out into the river some seventy-five feet below.

Afterwards the critics told us that the rush of water took everything: gold, gravel, dirt and all. If there had been enough coarse gold we might have captured some with long enough boxes and coarse enough screens. But fine gold went right on over into the tailings pile in the river.

We kept panning and were getting lots of colours so figured we were getting richer by the minute. But we delayed the clean-up till we had been working a month to give us time enough to have worked out enough to split six ways. Expenses were to come out first and between us we had put close to thirty-five dollars into the jackpot to buy the grub for a month and the material to build sluice boxes and water wheel. Finally the big day came and Mac came around to engineer the clean-up as none of us knew too much in this line. Man, oh man, did we gather round and crane our necks watching that last panful getting worked over. Mac didn't seem very enthusiastic and we soon found out why. For all our month's work and thirty-five dollars invested we got twenty-six cents, more or less, than we had invested. It didn't seem to matter too much and I never did remember if we had twenty-six cents to split between six of us or twenty-six cents to dig up!

The saskatoons were ripe by then and there were lots of bears in the blueberry patches so we lived on berries and bear meat. The Shook boys pulled out and left the country. Soon a Hawaiian named Al Nani came over and put another mining proposition to us. This was further up the river and then up Beaver Mouth Creek. We were to build a wing-dam in the creek to head the water into the sluice boxes. The gold wasn't very deep and was coarse. Also he guaranteed wages, or a share of the clean-up, whichever was most acceptable at the finish. This sounded like a pretty safe bet and Art and I moved up to his set-up. He also had three or four high school boys working with him testing ground. We went to work scraping gravel in as soon as we got the wing-dam built, and they had the sluice boxes ready.

By now we could do a pretty fair job of panning and this gold really looked good to what we had been working on, so we were pretty confident that we were in the chips this time. We wanted them to clean-up after two weeks work, and the other boys did too, but Nani kept stalling it off till we had worked about a month. Then he said he was going to town and would clean-up when he got back the next day. Art and I had a camp something like half a mile from the workings for horse feed. The other boys were camped three or four hundred yards from the workings and every evening they would all come over to our camp to get us to tell cowboy yarns. The clean-up went according to schedule next day, except that Nani didn't show up and none of us saw him again. He must have come back in the night, cleaned the works and skipped the country leaving us with empty boxes. We got a twenty-five-year judgment for wages due us against Nani but that didn't do us any good either.

We did work some more there hoping to earn a little, or that Nani might show up, and we could take a little out of his hide. The patch of ground was pretty well worked out so there was very little we could do there. I think we got about six dollars apiece.

While we were working on Al Nani's layout I had shot a bear away up the Beaver Mouth Creek and, as meat was powerful scarce, I wanted to pack it in. Also, as it was my first bear, I wanted the hide. I took little Fanny out to pack it on. She was pretty snorty and I was expecting plenty of trouble as a lot of horses hate the sight and smell of bear. I wasn't a first-class packer then and not too sure how to tie it on, so had left the hide joined together between the quarters so I could flop one quarter over the horse and the hide would hold them both up in place. I brought plenty of rope with me, partly to tie on the meat, but enough to tie the horse every which way.

I found a ledge of rock about five feet below another ledge with nice standing room for a horse, so I hobbled and blindfolded Fanny, then hauled the bear down to it. Fanny never even snorted so I oozed it gently onto her and tied it on. I took the blindfold off, then the hobbles and she stood just as quietly as if nothing unusual had happened. She packed it in without ever batting an eye.

That was an easy one, but another horse I tried the same stunt on acted altogether differently. She smelled bear before she got to it and started to snort and quiver. I couldn't get her close at all and had to throw her and tie the bear on solid before I let her up, even blindfolded. She kicked, squealed, bawled and bucked but once I got it tied on she couldn't win the argument. She was just about as bad to pack a lynx on, and whenever I caught anything on the trapline I had plenty of trouble. I found I could hang fur up in a high limb and ride under it, pick it off and tie it on. But when she found out, I sure had to ride.

After this abortive prospecting, an old feller name of Bill Hollin from some ten miles up the creek hit me up to go and help him stack some hay. This was right in my line and I went up next day. This was the first ranch I ever saw or heard of where there wasn't a horse on the place. This old feller had got a Holstein cow some twenty years before and she had a bull calf from somebody's Hereford bull.

Old Bill didn't like civilization or people, I gathered, and he had holed up in this picturesque little high-walled valley on the creek. The high, steep hills were all the fence he needed to hold his stock in there. This old swinging-bagged milk cow and her bull calf produced a herd till he had nearly forty head the fall I was in there. He had never sold a hoof of stock in all that time. In haying time he hired a man and team, and that was the only time there was a horse in the valley. He had a bicycle to travel on but he didn't go out more than two or three times a year to get his closest neighbour to bring in a few supplies for him.

Definitely he had lived alone too long. The day we were finishing the stacking it started to rain and he let out the worst string of cussing I had ever heard. He went into the house and got his rifle, then came out and shot several times at where the sun should have been.

I headed back down the creek, nearly fifteen dollars to the good after that haying deal. Art and I decided best I take a team and go back to Quesnel and go on out to start putting up the hay for our horses. He would try to get work up Barkerville way as he heard there was a little activity up there. That worked out pretty well. Art got several little jobs packing with one to five pack horses and made us a winter grubstake.

CHAPTER XI

Haying, Hunting and Horse Trading

I took old Jean and Smokey on the wagon and Red for a saddle horse, then hit right on through town and on to Ramsay Creek. While we were waiting in town that spring for some work to show up, we had made a deal with Lannie Torgerson to buy an aged registered Belgian stud for a hundred and twenty-five dollars. We had been getting all the mares we could acquire by hook or by crook with this in mind, figuring the well-bred mares would raise us some saddle horses and the cayuses would raise something to work. Colts from them crossed with a work horse stud would get us into decent work stock. We had made a rush trip out with the old stud and built a brush fence around a fairly high ground meadow we had discovered on one of the Ramsay Creek tributaries. We put Black Tiny, a well-built Percheron-and-Arabian mare we had got from Butch, Klooch and Pierre's old Kate in the pasture with the old stud for the summer. We would have liked to put all the mares we had in with him but hoped to be able to get work packing with them.

One of the first things I did on my return home was to go over to our "stud pasture" to see how the little herd was doing. They were fine, happy as clams, all in good shape and the mares were looking after old Duke just like he was their baby. But the feed wasn't too plentiful and I thought best to let them outside where there was such an abundance of feed which would be going to waste.

We had built one side of a pasture at Ramsay Creek, trusting to the boggy creek to hold the other side and keep what we wanted in. I got Klooch out of the bunch and so had Jean, Smokey, Klooch and Red in the pasture. Up till nearly dark everything stayed put but Red was determined to get across to the bunch. Finally he made a crossing, like a coyote, on a dam we had built to flood the meadow if it was too dry. He proceeded right away to cut the mares away from old Duke and herd them away. I caught a saddle horse and tried to catch up but it got too dark and I had to give up the chase till morning. I found the bunch back in the stud pasture but old Duke wasn't with them. I hunted for five days for him, thinking I might find him either lost or bogged down. On the fifth day I got a whiff of dead flesh in the air and followed that up and found the old stud.

Apparently the bunch had got ahead of him going around a neck of swamp and he had tried to cross the neck straight to them. He started bogging down in the middle of the swamp neck. Had he kept going straight across he would have made it easily as he had such a little way to go. But he swung at right angles and wallowed straight into the middle of the worst part of the swamp. He had ploughed his way for close to seventy-five yards up into it and it must have been away up on his sides, judging by the trench he had left. If he had gone at right angles either left or right, he would have made it to solid ground in the same direction. But no, he could see wide open space ahead and that must have been what he was looking for. Only his head from the eyes up and the line of his back and neck were above the surface. However, all our mares were in foal. Pierre's old Kate gave birth to twins in the spring but both died soon after birth. Klooch mothered "Beaut" and Tiny had "Babe." Beaut and Babe were our skookum little Belgian team for a good number of years and, more important, they were the mothers of quite a little herd of darn good horses from a grade stud we got later from Joe Elkins.

After the sad and discouraging episode with old Duke I went to work on the haying. I didn't like the idea of pitching every forkful and so built a sort of cross between a bucking pole and a sweep. With this I could push hay into large bunches and then round them up or cock them enough to be fairly safe from the weather, and then go on cutting and raking before the hay got frozen too much. Later I tried pushing these big bunches into stackyards and up on poles laid on the stack and raised as the stack raised. I got a lot of hay into big piles pretty quickly, but it wasn't too successful as I couldn't get hay high enough to make good stacks. So, for the last big stack I set up the derrick to put a good top on the pile I had pushed in. I had got quite a high stack nearly finished right up to the last two or three loads when I had to go up on top of the stack to place the load and trip the slings instead of tripping from the ground. I was using Jean and Klooch for a team. Jean never did pay too much attention to "whoa" and old Klooch was a little deaf, probably from having a rifle shot too close to her ears. She waited for the other horse to stop before she guessed it might be a good idea to do likewise. This time they let the load down so it was sitting tight on the stack before I got up on top. So I took a chance and hollered at them to take it up a little. I finally got them started but "whoa" at that distance didn't mean a thing. They took it right on up to the top of the derrick poles and were starting to pull the poles over when I caught up to the lines after jumping thirty feet off the top of the stack and running the full length of the hoist cable to ward off the disaster. After that I drove a crowbar into the ground and staked them so they couldn't go ahead or back after I left them.

When I went down to the settlement after haying that fall, I found Tibbles and Paleys finishing their last stack and so I stayed and helped finish it. Pierre and Jessie were down there too with their youngsters and the ladies all figured that this would be a good time to get some more blueberries, so I joined the blueberry pickers for a day. There was Lizzie Paley and her sister Elsie, Emma and May Cooper, and Jessie and Pierre. We had quite a berry picking bee and blueberry pie and sauce for reward. I had hardly guessed there were that many women in the country.

Art and I got quite a few traps that fall. We got a Hudson's Bay book all about trapping methods and hints; pretty good tips too. It gave pictures of the different animals so we would be able to make a pretty good guess on what we caught.

We couldn't afford eggs for ourselves but we got a dozen and broke some into a tobacco can we kept under the stove. In a little while it got pretty high and we set out some fox traps baited with it. We hit it lucky. The bait was just right and foxes just had to investigate. But our trap sets were too crude and the animals got wise that everywhere they smelt this rotten egg there would be a trap. You'd hardly believe how smart those little devils are. They would dig under the trap, if it was set in snow, until the trap tipped over. Where it was on the ground, they did pretty near everything but get into it. But we smartened up too. Sometimes we set a trap in plain sight and further back we covered one well. They would go right into the unconcealed trap and try to tip it over to get around it and never think of the other. If we hadn't put too much covering on it we would get a fox, but with too much covering it threw their foot out.

My first fox was a black one, the rarest of any, and the only black one we ever got. At one time a good black fox was worth fifteen hundred dollars. This was a good one, but the art of make-up had entered the fur business and fifteen dollars was all we got for it. Hoy said, "He all a same red fox, just dye red fox fur and you have black fox." Red fox, being the commonest, were worth only ten or twelve dollars then.

We got a few coyotes, weasels and the odd marten and lynx, but not much for all the work we did, riding and looking up the best fur country, blazing trails, riding long days with a saddle full of snow and shivering all the way home in the dark. But the experience was a big gain for us. Next year we piled up quite a catch and most winters from then on till the bottom dropped out of the fur business.

We didn't make a very good guess on how much kerosene the old lamp would take and it was quite a ways from spring when we had to make tallow bitches. Art wasn't much of a reader and put in most of his evenings rawhiding, building hackamores and such. He was quite ready to bed down any time from eight-thirty on, but I had to read. We had gathered up some old magazines and papers and a book or so, mostly from Tibbles, and I read and re-read them all, even the ads, the latter so much that now I hardly look at ads.

Before coming in that fall I got work at the Baker boys' ranch just out of Quesnel, picking up spuds and helping thresh. I took some of my wages out in vegetables so we didn't have to eat straight beans, rice and meat. I did most of the cooking. I had had a load of stomach troubles due to my typhoid fever and ulcers. I always had to be careful to have food well done, very little grease, bread rather than baking powder biscuits, and not too much fried stuff. Art just wasn't a born cook. His mind was always wandering on something else and the bannock would have a lovely black shine on it, or be dough in the middle. The meat would be blood rare. "A little on one side and not much on the other," he would say. His coffee making was the ace in the hole! Nobody, but nobody, made coffee like Art did. We used to get coffee beans in 50-pound sacks and grind it, or in one-pound packages. Art would dump a generous portion in the pot, then peer into the pot. He couldn't see anything down in there so he would shake the package over it two or three more times and say, "Best give her a little more," or "That should do her." Likely all the time he'd be talking to you and be figuring out what to do the next day or next year, and wouldn't have an idea what he was doing. Then he'd boil hell out of the brew. Well, in the end, the stuff was so black and bitter it would curl your moustache just passing through, and Lord knows what it would do to your insides, but I feared it wouldn't be good. So, whenever I could get the jump on him, I made the coffee.

Whenever we weren't camped out I made bread. I had made my first bread when I was seven years old so this was nothing new. I made sourdough bread in camp sometimes but it seemed to be pretty delicate stuff to handle. If the wind blew a little it would fall and you would have to let it rise again, but it made delicious bread. I was beginning to have quite a reputation for my sourdough hotcakes, also my cookies. Our main course for all meals was meat; fried, roasted or boiled. We certainly consumed our full quota of meat for a few years. When we were working hard we would eat a good-sized frying pan of steak each at every meal, and it would be cut at least half an inch thick. One day we were both outdone in meat eating. Joe Elkins came in in mid-afternoon and I had just finished cooking. I had a pan eight by sixteen inches filled to capacity with a rib roast and Joe cleaned the works. Then we found out he had got lost and had nothing to eat since breakfast early morning the day before. He had camped out all night, quite a cold night with close to four feet of snow on the ground. I didn't know an Indian could get lost, but he is only half Indian so maybe that accounts for it.

Joe was a great horse trader and was never happy unless he made a deal. Art and I had bought a brown mare from Shorty. She was just the type of mare we wanted. She was plenty useful herself being about half thoroughbred and half Percheron. Old Flossy was her mother and we would like to have got a whole batch of colts out of that mare. Flossy had about as nice action as a saddle horse can have and a wonderful disposition, willing as could be, and very well built. She had one disfigurement which spoiled her good looks. Some way in her early handling by the Indians, they had broken her tail and it left a big hollow in what should have been the rounded portion of her hip.

Brownie was just right for us to breed either way, for saddle horses or work horses and, being very useful as well, we certainly had no thought of selling or trading her. But we needed work horses and Joe Elkins heard we were trying to get a stud colt from Duke Martin at Alexis Creek. So he came over and told us he had a work horse stud. He was pretty mixed up in his breeding, a little cayuse and Clyde and Percheron mixed. But Joe would trade him for Brownie and some cash. He had got some really nice colts out of his stud and now had enough. Besides, he had got an extra good saddle horse stud, an old race horse that had lost an eye and was banned from Vancouver tracks. This horse's name was "Terrifier." We had no trade notion at first. But Joe figured a little and worked it down to an even-up trade. Art had seen the stud and the colts; he liked what he saw and this sounded pretty good. We had to have a stud before the mares could raise us any work horses and our ex-saddle horse work bunch were an eyesore in harness. So we finally made the swap.

We called our new stud "Duke." He was a six-year-old bay, blocky built with a gentle disposition, weighing around sixteen hundred pounds.

About a couple of years later we made another important trade with Joe Elkins. I don't recall what we traded but it must have been good as we got a gentle broke roan thoroughbred gelding, a little past middle age. More important, we got a black yearling stud colt out of Terrifier. This youngster didn't look like much after Art had broken him to lead and led him fifty miles across country through quite a bit of snow. He seemed to be awfully lanky built, mostly legs. He grew to over seventeen hands tall. He was coal black with only a two-bit-sized white spot on his forehead and, being seven-eighths thorough-bred, was the makings of the type of saddle horse we needed. The name Tony seemed to fit him like a glove. He got to be my top saddle horse for a good many years, but he nearly got the best of me several times.

Lexie used to visit us in the winter too. He lived in the rancheree by Alexis Creek and ran a trapline between the Cooper meadow and Nazko River. At first he used to go through alone. Then he got smart. He'd bring another Indian with him on the first trip and help make the sets and show the other fellow the line, then let him run it on shares the rest of the winter. Lexie would then go home or drop down into the Nazko rancheree and gamble and do a little courting. He generally cleaned the other Indians out of their fur money too, so he had lots of trappers working for him. We undertook to educate him the first winter. He would always stop over two or three days both ways to make chin music with us. He was a great talker and one damn smart Indian, too. He saw the funny side of everything and would be just brim full of news when he came over from the Chilcotin. He was very interested in the stars and we told him all we knew about them, which wasn't much. Then he wanted to learn to write and we really went to work on him. But soon he would completely lose interest and start telling old stories his dad (Old Long Johnnie) and other old-timers had told him. Being our main contact with the outside world for five months, it was always an occasion when he arrived.

I ran a short trapline out four to eight miles on the trail he came in on. One night he came in with a lovely silver fox tied on, only about two or three hours behind me. I was plumb interested right away, guessing that he had got it out of a trap or snare of mine and sure enough he had. I had just made the set two or three hours before and made a catch right away. He often brought in fur out of traps when he was passing through.

Then one time we persuaded him to bring us a wild horse as he wanted to give us something for all the horse feed he was using. He caught an old roan mare out of the wild bunch and brought her over. She had a stud colt which we called Baldy. We kept him a stud and raised a dozen really good saddle horse colts out of our blooded mares.

Baldy was an awfully good pony himself, too. A natural cowhorse and, when he was a stud, I never saw a finer exhibition of cutting horse talent anywhere than when Baldy went to cutting a gelding out of his bunch and keeping him out. His bunch of mares did what he wanted or else!

During the early part of the next winter, moose were very plentiful reaching a peak during a thaw in late January. We could see several from the cabin all day long and see dozens in a day's ride. But we had meat enough, we figured, so just watched them and wished we had a camera to take pictures. Gradually they thinned out till, by the first week in February, there were very few in evidence. We still didn't have many traps so only had two short trapline trails broken out. Before long there was only evidence of one moose in the area we were covering and later Art found this one, an old skinny bull, wedged between two trees and frozen stiff standing up.

The snow got deeper and deeper passing the four-foot mark and there were two heavy crusts on it, one about eighteen inches from ground level and one around the three-foot line. A horse was helpless other than on a broken trail. By the middle of March we saw that our meat supply wasn't going to make it till break-up when the moose would come back.

Neither of us had ever used snowshoes but I had used skis so we decided to make skis. We hunted up a dry spruce and towed it nearly four miles home. Then we set up a whipsaw platform and whipsawed four boards off the log with an old crosscut saw. We concentrated on one pair of skis from there on and rasped them down with an ordinary shoeing rasp. Then came the bending. We didn't know how this was supposed to be done. The best we could figure out was to cut the side out of an old four-gallon kerosene can, then fill it with water and put the tips of the skis in it. We boiled them about three hours, then stuck the ski point over a ridge log and bore down and tied the other end down. They bent okay but split as they dried. The best we could do then was to iron them up. We took the framework off an old grindstone and screwed it on to reinforce them. Then we rigged up a rawhide harness, and the rough-and-ready skis were made. I hunted up some little dry spruce poles and made a sling for my rifle and a sort of pack sack to carry a little lunch. Next morning I started out east. There was a pretty firm crust on top by now and the skis stayed right on top. Even though entirely out of practice, I could make pretty fair time.

I never saw a track till I saw a moose, and that was not till late afternoon. By the time I got the rifle down, the moose was gone. I investigated and found that there were seven in the bunch. They had been staying in the thick little jack pines for quite a long time, eating the green needles and small limbs that the heavy snow had bent down. They were likely slowly starving to death. Apparently the heavy crusts on the snow made their legs too sore and they would not venture out into the willows and the open where snow was deeper and crust harder. It was too late to follow the moose and it was bright moonlight so I headed back home rather than camp out with no outfit. I had not figured to go that far till I had hardened my skiing muscles a bit.

I rested up next day, just limbering up a little on the skis. Next morning I headed out again. I headed directly to a point I figured would be just ahead of the moose. But I was off a wee bit and jumped them straight away from home without seeing one. I had an idea they wouldn't go far so I made a big circle and came back at them from the far side. One cut out of the bunch and headed north towards where I had jumped them the previous day. I kept well out of his sight and gradually bent him into a northwesterly direction till he hit Ramsay Creek and then I bent him up creek towards home. I saw him every little bit but decided herding him home would be easier than packing him. It worked too. Just about sundown I got him to our sleigh trail where we were cutting and hauling logs to build a barn. This was close enough and, rather than take a chance of his going down on a wrong fork of the trail, I aimed to shoot him as soon as I came in sight.

I came out into the open ready to shoot but no moose in sight. I couldn't believe that he had crossed so quickly and I stood on my skis wondering how he could possibly have eluded me, when I heard a rustling at the edge of the timber twenty yards from me. There was my moose. He had crawled in under the tent-like limbs of a big spruce, trying to hide. I shot him with one hand without getting off the skis. Something told me I didn't have much. The moose was poor as a crow. But that wasn't all. As soon as we got him in we put a potful on to boil up a mulligan. There were no tantalizing odours from that stewpot, but there was a horrible smell that drove us out of the house. We boiled and boiled it and changed waters several times to get rid of the smell of boiling jack pine. The smell got milder all right, or we got used to it, but the meat didn't get tender. It was tough as a chunk of rawhide and about the same as chewing on an inner tube, and we guessed no nutriment in it to amount to anything.

So I decided to go out again a couple of weeks later to try to find one that had been rustling on willows or, better still, coarse swamp grass. This was around the tenth of April. Snow was settled down quite a lot and there were even some bare patches on the sunny side of the creek, but still forty inches deep in the timber and solid except when it turned very warm.

I headed for a big meadow that I knew of which had lots of willows and I was lucky. There, away down the meadow, was a moose out in the willows. The crusted snow was very noisy with skis but I was hog-tied without them. So the only way I could figure out was to go away up the hill on the sunny side of the meadow, go down parallel to the meadow till I was opposite the moose, and then try to walk or slide or crawl down to shooting range. I did the latter, packing my skis till I got in sight of the moose at about four hundred yards. If I went any lower and closer, he would be out of sight below the willows and I couldn't cross the meadow with skis. So I had to take the four-hundred-yard shot or likely nothing. I made a perfect shot putting a bullet through his heart. He dropped so suddenly I hardly knew what happened. I had a good moose with even a wee bit of fat on him.

During this time it had turned cloudy and warm and started to snow, wet, heavy snow. It was dark before I finished butchering but I didn't plan to camp out with my meagre outfit so I headed for home. Before I had gone many miles my skis were sticking badly and snow underneath had softened up so much I would break through with one ski and upset. Laboriously I would get on top again and go a little further, packing a foot of snow on the skis instead of sliding freely, and then break through and down again. If I had had any brains I would have built a fire and called it a night. But I think I was afraid of the snow getting softer and being too deep to walk in and too soft, wet and sticky for skis. I had no ski dressing. I would be stranded and it would be almost impossible for Art to break trail with horses. So I kept on and on far into the night, going shorter and shorter distances between rests and getting a little panicky as I played out.

I never guessed it but all this time good old Art was fighting a string of six horses down towards me. He guessed that I would be dead tired. I had told him I planned to come back on the sunny side of the creek where the snow would be settled. So he tied six head of horses head to tail and set out to break trail to me. One horse would only break trail about a quarter of a mile. Then Art would take that one to the back of the string, saddle the tail-ender and tie the tired one on, and away again. It was three in the morning when he saw me and let out a war whoop. Man, oh man, was I glad to hear that holler! Maybe another of my nine lives gone?

I was packing quite a chunk of tenderloin with me and we had a big feed of it that night and fed on it a couple of days more before going after the meat. I went on skis and butchered the meat up in quarters and packed it all to the timber before Art got there. It was nice and warm with the snow soft and slushy and not sticky. The skis went down a lot but the horses waded through it okay and we packed the skis home. I aim to show those old skis to my grandchildren someday and tell them, "Them thar's the skis your old grandpappy run a moose down on."

We went to logging in a big way that winter of '33-'34. We had decided to build a ten-horse barn with floor, hay loft, peaked roof and all the trimmings. We located a good patch of logs, cut and skidded all the timber to a landing, hauled it in from about three miles and decked it near the chosen site. We split all the floor pieces and smoothed them up, and split logs for scoop roof and hollowed them out so as to be all ready to build when the snow went. We had no broadaxe, adze or wedges. Everything was done with two double-bitted axes, crosscut saw and lots of damn hard work and many long days of it.

Julius Quanstrom had showed us how to mark our logs for cutting the notches so the log would go down the right depth and the notch fit perfectly at both ends first try. Harry Quanstrom came up later and helped us build. When we shovelled snow off the logs we found they peeled slick and had a nice varnished look. The logs were 28" x 34' so we had to use horse power to move them around, and parbuckle them to roll them up. Art had to blacksmith out a couple of cant hooks. He made them out of old horseshoes and we put heavy spruce handles in them. They were awkward as hell but worked okay.

We really enjoyed the building and did a particularly good job on it. That was our best building job up to then with the use of all the tricks we had learned from anyone we had come in contact with. This was practice to make perfect for building houses later. As the barn went up we would stand back occasionally and admire our handiwork and say, "That ain't gonna fall down for a long time, I'll bet." Then when the roof was on we'd say, "Won't need to shovel snow off that, and bet she won't cave in like others we've heard of either."

Forty-odd years later the old barn was standing the test of time. It was something we would always be proud of.

CHAPTER XII

Incidents with Pack Train

We had brought all our outfit down to Burnstad's preparatory to go to town and on up to try to get work in the Barkerville country. So we pulled in there with all our broken and partly broken horses to pick up the wagon and other pack rigging and camp outfit. We knew that all the Nazko horses would head for Nazko at the drop of a hat if more than two of them got loose any time, so we had to tie some kind of rigging on everything to hold them.

Some practical joker had told us that horses stake better by the hind foot, don't tangle up so much and get around better. (I would blame it on Pan Phillips, he's just the type, but I don't think either he or Hobson were in the country then — at any rate we didn't know them.) Well, it sounded logical enough and as we had ten or a dozen head we had to stake, we had to try something. We decided this was the time and the place, a nice open flat with plenty of feed. We had lots of rawhide stake ropes about twenty-five or thirty feet long and plenty skookum. We took the ponies out of the corral one by one and tied a green pole about six or eight feet long onto a hind foot and turned them loose. We had an idea there was going to be fun. There was and plenty!

One after another as we turned 'em loose those ponies lit out of there like scared rabbits with their toggles just a-bouncing. Some of the gentler ones might have stopped and got used to it, but about time they got that idea another would come along and bounce a toggle into it and the stampede was on. We almost died laughing, it was so comical. They were hungry enough they hated to leave the good feed and before they'd gone off the flat most of them would have settled down to feeding if nothing disturbed them. They didn't go in any particular direction and each new stampede was apt to be in a different direction, but eventually by dark they had fanned out and up into the timber and it took us till noon next day with a really early start to find them all. None were hurt and all seemed to have got over the fright but from then on we went back to the orthodox method of front foot staking, and hobbling and side hobbling.

The high water caught us short about this time. The horses were all in the flat across the creek and in the morning, instead of being a little stream, the old creek was a boiling torrent. We didn't know of any good high water crossings. Some crossings were good on one side but had steep banks on the other. So we looked up one that was good to come out on our side and decided to swim them across. We could never have chased them into it, so we felled a big spruce tree across the creek for a footbridge. We packed a bunch of hackamores and some salt for bait, caught the whole bunch and tied them up. Then we tied pack ropes and lass ropes together till we had enough rope to reach. Art went back over to the cabin side and I tied the first horse on the long rope and heaved the other end across. It took a few tries to get the knack of throwing that much rope that far, probably a hundred and fifty feet. An ordinary lass rope is forty feet.

When Art got the rope end, I let loose and got in behind the horse with a good switch. Most of them pulled back a time or so and nearly hauled Art into the raging stream. But after we got a good saddle horse across, Art saddled up and worked off the horse. Most of the horses, after pulling back, would come up on the rope and take a mighty leap out into the stream. They would go right under and come bobbing up, looking like drowned rats, blowing, snorting and shaking their heads and swimming as fast as they could. The current whipped them downstream like twigs but we had picked a good spot on a bend where the current crossed over to Art's side with a nice easy grade out. Once into the current there wasn't a chance but what they'd come out okay. Some of them were nearly rolled by the strong undercurrents and, watching each one, we could pretty well guess which would be the best high water swimming horses. We were plumb ready for the bannock and beans by the time we got our sixteen head across.

We tied the rigging on our sixteen head that first spring and with a four-up on the wagon we headed for town and on up to Beaver Pass. There was lots of feed and room for our sixteen head of horses. We turned them loose and hoped for the best. They took root right there fine and were easy to round up any time we got work for any of them.

Work was mighty scarce though. Every so often we would get work for one or two pack horses moving a prospector up to the hills somewhere. Some had the price and some didn't but as long as they seemed hopeful and we weren't busy, we packed them in anyway. We were promised shares of clean-ups, or they would stake a patch of ground for us if it looked good, or just pay if they made it. Only one outfit never looked us up again.

There was one outfit doing assessment work and such like on a company claim. Some of the big-wigs were coming in and sent in quite a pack train of supplies to be delivered. The ponies had been doing nothing for quite a spell except get fat and sassy. There were two "delicate" packs. We picked a couple of our gentle saddle ponies for these packs and let the broomtails take the picks, shovels, tents, candles and what have you that wouldn't take too much damage from a little buck jump. Imagine our surprise when the "gentle" ones started up Beaver Pass valley on a gallop with the odd buck jump thrown in for good measure. The others lined out like trained pack horses behind them with nary a jump. However, even the eggs made it into camp okay.

We got flooded out of our tent camp one night after too many heavy rains. Harry Quanstrom was with us this time. Lightning Creek went on the rampage and broke out of its banks and away in the black of the night we felt the water coming up in our beds. There wasn't much we could do till morning but perch like ducks on windfalls and hope the windfalls didn't head off downstream. In the morning we moved to higher ground and built a little shanty affair; no hell for fancy, but it served the purpose for a short spell. But it was down too much in the shade and always damp and dreary so we moved up to the old Beaver Pass buildings where Gardners used to run a stopping house and sawmill back in the days of the stage coaches. There we found an old "buckboard" as we called it. Jack Gardner stoutly maintained it was a "Mountain Spring Wagon" and he wasn't guessing, he knew what it was. We bought it from him for twenty-five dollars. It was a really well-built rig, a Studebaker no less, and in good shape yet. It looked mighty good to us for the long trip home (a hundred and thirty miles) and for future trips to town and back (seventy miles each way from Ramsay Creek). The old iron-wheel wagon was to be relegated to hauling haying machinery back and forth to meadows and the very odd town trip when we might have too big a load for the new spring wagon. But the plans of mice and men don't always work out as we found later.

There were also the remains of an old BX freight wagon, a McLaughlin top buggy, fancy cutters and sleighs, all the trappings of the passing era of the horse vehicles. Gardners were still in the lumbering business but mostly mechanized. They still used a few horses for skidding in the bush and on the landings but the era of trucks, tractors and cars was taking the place of the old horse logging and travel days.

We got a few pack trips out of Wing Dam and then several trips out of Stanley and we moved camp up to Stanley. We had quite a lot of stuff to pack out of Stanley first trip before we moved up there. Having to ride seven miles there first from Beaver Pass, we had to start operations right early and were very short of time. We had Black Tiny, who was pretty snorty yet. So we made up a pack of lash cinches and canvasses and such like pack rigging and very carefully and gently tied that on her at Beaver Pass, figuring the seven miles with it would educate her quite a little. Stanley seemed pretty much a ghost town except occasionally at night it would come to life. But mostly you'd never guess there were over half a dozen folks living there.

We went to packing in a hurry when we got there. We saved out a pack for Black Tiny that she wouldn't hurt much if she blew up and, after packing all the others, went to finish up on her. It consisted of boxes of candles, picks and shovels, and odds and ends of all types. There were too many pieces in it. We did get it all on and tied with the sling ropes, but hadn't got the lash cinch onto it yet, when Tiny figured she wasn't going to suffer any more indignities. I was holding her head and helping on one side with Art doing most of the packing. Neither of us had taken time to take off our spurs. Tiny made a jump ahead and planted one foot on my spur and at the same time ran the corner of a box of candles into my back and, not being able to get my foot loose, I couldn't swing on her head and hold her. I had to let go and the box knocked me down under her and she lit into bucking.

I think she did a couple of jumps right off my back before she got clear of me. Another of my nine lives gone, but I didn't even get hurt that time. Shovels, picks, tents and, finally, candle boxes came flying in every direction. But what was more surprising, out of every ghost shack came people; and in less time than it takes to tell of it, there must have been an audience of fifty all around.

Art hung onto the long end of Tiny's rope, got it onto his saddle horn and wound up by upsetting Tiny in the mess she had made. We hogtied her and left her there all day while we made the pack trip. We threw her pack here and there on top of the other packs and made the trip out to the camp.

When we got back to Stanley in the evening we decided it was time Tiny was broken and Art clamped his saddle on her and let her loose with him in the middle. She had the conceit pretty well taken out of her for that day and didn't give the folks much of a show. But she was a real good pack and saddle horse from then on except for one trip on the trapline back at Ramsay Creek the next winter. She went to bucking in deep snow and threw herself. Art got tangled up in the snow and couldn't get away. She had landed the saddle horn right on his face and made a bloody mess of it. There was so much blood we couldn't figure how badly hurt he was, but he got aboard and rode her home seven miles, partly in the dark. If Tiny had ever looked back at him she'd have died of fright. He sure looked wild and was plenty sore to go with it.

There was a lady prospector down by Beaver Pass, a Miss Taylor. She wanted to get her rigging packed some twelve or fourteen miles up Beaver Pass. This lady had very strict notions on the fitness of things, or what was and was not proper for a single lady to do. According to the creed she ran on she couldn't contact us bachelors directly. She therefore left a message for Art at the local Beaver Pass store to the effect that he was to meet her there at a specified time to arrange to take her belongings to her new prospecting territory.

The meeting was duly chaperoned by the storekeeper and the arrangement, after some haggling, was that Art was to go in to her camp at eight-thirty a.m. She had specified ten a.m. but Art said he would have to make a return trip and ten would be much too late, so how would seven a.m. do? No dice. So they compromised on eight-thirty. Everything was to be in readiness and set out where Art could easily see what was to be taken. Two horses would handle the job. She would be away. (It wouldn't be proper for her to be there with a young bachelor!) But things didn't go as planned. When Art arrived on time, the good lady was still there and in great difficulties trying to get her junk into big and little boxes. She apparently thought she had too few boxes but to Art she had too damn many.

Art wanted to get on the trail but sat outside and gave the poor woman a little more time. Then he hollered out, "How're you gettin' along with your work? About time we got the outfit packed and moving." The lady was about driven to distraction by then and decided the whole situation was too much for her to cope with. She sat down on a box of her junk and gave vent to tears. Art decided she needed help and asked if he could come in and help her pack the rigging, seeing as packing was maybe more in his line than hers. She unlimbered the cast iron code and told him he could try.

Now any good man would have patted the poor distraught woman, wiped her tears away, told her to leave everything to him and brew a cup of coffee to cheer her up. But the story Art tells me doesn't take that line. He claims he told her she never could get all those boxes tied onto two horses and still get them up a narrow pack trail and if he didn't get packed pretty sudden, he couldn't make it that day anyway. Apparently this dried the tears up and the lady got a mite peeved, grabbed boxes right and left and emptied them out on the floor one after another and told Art to go to it, he knew so much about it! She left him and went on her way talking to herself.

Usually she tied a bell around her neck, and apparently she did after she got a little over being mad.

Art tied into the riggin' and had it all packed, boxed and lashed onto the horses in a little while. When Art caught up to her he nearly bumped a pack horse into her, waddling up the trail with her bell ding-donging away. Suddenly she looked back and said to Art, "Oh, I thought you were a cow!"

Miss Taylor led the way from there, seeming to have relaxed her code to the extent of allowing her packer to accompany her on the trail. But when she got to where the trail left the main trail to cross the creek and up the other side, Art balked. There was no place he could cross the boggy creek and swamp to her intended camp with a horse outfit, and it was much too late in the day to help her across by hand. So he went to unpacking and told her that was as far as he could take the stuff. She stamped her feet and said, "This is not my destination" and repeated it several times.

By this time Art had lost most of what patience he had started out with and told her, "I don't give a damn if it's your destination or not. It's as far as I can go and it's my destination!" The argument was getting pretty hot when an old-timer came along. Miss Taylor apparently knew him quite well and seemed to have more faith in him than she did in Art. He told her that Art was quite right and couldn't go further with the horses as he had to get them back to feed. As night was fast approaching, it would be best she set up her camp right there for the time being and call it home.

That ended the trip and the argument. Apparently the poor woman didn't strike it rich or even enough to grubstake herself. But being so independent and afraid of men taking advantage of her helplessness she nearly starved to death before folks got wise and helped her out of the country.

Things were pretty quiet around midsummer and I went out prospecting with an old Swede, Andy Hansen. We went south from Beaver Pass first and wandered all over with light back packs of camp outfit, grub, shovel, gold pan and light pick. Apparently the area had been prospected pretty well before, as just about every place Andy decided we should dig a test hole and do a little panning, we would find an old prospect hole nearby. We nearly always got just so far digging before Andy would say, "Not good enough to work," and we would go on again. Andy was a great storyteller and had been mixed up with prospecting most of his life. He had been in the Yukon gold rush in '98, also up in Alaska, and pretty well all over the Cariboo gold fields. He told great tales of the "Lucky Swede," the Cedar Creek strike and many more. I have a poor memory for yarns and jokes but I think it was Lucky Swede who imported enough milk for his lady friend to have a bath in. That was away up in the Yukon where milk was likely about two dollars a quart at the time, if you could get it at all.

We went over the top of Sovereign Mountain on the first of July and there were snowdrifts eight or ten feet deep on the shady side. Quite near one I nearly stepped over a deer fawn before I saw it. It was only a day or so old and didn't run. We petted it a little and then went away a few yards and watched. Sure enough, the mother came out of hiding and claimed her baby, then took it away all very quietly and sedately.

Andy and I crossed the valley and went up Beaver Pass and up and down a few more creeks. We finally found one that Andy figured we could make wages on but it was against Andy's religion to work a claim. He wanted to make a "strike" or nothing.

Art had taken some of our blooded mares in to town for the July 1st races. Pierre and family had gone in and somebody talked Pierre into riding in the Roman race to make a little more competition as there were only two teams. So Pierre hit Art up for horses. The best outfit he could rustle together were Fanny and Flossie. Neither of them had ever been raced before, let alone in a Roman Standing race. But Pierre got up on them and, although he never got them out of a fast trot with the odd little buck jump thrown in for good measure, he made it around the track without coming down and got second prize as one rider had been disqualified for coming down for a second. The crowd got quite a laugh out of it and gave Pierre a real hand.

One night in the little cabin at Beaver Pass I got a terrible toothache. The only dope we had around was Sloan's Liniment. I poured some on my finger and dabbed it all over my gums. Then, half asleep, I rubbed my eyes. That cured the toothache right then! I was wide awake pronto. Talk about a counter-irritant! That was it, the genuine article. Try it sometime. I couldn't keep my eyes shut or open but had to blink steadily. Art rared up and got a bucket of water for me to dip my head into but it took a long time for the stinging to subside. But "it's an ill wind . . ."; the toothache was completely gone and didn't return.

Art cut his knee pretty deeply with an axe up at Beaver Pass. He asked me what we had to put on it. We had forgotten the iodine. Salt was all we had. I gave him quite a lecture on the healing and antiseptic qualities of salt, which I learned from the lady druggist back in Alberta. This lady claimed that if folks knew all the healing properties and other things common salt was good for, there would be no need for druggists. For Art's cut knee there could be nothing better. Art seemed to have plenty of misgivings, but finally let me pour a generous sprinkling of salt on the wide-open raw cut. I moved cautiously to the door end of the shanty right quickly. It turned out to be a good idea. I didn't figure it would be a wise idea to stick around and be in line of a riding boot heaved with murderous intent. Art grabbed the closest heavy fry pan and started after me, cussing all lady druggists and drugstore cowboys about as well as they could be cussed! But I had made it to the great outdoors, well out of harm's way, and kept my distance till things cooled down a bit. The protest was vociferous and educational and, I might add, blasphemous. The cut healed very nicely and quickly.

CHAPTER XIII

The Daddy Wolf —
Building Cabin in 50 Below

Back at Ramsay Creek, late in October of '34 after haying was finished, I was mudding and banking the house for winter. I had Duke and Sis in the barnyard. All of a sudden they let a whoof out of them, lit out across the barnyard, and jumped the creek. They stood on the little patch of ground on the far side between the fence and the creek, snorting with their heads as high as they could hold them, looking up the road back by the barn.

I went around the corner to look see and there, coming along the road towards the barn and house, was a huge animal, the like of which I have never seen before, or since for that matter. It stood higher than a buck deer, but had very long hair and a great long shaggy mane. It was a fairly light grey colour with massive legs and head. It just had to be a timber wolf. Although I have seen many since, I've never seen another nearly as big. Before that, I had only seen one, up at Lesser Slave Lake in Alberta, but it was only half the size of this one. I ducked into the cabin and got the .32 Remington. I came out all primed to meet him face to face right outside the cabin which was where he'd have been if he had kept coming the same direction.

I saw he had turned off to go out around the barn and, when I got a bead on him, he was passing a big leaning windfall so that his brisket came out first. I didn't wait for a more vital spot to appear but let him have it. That shot was a little too low to drop him, but he came out further and revealed his whole front end and I got a shot dead centre between lower chest and top of withers. He dropped and I ran up. Shorty did too. He was only about fifty yards away.

Shorty really had him a big dog to yap at this time. That brave little devil was right up nipping at the wolf's hind end. The wolf was paralyzed now from the shoulders back but, big as he was and wounded so he couldn't get away, as I came up to him he raised up on his front legs and tried to drag himself away. No thought apparently of defending himself. He paid no attention to Shorty at all. I shot him again right dead centre in the backbone between the shoulder blades. The bullet tore a big hole coming out of the front of his chest low down. The middle shot had gone right through and had torn a hole in the far side. Both of the last shots should have been fatal, but that big old dog just flopped down and barked and then howled.

I knew he was harmless but that howl right up close made me feel that I had long, stiff hair all up my back and neck and over the top of my head, and that it raised right up and made me tingle. I have had the same feeling since when wolves howled close and others I have talked to have had the same experience. This makes me think that at one time before man had efficient weapons, timber wolves were his natural enemy. It is an instinctive fear that one has no control of. You may be inside a log cabin and know you are perfectly safe, as I have been, and know that the howling wolves are much more afraid of you than you are of them, yet you have the feeling that hair raises all up your back and neck and over the top of your head.

When this big wolf went down the last time he grabbed limbs on a windfall by him and snapped limbs, the size of my wrist, like matchsticks. Those powerful jaws could pulverize a cow's leg bone in one bite. I had to chase Shorty away, I was so scared he would get in reach and one bite would cut him in half. I even made him go back to the cabin with me as I had run out of ammunition and had to get the .22 to finish off the big dog. It took three shots with the .22. First I shot for the heart with the rifle only six feet from him. No effect. He just snapped off more limbs and howled. Then I put two shots into his brain. That finally put an end to the daddy of timber wolves.

I was pretty skookum in those days but I couldn't lift him. I had to drag him over to the house and then I had a dickens of a job to hoist him up by the hind legs to a ridge log with a long rope so I could skin him more easily. I had no boards to make a stretcher so I cut two little green poles and nailed wedges on them, a very poor makeshift stretcher and so flimsy that I couldn't stretch it as wide or long as it should have been. But even at that, just pulled loose, it stretched eight-feet two-inches long and over two feet wide.

I think anyone who has hunted and made a kill or successful hunt, feels the need to tell someone all about it. The telling and retelling of the story seems to be a big part of the thrill. Here was I, all alone forty miles from anyone, and just bubbling over with my yarn. My first timber wolf, big as they come, and I ran out of ammo with him still howling. My chance to tell it was closer than I guessed. About three days later a stranger rode in leading a little buckskin pack pony. Old Sis and Duke gave me plenty of warning this time. I guess they figured that little buckskin pony was another wolf sneaking up on them and they spooked again. I was working on the cabin, and I grabbed the cannon and went out to meet the foe. I met him before he even got to the barn, right where I had first seen the wolf. Well, when I saw it was a man I guess likely I lowered the gun but, without any further preparation or the amenities of introduction, my wolf yarn just came a-bubbling out of me. I told him the whole story, with the guy just sitting there, hungry as hell, and didn't know me from Adam's off ox (and likely before I got through wasn't sure if he wanted to). I hadn't even said a "Howdy," or "Did you eat lately," or "Get down and rest your hind end and come on in." I'm plumb sure he figured here's a guy who's been in the sticks too long alone. But I never let him get a word in edgeways till I was finished. He just had to stay put and listen.

Then it hit me like a bat on the head that there were other things I should have said first. I gave the poor feller a chance to introduce himself, and let him come on up to the place and get unpacked. George Wilcox was his name and it turned out he had ridden across from Alberta via the Goat River trail, mostly a goat track, into Barkerville and run into Art there. It was pretty late in the fall, no work available and he was worried about wintering his ponies. Art told him to come out to our layout and he and the ponies could winter with us. Art told him he might find me stacking hay alone and be able to give me a hand. In any case, he would be welcome to stay. Art said I'd be tickled to see him, having been alone two or three months. Little did Art know just how tickled I would be. I hadn't got used to living alone yet (does anybody ever?) and I guess I talked about as much as George could stand to listen to. I talked as late as he would stay awake at night and all day when we were together for the first while.

George was a pretty good talker himself and, after I got winded a bit, I found he could run me a close second. He was quite a man for his tea. Art and I mostly used coffee in those days and we didn't have much tea around any time. Even after Art got back in later we were short of grub, and tea especially. George never said anything about it. He built a couple of chairs and a pair of snowshoes and set some traps while Art and I were building a little cabin for a stopping place down at the Cooper meadow. One of his chairs was a masterpiece. It was made out of three big blocks, all hewn to shape, with auger holes drilled into them to hold legs. The back piece is the outstanding part. It fits the form perfectly without any padding and is really a comfortable chair. But you need a block and tackle to move it around the cabin. Consequently it doesn't go over so well with the womenfolk when they go to chasing dust or rearranging the furniture for better effects.

We had bought quite a few traps by now and after Art got home we went to work setting them out, opening up new trails and blazing them. By Christmas we had caught quite a lot of fur. But we had started building the little cabin at the Cooper meadow and we wanted to finish that and a barn before we made the long trip to town. Pierre came up one day and he and Art went out hunting and rode all day without getting anything. It had been snowing heavily and the timber was loaded with wet snow. Art had ridden Sis and he felt pretty sorry for her so decided to dry her off before turning her out. He stood her alongside the campfire. This same campfire was cooking our supper. Camping in the winter without much grub, most everything is in one kettle, a "mulligan." Meat, beans and rice were in this one, and the last of our meat too. The heat of the fire was too much for trail-weary old Sis and she fell asleep and flopped almost over into the fire, knocking the mulligan pot hell west and crooked, spilling the whole thing into the ashes. Art forgot all sympathetic feelings for Sis and jerked the riggin' off her and slapped her hind end with the bridle reins, with a "Get the hell outa here you old sonofabitch and forget to come back."

At the time, being desperately hungry, nothing cooked and not much left to cook, we never thought of any pictures. Later we remembered the Charlie Russell painting, "Bronc to Breakfast," which hung in our old home living room back in Alberta, depicting the old round-up cook with his pans of bannock, sowbelly and coffee pot over the campfire at the tail end of the chuckwagon. Into the works the horse-wrangler is riding a bucking bronc, knocking the cooking outfit every which way, and the cook is threatening to do murder with a long butcher knife.

Art got a good moose next day so we were well away. Then the weather turned cold — bitterly cold. We had no thermometer but later we heard reports of all the way from 50 below to 70 below F. My sourdough, instead of being all live and bubbly, was frozen solid. The only way I could make hotcakes was to put the sourdough pot into another pot of water, set the works right on the fire and keep the water boiling steady while I mixed and dipped batter out. Luckily we ran out of flour in a day or so or we never would have got anything else done. We cut steak with a double-bitted axe and threw the chips into the smoking fry pan to thaw out and cook. We sure didn't take off any clothes to go to bed either. Had to wrap our heads in gunny sacks to keep our hair from freezing stiff and breaking off, making us bald headed!

We got the cabin walls up, the gable ends in and ridge logs all set but the top one. Rolling it up we broke an end log right off short inside the notch which meant taking the whole works down to replace the broken log. We figured it was just too cold when nearly a full-size log broke off that easy, and so we quit. It was only a day or so to Christmas anyway, so we packed our blankets and some meat up to Ramsay Creek and George Wilcox. But we left the tent standing so it would be easier to come back to, or so we thought. We had saved out some flour, sugar and a few dried peaches and Art had vowed he would make us a peach pie for Christmas. I had some misgivings — if it was anything like his coffee making! However, there wasn't enough of anything to argue about and on Christmas Day Art tied a flour sack around him to look the part, rolled up his sleeves and went to work with a gleam in his eye. Neither one of us ever did much fancy cooking. We just didn't have the time and always seemed to be hungry enough that plain grub tasted plenty good enough. When we had the makings, one of us made what we called "high-toned bannock" on special occasions. This contained most everything we had in it: raisins, sugar, cinnamon, vanilla, fine rolled oats, sometimes coconut and, of course, flour, salt, baking powder and a little moose grease. Some magazine which Art got hold of told how to make icing that was different. You just spread brown sugar on top. So one time Art did this and when he took the creation out of the oven, it looked so good he decided it required special care turning out of the pan. Thus he rolled up his sleeve and tipped the cake with the lovely bubbling brown sugar icing out on his bare arm, so he could let it down easy. Well, when that bubbly icing touched his arm and stuck full length, Art forgot all about the delicate reverence in handling the deal and let out a whoop you could have heard halfway to hell. I never would have guessed what an agile dancing brother I had without this incident.

Getting back to the peach pie. Art kept a one-track mind through that performance, and darned if that thing didn't turn out to be a masterpiece. Talk about what mother used to make! Shucks, if she could have made pie like that she'd have gone into the catering busines right sudden. Rich, golden brown, flaky pastry and delicious flavour, not the least bit soggy from the dried peaches having to be soaked overnight and cooked some before putting on the cap. Not too wet and yet nice and juicy; in short, just perfect.

I had roasted about the best cut of the moose and no king ever enjoyed his Christmas dinner any more than we enjoyed that one.

Don't think we didn't appreciate being inside looking out at that 50 below weather. We could really "hot" that old cabin up and feel heat all around us; no ashes in the grub and no squatting on the cold, cold ground. It makes you feel like you amount to something to sit up to a table in a chair after long sessions around a campfire. We even laid off the beans and rice as we had saved out enough spuds and carrots for the big spread.

But they do say all good things come to an end and for damn sure ours had. About all we had left was plenty of good meat, coffee and tobacco. We stalled off going back to the campfire for a few days, hoping it would turn mild. But it didn't and a couple of days before New Year's we took off again. Art took a team and sleigh down and I rode down as I had the odd trap and snare set a little way from the road. If we'd had a thermometer we'd likely have had brains enough to stay put. But we wanted to get a load of grub in before the snow got too deep and wanted to have this "halfway to Tibbles" stopping house and barn ready first. Art got there first and was across the meadow getting a load of hay when I got in and learned of our misfortune. We had let Burnstad use the meadow and he had brought up his cattle and turned them loose. They decided our tent was just what they needed and crowded in, knocked it down and now it was frozen solid in manure. Before I took this all in, my feet started to come unfrozen. I had frozen all my toes and soles of my feet, not deeply, but plenty to put the run on me. They hurt so much I ran across the meadow and back three times before I could hold still.

Our only out was to cut the doorway into the new cabin, build a fire in it and move in there. Art got hay for under the beds and when I could stand still long enough to chop a tree down, I cut some wood and we moved our outfit into the unroofed cabin. There was practically no dry wood left around that we could find in the dark anyway. We had to use green wood with a little dry to make it last, as it was too dark to locate more dry wood. This made everything just lovely. Ever try burning green wood inside a shack with no stove or stove pipe? Try it! True enough there was no roof on it but that smoke didn't seem to want to go out in the cold anymore than we did. We were like between the devil and the deep blue sea. We couldn't stand the cold without the fire and couldn't stand the smoke with it. We were smoke cured plenty by morning; we couldn't keep our eyes shut or open.

There was a little B.C. heater campstove down at Burnstad's ready for the cabin so we went down after it first thing in the morning and that made a world of difference to the setup. With good wood we could keep quite warm and we put in our evenings chinking the cracks with moss.

We got the roof on in a big hurry, called the little ten-by-twelve shanty good, and switched to building a five-horse barn. For it we used a lot of the logs that had been cut for the cabin we started the first year. The weather turned mild and Lexie and his partner came over and gave us a day or so help. We had that barn up and a pole roof covered with hay in about four days. That was all we needed for the time being. We had a good, warm cabin for ourselves and a barn and feed for our horses.

George had caught some foxes, weasels and a coyote or two, and Art and I had a little bunch of fur and my big wolf hide. So George and I rigged up our outfit and took a team and sleigh to town. I felt sorry for Art going back to trapping alone while we went out to the great outside world. We would be sampling other folks' good cooking and making chin music far into the night along the way.

Our first stop was at Paley's where I got Alec to price my wolf hide. He was buying fur then and shipping it to Seattle Fur Exchange. He looked up his price lists but wolves weren't quoted on it. Alec said it was a good one and worth somewhere between thirty-five and fifty dollars likely. Then he said it would be fairer to both of us if he shipped it to Seattle and gave me what he got. I let him do that. There was no bounty on them until some years later. Imagine my disappointment when the returns came back and amounted to five dollars and fifty cents. I would never have sold it had I known that was all it would bring. But, being out of grub and very short of finances, if there was a chance of over thirty-five dollars I just couldn't hang on to it. I have killed over forty wolves since, and seen many that other people got, but never one nearly as big as that huge old dog. His hide would really have been a valued souvenir.

The price of other fur wasn't very good either, so I only had enough to buy the bare necessities in grub and what clothes we needed; there was nothing to tarry in town for, so we were on our way back to Ramsay Creek in short order.

We put in a day in the house when we got home and built some fancy bannock and bread, cooked fruit and had ourselves quite a feed. Art got the lowdown on all the neighbours' doings. George dug a little aluminum teapot out of his pack and produced plenty of tea he had bought, and we were to see just what dishwater we had been giving him for tea. For the first pot of tea he took all the tea leaves he could hold in his cupped hand and dumped them in the pot. Then he poured in about two cups of boiling water and set the pot on to boil awhile.

Mostly he didn't drink more than a cup or a cup and a half of this brew at a sitting. The pot was always left on the stove where it was boiling or near boiling from then on. When there were too many tea leaves in it to hold a cup and a half of tea he scooped a handful of leaves out. But for every sitting, a handful of fresh tea was dumped in and she boiled merrily away.

We used to hear Arthur Godfrey's talent scout program on the radio when it was sponsored by Lipton's Tea. Apparently he didn't always make the cup of tea for his talent show in quite the orthodox method. There would invariably be either caustic comments or witty remarks made by some discriminating tea maker. Well, if some of those folks had got an eyeful of George building his brew a few times they'd have said, "Now I've seen everything!" and figured Arthur Godfrey was a pretty fair tea maker as tea makers come.

George was good company all winter but come spring he got itchy feet right early. He packed his little old teapot and his riggin' on the buckskin pony and headed north. We never heard of him again. I've often wondered if the inside of his stomach wasn't pretty well tanned.

We had two or three colts the previous summer and had weaned them and were letting them run in the barn when it was cold. That helped put a little interest in our home life. We were both born stockmen and, not having any cattle yet, it was sure nice to have a few colts to monkey with. In the spring we broke them all to lead, handled their feet and branded them. We had got a brand registered for horses and cattle. It was our first choice: Lᶜ, denoting Lavington Co. — left ribs on the cattle and right shoulder on horses — and that was the beginning of the Lᶜ ranch as it was to be known.

Not long after we had built the little shack at Cooper meadow and made our trip to town, a chinook came along and I went out on the trapline and landed at Cooper meadow. Pierre and family had moved into that little two-by-four shanty to feed their few cattle and some he got to winter for the Websters. Hazel Rawling had come up to stay with them a few days. I got in there at night and talked Hazel into riding with me next day. I figured we would ride down to what was called the Big Flat, about two miles up Baker Creek from the Burnstad place. I had a coyote bait there and we hoped to find a fresh track of a coyote or fox, and try running it. I was riding Brownie and had a little pack on Flossie. But I only had hackamores on them, no bridles. I staked Hazel to Flossie with Pierre's saddle and we were away.

We struck a fresh marten track only a couple of miles out. We tracked it back and forth this way and that for twenty minutes and decided it was too tough on the horses and looked to be too long a job. So we quit tracking and headed straight for the Big Flat. We had only gone a quarter of a mile when we ran onto the marten track again. I nearly crossed it and left but I noticed it went up on a little open sidehill with hardly any trees and I couldn't see any track on over the hill. I went over closer and still no track so looked up and there was our marten, sunning himself up in a spike-topped tree. I was so excited it took three shots to get him.

We went on down and looked at the coyote bait. But the snow had been too soft, wet and deep for coyotes to tackle going out into the open, so there was nothing there.

The previous fall we had built a log wall two rounds high and set our small tent over it. With an airtight heater inside, it could be made quite comfortable even in severe cold weather. I made a cup of coffee for us there. We hit back a different way and struck a red-hot fox track and took after that. We only went a few yards off the road before we came to the fox's bed and it was right fresh. So away we went with a hoot and a holler. Inside of two hundred and fifty yards we came up on a red fox. I got my .22 out, unlimbered my holler and in no time Brownie was right up on him and I took a one-handed shot at the galloping fox. No harm done, so I jumped off and tried again. But as soon as I stopped and quit hollering, the fox slowed to a trot and weaved back and forth, instinctively seeming to keep a tree in line. He could travel faster trotting rather than jumping because he could pussyfoot along at a trot and only go down a few inches, whereas jumping he would practically bury himself in the soft snow every jump.

I had to mount and ride again to catch up. By now the fox had got into one of Brownie's tracks and was making better time. But her tracks had gone every which way and every little bit I'd see the little red fox bobbing along and almost coming towards me. I would cut across. But the funny part was that Hazel couldn't get Flossie to cross over and sometimes we passed going in opposite directions. It worked out in one respect. I dropped a fur mitt here, and another there, and a hat yonder and she picked them all up. Every time I caught up I'd get in a shot from the horse and then get down and get in another shot from the ground. But I missed every time. I couldn't take time to get a club and couldn't reach with the .22. Then I got off to get in a ground shot, forgot to throw the hackamore shank down, and Brownie kept right on going over to catch up to Hazel on Flossie. I was a-foot with the gun empty and the fox carefully trotted away, got into a rock canyon and on to freedom. We didn't get the fox but we sure had fun.

CHAPTER XIV

Getting Crippled in '35 —
Horse Funeral in Stanley

In the early fall of '35 we were camping at Beaver Pass. Packing jobs were very scarce and I left pretty early to go haying. I had four or five horses and the wagon and made camp first night on my way down at Cold Springs, some seventeen miles from Beaver Pass and seven miles from the old Cottonwood stopping house. I staked and hobbled my horses pretty well as they were apt to go in either direction. I made camp on the Quesnel side of the little meadow, a hundred and fifty yards or so from the meadow and seventy-five yards from the road. Some time around four o'clock in the morning something, likely a bear, stampeded the horses. They got badly scared, broke loose and headed onto the road and then for Quesnel. I heard the commotion, bell-jangling and snorting soon enough to jerk my boots on, and ran out onto the road to head them off. Old Smokey was in the lead and passed me but when I cut the others off and stopped them, he doubled back to the bunch and they all stopped momentarily.

In the dark I caught the end of the rope that was still on Smokey's foot. But in turning back, the rope was doubled and there was probably fifteen feet of slack in it. Before I got time to take up the slack they stampeded away from me towards Beaver Pass. When Smokey hit the end of that rope he was really travelling. I had set myself to hang on but it buckled my knee and threw me down. It was just as though my knee was broken. It was absolutely powerless and painful as hell. I crawled back to camp to figure things out and get a coat or something. I figured the best I could do was catch the first truck whichever way it was going. If it went to Quesnel I would go to a doctor but if going up, I would hole up in camp. It wasn't long before I heard one and I started crawling back to the road again, but I couldn't crawl fast enough and it went on by. But once they started in the morning I knew they would soon be coming from both ways as these trucks were the only means of taking supplies to Wells and Barkerville and way points.

I put on a coat and hat, then crawled out to the road. I sat and waited for the next truck and hailed it. It was Ole Fardell, going to

Barkerville, so I got a ride as far as our camp and gave Art a holler. He jerked his britches on, came up to the road and helped me down into the little dark, damp cabin below the road, and there I stayed for two weeks.

We figured it was just a sprain and would soon get all right. It swelled up like a stovepipe and stayed that way. All we had was a bottle of turpentine for cuts or caulk wounds on horses, but we'd heard of using it as a liniment. So we rubbed the turpentine in several times a day, every day, and almost blistered the hide off trying to get the swelling down and relieve the pain. Folks stopping by all figured that was good. Some suggested hot fomentations and others said cold packs. We tried both but to no avail. I was hardly able to sleep all through this session because of the pain and finally we decided I had to get to a doctor, so I caught a ride into Quesnel and got hold of Doc Baker. He was pretty badly upset; said we should have come to him right away, whether we had any money or not. He said the turpentine was the worst thing we could have used. The cartilages and ligaments were all torn and turpentine tended to shrink and dry them and thus create more pain, drawing my heel up and drawing on cords right up to the base of the spine. He was afraid the damage would be irreparable and that I would be crippled for life. He wanted me to go to hospital but I wouldn't.

Anyway, he taped it all up and rustled me a pair of crutches and told me to come back in three days. I had brought a little camp outfit with me and hobbled over to one or our old camping places. We had always made friends with all the town youngsters who came around our camp. We let them ride horses and lead some to water, shod their ponies for them and let them sample the sourdough biscuits and rice or whatever. Now I turned the tables on them. They helped get my riggin' over and set up, get wood and water for me, and were just as busy as little bees helping me get settled. They hated to go away and leave me, but I told them I'd be okay. I was supposed to rest and didn't need any help to do that, but they could sure come again. Also I got word to Art to bring team and wagon and saddle horse down so I could go on out haying. The swelling went down quite a bit before the three days were up and the pain eased off. I caught up a lot of sleep in a little while.

Doc took the tape off, then gave me a bottle of olive oil and told me to go to rubbing and massaging with lots of the oil. Then he taped it up again, but when I said I wanted to go on out home he shook his head and said "crazy." But he gave me more tape and oil. As the swelling went down, I was to take off the old tape and put on the new after a good massaging with oil. But in no uncertain terms, he said I must come back in two weeks.

So I loaded into the wagon when Art got it and headed west. I had to make it to someone's place for every overnight stop to get help taking care of the horses. I had never been very badly hurt before and, other than my haywire stomach, took quite a little pride in my physical fitness. Now I was kind of ashamed of being so helpless and I resented the thought of being crippled, and so dependent. I guess I was extremely sorry for myself and damn near cried myself to sleep. Not to be fit and independent of help to do anything, I aimed to do what was about the worst thing I could have done. I fought it right from the start. I would suffer no end of pain to make light of it and try to stop anyone thinking I needed help to do things. I went to Burnstad's and propositioned him. I would run mower or rake or any job where I could sit or stand still on one leg. So I would help him with his haying all I could if he would help me and do the jobs I couldn't do. He was agreeable and we went to work and put up hay for him on his place to beat everything. Then I had to go in and see Doc again. I figured when I came back again we should go up and get a little early hay for us and then either finish ours or Pierre's whichever seemed best. That didn't sound good to Pierre. He wanted to finish his first and save moving between jobs.

Well, I got my back up. Had I been normal I would have thought nothing of it. But as I was, there seemed to be an awful urgency to get started on our own hay and I figured Pierre was just taking advantage of my being so helpless. I thought we would take up most of the haying season putting up his hay and we'd just have a lot of late frozen junk. All this was unreasonable, but I had to assert my independence and I wasn't going to beg anyone to help me.

I rode off for town on my faithful and very gentle old Jean in a bit of a huff. I was lucky and after riding some sixteen miles I got a drive in with a hunter in a car. He was staying in town till the next afternoon which would give me time to get fixed up. I left my horse at the neighbour's till my return.

Doc had told me to call him any time I got in, but I met him on the street right away and he took me to his office and sized up the deal. The swelling was all down and not much pain, but my knee was bent and my heel raised up three or four inches from the floor. He made the decision to straighten things out and sat me on one chair and placed my heel on a cushion on another chair.

Then in his inimitable way he says, "This won't hurt a bit. Won't hurt a bit." This was a stock phrase of his whether he was pulling a tooth or cutting off an arm. He knew damn well he was lying, and just before he did anything he amended it. "Yes, it'll hurt a little bit but you're a good man. You can take it," and down he came with all his weight with both hands over my knee. I nearly hit the roof and let out a yell you could have heard plumb across the divide, and started to use up a lot of my good stock of cussing. "I had to do it," Doc says, "had to do it. Don't want you to be a cripple. It had knit all crooked and had to be broken. You'll be all right in a little bit. Here, have a drink, have a drink." He dug out a bottle of whiskey and handed it to me. "Good man, hurt like hell, didn't it? Be all right soon, be all right soon. Sit down and rest a bit." Doc used repetition for emphasis a lot, but I think everyone who knew him loved our good old Doc. He was never too busy or too tired to help you whether you were wealthy or flat broke, Indian or white man.

When, quite a number of years later, he passed on over the divide, we folks in the Cariboo felt we had lost one of the most precious things in life. Many are the stories that are told of our Doc. Now we have a large, modern hospital named after him and he lives on in memory. Doc gave me another drink and then told me either to get someone to sit on my knee for one or two hours every night, or put a weight on it to hold it straight to keep it from knitting all bent again. I was to swing my leg as far forward and back as I could, trying to keep my knee straight. In the winter, skiing would be good for this, also snow-shoeing. Then he turned me loose telling me to be sure to come back if it knitted bent again. I promised I would but also promised myself I would really work on it to keep it straight so he wouldn't have to break it again.

Slim Montgomery and Florence Marsh were married that day and I went up to the reception at Marsh's for a few minutes, but I was in too much pain to take in that kind of a deal and I hit for the roost right quickly.

We got out to Tibbles in time for me to ride on up to Burnstad's next day. This was in the moose running season and I heard a moose grunting. I wanted to see how well I could imitate him, so I started to grunt. Knowing how cantankerous bull moose can be in the fall, it is plumb foolish to call one unless you are armed and want the meat. I got action right quickly and more than I had reckoned on. The old bull came right out and gave chase. I had been riding slowly and even that was painful but now I had to ride on a fast gallop for a whole mile with one leg dangling. This is the only time a bull ever chased me like that. They have bluffed me off the road and such like, but this one was right out for blood and I just had to grab the horn and cantle of the saddle, then hang on and grin and bear it. I had no gun and no desire to shoot the moose even if I had, but I would like to have blown a blast of buckshot in his face. He got right up close before the old mare got into her stride. I wondered if it wouldn't be easier to stop and let nature take its course. I was about to faint with the pain before he gave up the chase. Sure educated me, and before I did any moose calling I had the cards stacked my way. From there on in I rode at a much more sedate pace.

The Burnstads had a youngster staying with them, a boy about eleven or twelve by the name of Harold Fleming. I talked him into going up to Ramsay Creek to help do the chasing around jobs so I could get away with walking as little as possible. I rested up a day and got my outfit lined up and took off to do my haying on my own. The first obstacle I hit, we broke through the second bridge up. The high water had taken some of the covering off and, being crippled, I didn't fix it well enough before driving on. The team went through and both horses flopped down with their legs through the covering, struggling to get up. I was afraid one or the other of them would flop onto me in their struggles to get up. They were jumping and plunging with legs flying every which way, and I was so awkward on one leg trying to unhook them, I had little chance to jump out of the way. I was afraid to let the youngster get close to them. He was nimble enough, but not experienced enough to know when to jump clear, and when to get in and do things. However, I finally got them unhooked and uncoupled and they floundered their way back to the side we started from.

Then I had to cut windfalls, willows and the odd tree to clear out an approach to a place we could ford the team across. Then I had to ride the team over and hook them together, tie ropes, chain and whatever we had together, enough so that we could tow the wagon on across the broken bridge. By the time I got the outfit across I could damn near have wept, I had hurt myself so much, and everything I had to do was so painful and hard to do. We still had a long rough road to Ramsay Creek, the team to take care of, supper to get, our grub and everything to take in and beds to make. I knew all these little things that ordinarily seemed hardly worthy of mention were going to be pretty tough to work through and the youngster would be hungry as a bear and dead tired by the time we got in.

Some way we got it all done and then the glorious moment when I could lie down and rest my weary and painful bones. That old bedroll wasn't much for fancy, but at times like that it seemed to mean more than a million bucks in the pocket. I had to take one of the three or four dope capsules Doc had given me in case the pain got

145

too rough, and I have to admit I didn't get a very early start the next day getting organized to begin haying. But it was a rest to get on a mower and rake. That part was easy for me.

Bert Foyle had told me of a sort of cross between a buckpole and sweep that he figured would be a big help in piling the hay up, on one leg. So I got Harold to whittle down the timber and skid it out. He was plumb happy taking his time doing that alongside where I was mowing. We had wonderful haying weather and as soon as we got a little patch of hay raked and bunched, I put the team on the go-devil rig we had built and pushed and piled the hay into the stackyard. Then I forked it up as high as I could reach and got Harold up on top to tramp it down, and we were doing fine.

Then one day Hugh Wilkinson rode in and told me Art had sent a letter out to him with a little money and asked him to come up and help me. I had got to know him and the family as they lived right close to the road nine miles out of town. Jack, his dad, was a foreman on a public works crew, and had told us to stop in there any time we were passing by.

Hughie was only a boy about fourteen then but he sure looked good to me. He had been helping "Ski" Prosser haying. Ski and his brother "Con" had come across the Goat River trail with a little pack train over to Barkerville and located about twenty-five miles from our Ramsay Creek layout in '34. Con had cancer and didn't last long, but Ski was a neighbour for many years till his death about '69 or '70. Ski was quite a character. The name Ski was supposed to be short for Whiskey, Guy being his correct title. Ski had been running a little pack outfit, and renting saddle horses and guiding tourists on hunting trips down around Waterton Lakes Park. Now he had decided to go into cattle where there was open range. He brought a lot of jokes, yarns and expressions that were plumb new to this locality. I always figured Ski should have been a salesman. He could sell snowballs to a trapper in Alaska.

Ski had been rolling Hugh out about 3 a.m. to a feed of burnt or sour beans and bannock. Ski just wasn't handy at all in the cooking line. His cooking was quite a little like Art's coffee making. He would always be talking and never a thought of what was going on at the stove, till smoke started rolling out of the fry pan or oven.

I stayed with the push-pull buckpole sweep and put Hughie to cooking or stacking. Weather had turned a little wet and I was having trouble making the rig pick up hay. I got out in front of the main squared timber and frame backpiece, and was trying to tip the points

146

of the teeth down by getting my good foot as far ahead on a tooth as possible with a hand hold to steady me on the back piece.

The inevitable happened. My foot slipped off and went down under the cross-piece and sprained my ankle, and my haywire leg got a bad twist too before I got the team stopped. If I thought I was helpless before, I sure was now with both legs crippled. About all I could do then was talk and tell the boys what to do. Hugh got the team unhooked, then hauled me out and boosted and heaved me up onto one of the horses and steadied me all the way down to the cabin.

Pierre and Jessie had come in with their haying finished and ready to help me. So we had supper cooked and it was really delicious. I ate mine with my sprained ankle in a four-gallon kerosene can of cold water. I kept up the cold water treatment till bedtime and the ankle wasn't sore and never swelled up. But in a few minutes after I took it out it swelled like a stovepipe and I had to stay on the inside looking out, for a week or better.

It was time for Harold to get back home to school and, as we had nearly finished, and with Hugh's help had things under control, Pierre and Jessie took Harold and headed out for town. They had had quite an experience coming in. They met a big bull moose on the road. Jessie was riding ahead and this bull got up from the middle of the road and came right towards her, grunting and looking pretty tough to get along with. Jessie didn't stick around to argue who had the right of way. She headed back for the wagon on the double. Apparently the rumble and rattle of the wagon was enough to make the bull give ground enough for them to detour through open timber around him. Pierre was holding the rifle on him in case he changed his mind. They passed close enough to see that he must have been in a pretty tough battle and was all scarred up with raw horn slashes all over him.

Later on I ran into him in about the same place on the Corduroy Mountain. When he got right in front of my saddle horse and started for me, I figured here I've let myself in for another of those joyful fast rides — but with both legs dangling this time. I turned back and off into thick scrub brush and timber, then made a big circle out around and he stayed put. He didn't want to move or be moved. He stayed there for quite a long time after, and held the right of way on anybody headed through.

As we needed meat, we took the mountain spring wagon, went up as far as we could on the road and then worked our way up a neck of swamp towards some lakes two miles from the Ramsay Creek cabin. There, right out in the wide open swamp was our moose. Hughie unloaded me and got the old cannon for me. I took careful aim as it

147

was a long shot. Being so close to home where we could get the rig, I wanted to be sure of it. I dropped it dead with one shot and from there on Hughie was on his own as it was away too soft for saddle horses and almost too deep for Hugh.

He worked like a beaver butchering that critter up and quartering it all alone; then he had to drag the quarters quite a long way across the swamp by hand to where we could reach the rope with a saddle horse. Then I towed them out to the wagon. We loaded our meat on the wagon and got home after dark, very weary but plumb tickled with having a buckboard load of prime fat meat. We took on a mighty hefty feed of steak that night, too, before rolling in.

Pate Booth, a tillicum of Hughie's, came up and the two boys finished the stacking and fencing. I did the cooking and what little I could do puttering around on crutches. We had quite a time. They had mouth organs and right after supper they'd stretch out on the bed and play, sing, laugh and chatter, and I got a great kick out of it and wished they had been my youngsters.

The powers that be at Quesnel had decided to use water power for the area. Storage dams were to be built on several lakes in the area. Small earthfill dams had been built already, but a second dam was being built on Tibbles (Puntataenkut) Lake that fall. When I finished haying I came down to get on the job. I was still having to use crutches. Old "Red" Sears had a subcontract to get timber out and he gave me a job peeling logs for the dam, right on the dam site, so I didn't have to move around much. I peeled logs for days and days standing on one leg. I would get so tired by night I could hardly eat, but I think I peeled every log that went into that dam.

I told old Red to fire me if I wasn't cutting the mustard good enough. When I hired out I wasn't a bit sure that I could. But Red complimented me afterwards saying I could do better on one leg than a lot of guys could on two. We had plenty of use for any money we could make on the side. They only used water power in Quesnel till 1947 before switching to diesel motors, and the whole construction was left to rot. But it made a great difference to the fishing in Tibbles Lake. They never got fish bigger than about 12 inches before, but after the dam was built the fish got up to 18 and 20 inches.

We had wintered a couple of ponies for a Swede by the name of Gus Edwards up at Beaver Pass. Gus was quite a skier. He told us he and a tillicum of his had gone into Quesnel and back on skis, an eighty-mile trip, just to buy a bottle one day! That gave us an idea. Instead of getting cash for the horse wintering, we got him to make us two pairs of skis. Remembering how good Doc Baker had said skiing would be for my knee, one day I decided to start working my way up to the lakes two miles or so away from the cabin. It took me over a week to break the trail up there, even though Art gave me quite a boost by making one trip. I didn't get far the first day and wondered if I'd ever make it. But each day I could go further and then return on my track and finally I made it all the way. Then I got a few mink and marten traps set around the lakes and gradually worked further on till I got a circle made about seven miles long, beginning and ending at the cabin. I ran it for the rest of the winter.

I could do much better on skis than walking. When walking, I had to be careful so that my heel didn't come down over a hollow or my toes on a hump. When I did this, everything gave way and I would have to fall to prevent the extra stretching. However, the haywire pin got stronger day by day. My big trouble was that as it got better, I would be more careless and soon wind up on the bed for a day or so and have to start over.

Some years later we were branding colts in the spring. We threw one of the colts and the instinct to get down on him before he got up was too strong. I jumped the rope and sprained my leg again and that session I was laid up for ten days, with my bottle of oil to keep me busy.

For years after, I had a slight limp. There was a spot on the inside of my knee about the size of a four-bit piece that stayed as sore as a boil to touch, and I had wind puffs all around the knee like a bog-spavined horse. That sore on the inside of the knee was bad for riding. I put one or both hands on the pommel of the saddle and took as much or more weight on my hands as on my legs when riding fast on a trail. Roping or anything like that, where I needed my hands, I just had to glue my legs to the saddle to keep the knee from batting against it any more than I could help. I had to let Art do the topping off for me on any new ponies but for awhile we didn't have any to break until our colts grew up.

In between jobs at Stanley in 1936, we decided to build a cabin to pass the time. There were lots of old shacks there and we thought another new one would improve the looks of things, so we built a nice cosy little log cabin about twelve by sixteen. Soon after we got it built we got work for two horses but no work for either of us. We just rented the horses out and we sat in the cabin like real important office boys and got a cheque for horse rent every little bit. Made us feel like two-bit millionaires. Later we rented the cabin for a year or so and I guess taking it all round we came out about even on the venture, taking into account that no high-priced materials or labour went into the building.

Tragedy struck one night. A buckskin work horse we had was pretty mean and he must have kicked Sis in the night. In the morning we found her with a broken hind leg and in terrible pain. The break was up in the stifle and looked hopeless to patch up, so we had to shoot her. This was right in the heart of Stanley. After breakfast we had to figure out where to bury the remains. By this time Stanley was out in full force as Sis had become quite a favourite around the town. Actually all our horses were pretty much pets and the folks made a great fuss of them, feeding them sugar, salt, grain and trying hotcakes and most everything else on them.

The upshot was that the folks decided we would have a full-course funeral. This was in all seriousness. Everybody felt badly about it. Sis always got called "Old Sis" but in reality was quite a young mare, and a good one, really nice and gentle in disposition yet full of life. She loved to run moose, bear or deer and seemed to like the chase; it just made her eyes sparkle and she was swift enough it didn't take her many jumps to catch up on anything. She was very tall and a windfall had to be pretty high to stop her jumping over it.

Young Nellie Baker and Bill McGinnis took charge of the funeral arrangements. Nellie owned one of the two hotels and beer parlours in town. She was always called Young Nellie to differentiate between her and her mother who was also Nellie Baker. Bill McGinnis was the town barber (and bootlegger). They figured out music for the funeral march and Bill was to read the last rites at the graveside. Art and I, of course, were the chief mourners but one of us had to drive the team to tow the carcass down mainstreet and out some distance from town to an old abandoned mine shaft and then roll her in.

Everybody in Stanley got in the procession: prospectors, miners, Chinese, the few business folks there were, and all the ladies. Quite a few of the ladies were dabbing their eyes with hankies every little bit, especially at the graveside service which Bill read off as Art and I rolled the old girl over into the hole. To the "dust to dust and ashes to ashes" we rolled rocks onto her to keep the body down below the water level and then shovelled dirt in on top.

Then the whole procession marched back to town and most of the folks swarmed into Nellie's beer parlour to hoist a few and drown the sorrows of the occasion. From there on to Bill McGinnis' supply which was soon exhausted, but most folks had their sorrows pretty well drowned by then.

150

Bill was quite a bootlegger. You never bought a bottle and just walked out. Bill was too good company for that. Mostly you made your purchase and drank it right there with Bill and your friends. The drinks were on you that occasion. Next session Bill stood the drinks and most everybody seemed to be welcome. End result: no profit, but everybody happy both sessions.

You would wonder how a little ghost town like Stanley could support two beer parlours. They didn't do much business in the daytime but as the shades of night fell, and on till dawn sometimes, they were apt to do a roaring business. People got wise that there were no police, no town by-laws and they could really let their hair down if they were of a mind.

There was a lady who used to come down from Wells every so often. Mickey Lunn, who ran the post office, always told us when this occasion arose, as both he and I were ardent admirers of the lady's talents. After she got appropriately mellowed she'd get up on a table at one end of the parlour and recite the old mining ballads and tales. She had a spellbound audience for hours sometimes when she was really in the mood.

For all the lack of law enforcement I don't recall one case of anyone passing out or being really drunk and disorderly at sessions like these. Folks came to have fun and the entertainment they had with their drinking seemed to act as a measure of control. Generally there was someone who could play and some danced to the music, some step danced, some sang or recited either from where they sat or on the floor or on the table, as they wished. No doubt to the old-timers it brought back memories of the good old days when Stanley and Barkerville were wide open booming mining towns.

This brings to mind two ladies of more or less ill repute who lived in town. They were known as "Diamond Lil" and "The Red Head." On the occasion I recall, jealousy got the best of them. The Red Head had apparently stayed the night in a Swede's cabin and this particular Swede, Diamond Lil claimed as her own. In the morning she got wind of the goings-on and came around to the cabin with her 30-30 rifle at the ready. There was quite a little hollering back and forth and the language wasn't polite or ladylike by any manner of means. Finally a shot rang out. This was right in the middle of town in broad daylight, likely around ten in the morning. I guess most everybody was alerted but nobody in sight. Nobody interfered, asked any questions or seemed to pay any attention but there was plenty of curiosity, and I think most of us breathed a little easier when later neither the Red Head nor the

Swede seemed to be suffering from any injury. But there was a bullet hole right through the cabin door!

We got quite a little work that summer. There was a fairly large camp up on Burns Mountain, another on beyond on Amador Mountain, and Murphys and Leroy Biggs got us to take in some rigging to their diggings. There was another outfit below Stanley a few miles and a forestry outfit up on the Swift River. We could use our two-horse tandem on the two-wheel cart taking supplies into the Burns Mountain camp and the one below Stanley, but the others were all packing jobs.

Mrs. Murphy and her daughter Francis were the lady prospectors in Stanley. They had two or three husky dogs they used packing supplies in till there was snow enough to use a dog sled.

There was nothing much doing around July 1st and we had a little stake, and hadn't let our hair down to amount to anything for several years, so we hit for the horse races and dances and what-have-you in Quesnel. Eddie Boyd, who had been raised on a ranch out in Chezakut quite a ways west of us, was travelling with us and there was a loud-mouthed jigger trying to demonstrate how tough he was who kept tagging along with us. We figured it would not be too hard to ditch him in Quesnel but he froze on tight when we got to town. So we decided to give him the knockout drops. We got a bottle of pretty high-powered rum. Art passed the bottle to this clinging vine and he went to pour one in. He couldn't have known straight overproof rum wasn't too easy to take. He gagged and gagged. Art, Eddie and I took a round or so each and figured this guy should have another. We told him just to hold his nose and swallow fast and it would fix him up in a little bit. He made the grade this time and took a pretty hefty swig. That was enough to waste on him and we headed yonder. He commenced to follow but not for long. His legs started to go different directions and instead of watching where he was going he kept his head high and seemed to be reaching for something. Pretty quickly he got a hold of it. The ground had come right up to him and he grabbed big handfulls of it. Pretty drastic treatment but we had tried to let him know by subtler methods we didn't crave his company and verily we had ditched him.

We took in the races but that was only a starter. We danced all night three nights in a row and none of us went to bed for the three days and nights and then we went right back to Stanley. I think that was the first dancing I had done since our first winter in the country and Art had missed that occasion. So we caught up a little all at once. Eddie was right with us all the way and was sure good company, always full of fun, even though he was nearly asleep standing.

152

There was an outfit doing quite a lot of work up in Beaver Pass about ten miles away. Ken Langford was foreman on the job and he had his wife and family up from California with him. He told us there would be quite a lot of work for us with pack horses and go-devils (a kind of sled). There was no horse feed at their camp and we knew there would be times it would be pretty tough making the return trip the same day. Towards fall we would need a barn and feed there. So we went to work and built a ten-horse barn with a flat pole roof with deep moss on it. There were the remains of an old cabin there and we more or less rebuilt it and fixed it up pretty well so it wouldn't leak and could be easily warmed. Now we had a home in Beaver Pass as well as Stanley.

The work slackened off after I came back from haying and Langford told us if we'd fix up the ditch he would let us work the ground till freeze-up to make it worth our while to stay around and bring in what freight they still needed for a winter camp. This ditch had been built years ago by Chinese, I believe. Wherever it went around a sidehill the lower side was pretty well washed away and had to be built up. In several places new flume had to be built to cross coulees and such like. Then the whole ditch was partly filled with leaves, needles, moss, ferns and little trees. I think there was about two miles of it.

We knew the surface ground had proved out well. Some boys had been working a claim right alongside Langford's claim, and packing the dirt to the creek to wash it, and still making wages. There was coarse gold in patches, and right up in the grass and tree roots. Man, if we could just get that water running and rig up a dump and sluice boxes like we had on the Quesnel River, and scrape gravel in with a team for a couple of weeks even, we might hit a pocket and be wealthy overnight. We would be able to stock up our ranch with pure bred cows of the best and have registered Palomino saddle horses and all the trimmings.

We worked like a slave driver was standing over us with a bull whip. We got the ditch running twice but just got the water to the claim and there was a slide somewhere and we had to go back to fix it. Finally, we were all ready by noon one day. We took on a hefty feed and then poured in the gravel. We had to clear trees and roots out, but before night we got quite a few scraperfuls of the good stuff in, and had ploughed the surface and cleared trees ready for a full day coming up.

The next morning everything was frozen solid. Freeze-up had come with a vengeance. We had no inkling of it. We made some kind of a hash of cleaning up using boiling water and got six dollars for our

153

short afternoon run, plus more than two weeks working like the devil was after our hides. Apparently we wern't born to make our pile washing gold.

So we packed our outfit and headed out on the long, long trail home. We had wanted to make a grubstake for winter but there seemed to be nothing doing at all. We had eaten our way through most of what we had made. We wanted to take in enough grub for the winter so as not to have to buck travelling in deep snow when you could hardly freight much more than the horse feed you needed to travel on. Langford hadn't been able to pay us off, so we didn't have the price to do this. However, we decided to try to get jaw-bone partly on our own and partly on Langford's I.O.U. We went in to try out John A. Fraser.

John A. was one of the real old pioneers of Quesnel and had been the second school teacher in the country. He was Conservative member of the House of Commons for the Cariboo for quite a number of years. He was always very direct and gruff. It seemed kind of like he was trying to scare hell out of you to bluff you out. He would have nothing to do with Langford's I.O.U. "Don't know the man or anything about him. How much do you want? How much do you figure you're worth? How much should I trust you for? You tell me before I'll tell you what I'll do." Right then we didn't figure we were worth a hell of a lot with him shooting the questions at us so fast in his booming voice. His tactics caught us a little off guard, to say the least. Finally, Art piped up in a squeaky voice, "Fifty bucks." I'd plumb lost my voice.

"How long you gonna want it for? When'll you be able to pay it back?" We guessed we'd pretty sure have plenty of fur to pay it in a month or so, but didn't want to have to come in till late March or early April if he could wait that long. "That's not unreasonable," says John A. "I don't care a hoot how you make it, or when you make it, as long as you pay me when you say you will, and as much as you say you will. Go ahead and order your groceries and tell me how much the bill is when you're through." That was that. We had bearded the lion in his den and got fifty dollars credit if we needed it, and we did business with John A.'s grocery and drygoods store almost exclusively for twenty years. John A. was Quesnel's "Grand Old Man" and he was ninety-six when he died.

CHAPTER XV

Exploring and Locating New Home Ranch

We got curious to know what kind of spring range we had in these parts and took a camp outfit on a pack horse and headed away down Ramsay Creek, breaking trail through over two and a half feet of snow in shady timber, but bare ground on sidehills facing the sun. We were also looking for any signs of beavers, so we could make a few dimes trapping them. Actually we were a little early on both counts to make much of an observation. It was too early for there to be sufficient feed uncovered to camp horses on more than a few nights, and beavers were still under the ice. But we enjoyed the exploring. We could tell that we had any quantity of late fall rustling for hundreds of head of stock but the spring range was going to be quite a little on the late side. Later, and for the summer, there would be an abundance of feed again. This has meant that we can rustle grown stock till Christmas most years, and some years to the first week of January, but lots of years we had to feed the main bunch through to between the 20th of April and 20th of May. Our earliest turnout was the 18th of March, our latest the 21st of May in 1948 when it looked like we were going to have winter all summer. In that year most everything flooded for a time in the super-high, high water.

After that exploratory trip, we made two or three more. One was up the first creek of any size from the Cooper meadow to a lake some seven miles from where our road crosses the creek. The lake is about a mile wide and a mile and a half long in quite a pretty setting. There were fish in the lake, rainbow trout from fifteen to eighteen inches long. A pair or so of geese generally nested on a little island out in the lake. There were very few rats and no beavers so we backtracked and went up the main creek. There was quite a large lake on that, too, but all burned timber around and quite desolate at that time of year. It was quite a way from any good horse feed for camping, no beavers and no sign of rats, so we did not tarry there.

We went up the main stem of Baker Creek from Burnstads to what the folks around called "The Big Flat." Our horses had worked into it time and again and we saw more of it each time we had to round them up. There seemed to be an awful lot of swamp and most of it was brush covered and hadn't looked too good. But to this time, I didn't have a homestead and we thought maybe this was the makings.

We rode back and forth across this flat sizing up what could be worked into tame hay ground. We found that most of what had looked to be just moose brush swamp was solid enough ground and could be cultivated and likely would produce heavy hay crops. At that time it was choked with thick brush from four to twelve feet high. Some of it was so rough you could hardly ride over it. This would necessitate some special equipment for cultivating until it was levelled off. But it looked good and there was quite a big acreage, so we decided best I invest two dollars to homestead it and we could go to work on a brand new project.

The biggest attraction was that this place is about fifteen hundred feet lower than the Ramsay Creek meadow which makes a full month's difference in the spring. Snow on the Ramsay Creek meadows will be up to your stirrups yet, when there is green grass at the lower elevation. We decided this would be our home ranch. Plans started cooking from there on.

We had quite a string of horses to keep track of at Ramsay meadow that spring. We had brought some in from Barkerville to winter, some had come from Chilcotin country, some we were breaking for Shorty and some others we had acquired from the Nazko country. They all seemed quite satisfied in the early spring. There was lush green grass in the meadows we had cut, and this was good, clean, new feed and very attractive. We had built a small log fence pasture to hold a few, but had to turn the main bunch outside until we figured the time was ripe to head up into Barkerville country.

Right early in May it turned very warm and the mosquitoes came out in hordes. We were one day late getting started on the trail. The day we were ready to start, most of our horses had gone. Had they all gone in one bunch in one direction it would have been simple, but horses have a marvellous homing instinct and spring is the time they want to get onto their home range. They split and went three directions and split still more further out. The Barkerville horses had headed east and, as they didn't belong to us, we decided it was most important to get them first. Art took after them with no camp outfit whatever, figuring he could catch up right soon. If they had known the country and just been looking for feed, there would have been nothing to it. But they were fighting flies and were lost before they were any distance from the meadow.

156

We had run short of bells and this bunch had none, so Art had a straight tracking job from the start. They could make tracks faster than he could follow them. Instead of coming out to meadows on the creek that we knew of to feed at night, as a range broke bunch would have done, these lost horses just wandered any direction till they ran into a pothole back in the timber with feed in it. Art stayed on their trail for five days and nights. He had a .22, a salt shaker and a saddle blanket for camping. He got the odd rabbit, squirrel or chicken, dressed it, salted it, and barbecued it. That was living off the country in the raw. But he had to give up without ever catching up to the cayuses.

I had followed the old roan mare and two colts she had with her. They headed straight for her Chilcotin range. I caught up to them and got the colts turned back but I couldn't turn back the old wild mare. She would bluff my saddle horse out completely and I had to let her go to keep track of the others. I got them back and in the pasture, and took out on the trail of the main Nazko bunch. They had split at the Baker Creek meadow about seven miles down our road. Some of them had stayed there and fed, then followed the bunch into the timber a few miles and decided it was not in their best interests to go on. Then they had gone to wandering in a big burn, just as Art's bunch were doing.

I camped out one night without benefit of any grub whatever and tracked all next day without catching up to any. That was plenty for me. I was hungry and went back to Ramsay Creek that night. I got up early next morning aiming to take a little camp pack of grub with me and try some more. But while I was cooking breakfast here came some of my horses. They must have crossed my fresh tracks the night before and followed me in. We had been making quite a fuss of all of them, feeding them salt or grain right by the cabin to make them realize the cabin was home.

Sure enough they came right to the cabin door bumming for salt. But there were only three, an old Barkerville mare, a two-year-old wild stud colt out of the old roan mare, and one of our own horses. Well, I got hold of the two gentle ones and got them in the barnyard. The wild colt seemed quite gentle while the others were loose with him, but as soon as I caught them, he turned wild. I never saw anything like it before or since. He was almost in the notion of coming up close enough to eat salt with the others and then he seemed to suddenly revert to the wild state. A sort of nervous tension came over him and he practically danced, never seeming to have more than two feet on the ground at once, going this way and that, getting further away all the time and never coming as close again.

157

I put the others in the barnyard and he jumped in with them, decided it was no place for him and jumped right out. This was a six-rail log fence, plenty high enough to hold most horses, too. He hated to go away from there but was desperately frightened to come in around buildings or corralls any more. He circled the yard several times and came up the road from the far side each time. So I set a snare for him. But he never came up again. Then he went further out up on the meadow by himself. Two or three old standbys were up there but he would have nothing to do with them. I took the old Barkerville mare and staked her out in the open meadow. He came to her a couple of times and then left the country and we never saw him again. I knew I had no chance of corralling him or roping him. As soon as I went after him he struck into thick timber and once I lost sight and had to revert to tracking, I didn't have a chance. We couldn't have held him until he was old enough to break anyway. I'll bet he would have made a good saddle horse though. That candy dancing he did by the cabin was mighty pretty to watch and you could sure tell by his actions that pony knew right where he was putting his feet and really had control of them. However, we still had Baldy, his half or possibly full brother. That pony really earned his keep on the layout for all his useful years, till he deserved to be pensioned off.

The rest of the bunch had headed for their Nazko horse heaven, which entailed a trip over to Shorty's later.

The first few years we were in the country were quite dry to what we've had since. To get a good hay crop on the meadows it was imperative to build dams and flood or irrigate them quite soon after high water was over. So we built dams on every meadow around. Some we must have just built for the thrill of doing it as we only had that little bunch of horses. We didn't need the extra hay and never got any good out of them other than the practice of building. Several of them washed out in an extra heavy high water run off and we never rebuilt them, but we did learn from that that a good footing, careful construction, and the correct slope were very important. With some of them we tried a novel way of sealing the cracks. We had built them using split timbers with the round side upstream on some, the split side on others and alternated in others. Then we picked some fairly large trees with no limbs for ten feet or so up, skinned about five or six feet of bark off all in one piece, and laid this green bark flat against the dam timber before covering with dirt. It worked well. It would seal the cracks in the dam perfectly tight. In those we hadn't sealed, the water would soon wash holes through the cracks and then the dirt would wash away. The weight of water would tip the timbers out unless they were set in big rocks. Then the dry year cycle ended and wet years took their place and it has never been necessary to dam since. The main need has been for sufficient ditching to carry surplus water off and stop hay getting too rank and coarse, or prevent meadows from getting soft and swampy.

We did a little beaver trapping each spring from then on, when we could find enough beavers to work on. This always seemed to be mostly a damn lot of wasted time to me. We would have to take a pack horse or so with camp outfit and traps and sometimes have two or three camps, as our beavers were so far apart and couldn't be reached from any central spot. This meant setting up a camp and then wading through water as deep as possible, fighting through tangled willows for miles trying to find where big beavers were feeding. Then we'd have to go hunt up rocks the correct size to tie onto the trap to drown the beavers. Generally where there were beavers there were no rocks and we would have to pack them over a mile at times. A big beaver needs nearly a ten-pound rock to hold him and you couldn't pack them in quantity. Then you needed peeled poplar sticks for bait, and the best places seem to have nothing but willows. So more packing and aimless wandering here and there.

We'd get that batch of traps set and hit across to another colony on another creek and get that set up and so on. As we got each batch of traps set out we would have to return at least once, but preferably twice a day to check the set traps. Had there been lots of beavers, and all this work and time assured a good catch and financial return, it might have been more attractive.

But it seemed to be the wrong season for puttering around trapping. We wanted to be building something, doing something constructive rather than destructive, growing and planting or producing something worthwhile. But we needed every cent we could acquire for those years. Any gainful work was almost non-existent. Occasionally we did get a little excitement out of it all though.

One year Burnstad and I landed at a beaver dam just before sundown and there were two big beavers swimming around. I had my little "Shorty" dog and Pierre had a full brother to him. I shot one beaver and Shorty got him out on our side. But almost before I got the beaver safe on shore I spotted the other across the pond just showing a little and I got in a fatal shot on him. Shorty went in after him but, having been in the icy water for a spell, he hesitated and tried to tread willows before falling in and losing a little distance by the current taking him downstream. Then he couldn't locate the beaver and I had to shoot at it again to show him where it was. I was afraid it would

159

sink or get in the current before he got it, but he grabbed it and started towing it ashore, but across the creek. So I had to run upstream and get across on a windfall to help him. There was a ledge of ice away out into the creek with the water more than a foot below the edge. I knew Shorty couldn't get the beaver over as it was much bigger and heavier than him. In the time I was getting across, Burnstad's dog decided to take a hand in matters and I just got there in time to see Shorty do a backward jump, landing his hind feet up on the ice without letting go of the beaver. He first got up on top of the beaver and flipped his hindquarters up from there. But he couldn't raise the beaver out of the water.

That was where Burnstad's dog came in. He swam across, jumped up on the ice and carefully reached over till he got a grip on the beaver with Shorty, then they both backed up scratching and slipping, losing their holds and catching on again. It was such pretty teamwork to watch, I hated to move. But I finally had to pitch in and help them. They had to reach over too far and the weight was too much for them to bring up over the ledge, try as they might. I think that was the most fun I ever got out of beaver trapping, and two big beavers in half an hour besides.

That fall of '36, as Art stayed in Barkerville to work through the winter, I had to take the pack outfit home and winter alone. Art came with me to Quesnel. We decided we could afford a radio and bought a seventy-five dollar De Forrest Crossley set and a twenty-five dollar set of thousand-hour batteries. On the way home I stopped at Coopers, just three or four hundred yards across the creek from Tibbles. They hadn't had a radio before either, so we went to work and set it up using a bed spring for an aerial and it worked fine. I think the youngsters figured I was some kind of magician to get music and all, right out of the air. Next night up at the Cooper meadow cabin we had built, I set it up again. Pierre and family were staying there and it sure made a hit with them. I was tired and hit the hay after I had put them up to date on all the outside news I could think of, and they had gone through two or three months' mail. Jessie weakened pretty soon and went to bed, but Pierre sat up to read and listen till away on in the morning. He finally fell asleep with the radio still running.

A little before daylight a Mexican program came on and it woke Pierre and me up, and I heard Pierre say, "God, that woman can sing." We could get stations all over the States and Mexico, and it is hard to tell of the enjoyment we got out of that radio away back in the sticks where our only form of entertainment, for months and months at a time, had been reading old papers and magazines.

I could never play anything but had always loved good music and now we had music of all kinds from the best to the poorest, as well as news, sports, talks, speeches, church, theatre plays, ı..ystery stories, and soap operas — everything in sound practically right on tap, as long as the battery lasted.

When I first set it up at Ramsay Creek and turned it on I got Nelson Eddy and Jeanette McDonald singing "Maytime." I think if the roof had fallen on me I wouldn't have moved till it was finished, I was so enraptured. I am especially fond of organ music and stringed instrumental music, and I even like soprano singers. But for the early morning nothing seemed to fill the bill so well as cowboy music. By that I mean ballads of the range sung to guitar accompaniments, not the moaning, groaning, whining and howling noises these critters pass off as Western music nowadays, wailing of a lost lover, girl friend or divorcee and such like. What is "Western" about such cat wailing on a back fence? I don't know. There hardly seems to be any cowboy music played nowadays but lots of stations played it on their early morning programs then.

I didn't go to town for eleven months that year. I did get mail three or four times, brought out by neighbours. One year I made it to a New Year's dance in Quesnel. I had so much fun I figured that was a must for every year but I was never able to make it again. We had too much of a glow to slow down and by taking up collections we got the orchestra to play well into daylight the next day. By then the music was going round and round in our heads and we didn't need an orchestra any more. Some went on dancing out in the great outdoors.

Here I come to the end of the packing and freighting in the Barkerville country. I didn't go up for the summer of '37 and Art brought all the outfit home in the fall with a four-up on the wagon. We were putting in too much time travelling back and forth and there was not enough work to make any headway.

Each winter we had improved our ranch set-up as much as we had time for, with fencing and building. We would get in a little work each spring before heading up to Beaver Pass or Stanley. In '36 we ploughed up (with an old walking plough), worked down, seeded and fenced about a four-acre tame hay patch on the Big Flat. We got a whale of a crop of oats off it and from that winter on our moose got to like the taste of tame hay.

CHAPTER XVI

First Cow on the Ranch —
Beef Drive and Stampede

Hughie Wilkinson had worked for Coopers haying and got a cow and horse for wages. He wanted our Black Tiny. We wanted her too. He could have traded even up for some of our horses but not for Tiny. Finally we traded with him — Tiny for his horse and cow. The horse was just an inbred jughead but we got a little use out of him and finally used him for coyote bait. But we had one cow. Having just one cow, naturally she got quite a little attention. To begin with she started something. The first cow manure in that whole big district was hers.

She must have been a little lonely for a year as she had nothing but horses for companionship. But as she was about the orneriest cow one man ever told another about, maybe that didn't bother her any. I've seen a lot of cows but never one that was any ornerier than that old sister. We named her "Madeline." She was built for speed rather than beef. When she calved in the spring we decided right pronto we boys were going to have milk, something we'd had very little of since hitting the Cariboo.

We headed for the barnyard armed with lass ropes and a milk bucket. Old Madeline pricked up her ears at this business-like approach, and before we got very close she wound up her tail, lowered her head and proceeded to clear her private barnyard.

Nothing daunted, we rustled up a couple of saddle horses and tried again. She mighty nigh got the run on the saddle horses before we got a rope on each end and stretched her out. Who was going to be brave enough to get the milk for the mush? It seemed much more peaceful just to set and hold the rope. Art finally gave ground and volunteered. "You best stay put, Dude," he says. "Keep clear of that old gal on foot with that game leg. She's apt to beat you to the draw."

That was just the way I wanted it to be. I had no hankering to get down under that old sister. We found out later that her mother had been plumb mean, so she came by it naturally. It just oozed out of her. There were times we really got fun out of rassling her but when a man is tired and hungry, the novelty wears off. Of course, we didn't have to tie both ends after the first few times, but always had to tie a hind foot well back, or hobble her, and pretty regularly she got in some dirty work before she was tied. Man, oh man, could that cow kick. With her head tied to the manger and one foot stretched out three feet off the ground, I've seen her kick the barn roof with the loose foot, seven feet off the ground! You'd have to see it to believe it.

Art got to be a privileged character around her. He could chase her into the barn and snare a hind foot or tie hobbles on her and go to milking. But just let me try to chase her into the barn on foot and she'd light right out after me and tree me on the fence. She must have guessed I had more respect for her than she for me. Art got to saying, "She's a one-man cow." I'd come right back with "And I ain't that man." I never had any aspirations to be.

But several years later I milked what would likely be a great-great-granddaughter of our first cow. She was ornery as all get out, always went the wrong way at the right time, but was gentle as a kitten.

The next summer we went to work to tame some more moose pasture and enlarge our haying area. We cut between two and three miles of road from Ramsay Creek meadow to a big swampy meadow we called the "Moose Pasture." We built four stackyards and set up a camp there and put up the hay on it first. We started away early to have lots of time to go on from there. We put up the Ramsay Creek meadow next. Then we went to work to cut about seven or eight miles of road through a lot of pretty big timber to a big meadow down on Ramsay Creek. This meadow got the name "Sandy Meadow," not because of any sand in it but because a Scotsman from Alexis Creek, called Sandy Robertson, had cut about seven miles of road towards it, then decided it was too far from civilization and abandoned the project.

There was one patch of extremely thick little jack pine that would be really heavy cutting. We wanted to get through to bigger open timber in the shortest distance possible. So I went in from one side and Art from the other side to where we wanted to come out. We allowed ourselves time to get to correct places, and at a pre-set time were to start shooting. We both got quite a surprise and a nice one. We were within easy hollering distance of each other. So, instead of blazing a way through we chopped our way through right then, although it was really time to go home when we started.

Hugh Wilkinson came up before we finished this project and we obligingly staked him to an axe and he helped us finish. While we still had some widening to do on odd corners to get an outfit through, I thought Hughie needed a change and rest, and got him to drive the team and follow me up. It was pretty heavy timber so we didn't cut a tree more than we had to and some of the corners were pretty sharp. Hughie had not had much practice driving in thick timber or crooked roads, but was plenty young to learn. He didn't get far. There was a steep pitch with a sharp turn at the bottom. He made the steep place but got into high gear, couldn't bend the team around the curve and slammed into a tree with all the weight of the wagon and a load of haying machinery. He broke the neck yoke so we had to build a new one on the job with a double-bitted axe for a tool. He did a lot better after that pile-up for a lesson. As soon as the road was useable we moved a haying outfit down and put up a couple of big haystacks.

That wasn't enough haying yet for that season. The bug had bitten us and ambition was just oozing out of us, so we went down the road from Ramsay Creek and cut a little detour off the road into the Baker Creek meadow. We had to cross a creek with very steep banks there and had to slope them off with shovel and mattock to make a ford. This meadow we had always figured was too swampy to bother with. But every spring we threw a few matches into it and burnt off the old grass and short brush. We hadn't found any place to cross the creek until that spring our loose horses got down there. They liked the fresh green grass with no old dead stuff in it, and they had found a moose crossing that they could make. We had thrown lighted matches across the creek to burn the far side. Now we got across and found some really nice hay ground. When we cut the road into it we found our burning had paid off, and we had a heavy crop of clean green hay on it. So we put up a small section there just for the fun of it. We had far more hay than we needed for four or five years even.

The next bet was to try to get stock to winter or to run on shares. We tackled Paley first and hit pay dirt right off. He had been trading groceries for cattle to the Kluskus and Nazko Indians, staking them to a few dollars for July 1st horse races, or for a cow critter here and there, and getting Joe Spehar to winter them. But this meant a long trip in the fall and spring and wasn't too satisfactory. So he came up, sized up our haypiles and decided we had enough to winter the works and then some. He gave us the job for several winters.

We also got around twenty head to winter for Prosser for a couple of winters. We wintered Prosser's in return for cattle, and Paley's for cash. Presto! We were in the cow business.

In the fall we had three three-year-old steers, that we had bought that summer, to put in the Nazko beef drive. Of course we both went along. We joined Paley's drive at his place and helped him and Burnstad cut out and cowboy his, then joined the main Nazko drive at Quanstroms'. This included Joe Spehar, Harrington brothers, Julius

Wohl (running the chuckwagon) and Major Franklin. The Quanstroms threw in a few and Billy Quanstrom came with them. Shorty and Joe between them had three Indian cowboys. For around five hundred head we had seven cowboys, and a team and wagon; and Shorty going ahead in his truck, making feed and stopping arrangements at Cocky's, Nine Mile, and Holts, and stockyards and shipping arrangements at the P.G.E. station.

It was really good to be cowboying on a beef drive again. Art and I had sure missed these kind of doings for a few years. Art was riding Roannie, the thoroughbred gelding we had gotten from Joe Elkins, and I was riding a sorrel mare I was breaking for Nellie Baker. I was supposed to call the mare "Chloey," but that was too hefty a name for me to work with and I mostly called her "Cayuse." She wasn't cayuse though. She was almost pure bred Irish hunter and a really nice, gentle mare, with most of her education to be acquired yet.

Beulah Paul, an Indian riding for Flem and Shorty, had a big highstepping, showy thoroughbred of Flem's that we couldn't keep our eyes off. Flem had got a little past his prime for handling him and craved a gentler type. He was nearly too much horse for Beulah, too.

Joe Spehar had the most one-ownership stock in the drive and his old sorrel mare looked like this would be her last drive and she damn near wouldn't make that.

The big day finally came when we got the herd to town. The Fraser River Bridge was always a worrisome obstacle on the beef drives. Some drives just walked right on and others seemed like all hell wouldn't put 'em on. It seemed to depend a whole lot on the lead critters' reaction to hitting the first plank. If a couple of good cowboys crowded a little bunch right on, the rest came on fine and dandy. But if that first little bunch ever turned back, there was plenty of trouble to get another bunch to tackle it. Of course it was more fun when they broke back and you had to fight them up to it every inch, but it wasn't as good cowboying.

They sure did clatter and rattle when they got strung out all the way across the bridge, and the ponies with any life at all would be right up candy dancin' and rarin' to go. Most highlifed horses get a little nervous on a long bridge like that with cattle both ends of them, kind of wild eyed and rarin' to stampede. The old dogies didn't take long to get through the main street of town. This civilization right up close was agin their religion. Shorty and Julius got the police to stop traffic on the bridge and main street to let the drive have full right of way. Town folks were all lined up with cameras. This was their annual picture-taking time. Just a little further on from there and we got the works corralled in the stockyards.

Traditionally, when the drive is in the stockyards the cowboys are on their own for the night, with nothing but their saddle horses to take care of. They can put the nosebag on and take the wrinkles out of their bellies with restaurant grub if they are that-away inclined, or they can tie one on, and see the bright lights somewhat better with starry eyes.

Most are bachelors and some are even bold enough on the first night in town, but generally not before the second, possibly fortified with a glow from within derived from a gurgle or so from a bottle of scotch or rum, to go hunt up the female of the species, and escort same to a dance or show.

Well, Billy Quanstrom, Burnstad, Art and I hightailed it across to the Nugget Cafe. Our aim was to try to locate a bottle of any kind of giggle juice procurable at that time of night. We ran into Shorty and he had thoughts of such emergencies and took us up to his room where Julius and Alec had already congregated.

The bottle had made the rounds twice. Things were commencing to look brighter and brighter, tongues loosened up and everybody talking at once, and nobody paying any attention to what the other guy had to say. The rules of etiquette were about to be abandoned and we aimed to let our hair down. It was our night to howl after a long, long silence, when in burst Julius Wohl, more starry eyed than any of us, and all out of breath from the long half-mile run across from the stockyards. He had wind enough to holler, "Cattle all gone, cowboys all drunk!" We didn't wait for any explanations. Pierre, Art, Bill and I lined out for the stockyards in our high-heeled boots, clippety-clop, like a bunch of high-strung thoroughbreds.

This was a stampede, the genuine article. A train shunting on the tracks alongside the stockyards had spooked the cattle too much. They had piled into the side of the big holding corral and the force of the herd behind had broken the fence down and away they went.

Julius Wohl had his team and wagon right there and had started to cook his supper alongside the yards. We had tied our saddle horses to the fence and fed them. The cattle had broken out over everything. They would have pounded Julius to death but his wagon saved him. They mighty nigh scared that poor old Swiss chuckwagon driver to death. Our saddle horses were scattered from hell to breakfast up the flat. They must have run with the cattle quite a ways. Some had broken their shank ropes but some had long splintered pieces of plank tied to them.

166

We caught any horses we could locate in the dark. I got Alec Paley's pony. He was getting ancient but was a good stock pony yet. Joe Spehar and the Indians had tied their horses further down and they had been out of the way of the stampede. Joe got his pony and got in on the ride too but the Indians were eating supper and missed most of it. The cattle had headed north up the Quesnel River. Apparently the river held them on the one side and they raced up the flats alongside it for about two miles to where a long, steep bench meets the river to form a straight wall at the junction. They must have got winded enough to have slowed down, or this obstacle would have crippled or killed a bunch before they could mill to a stop. They couldn't go up over it and had come back a ways and milled round and round trying to find a way out.

But this natural corral had held one end, with the fear of what had scared them holding the open end. As soon as we saw and heard them, I called the boys to slow down and start to sing or talk quietly or call quietly. None of us had too much experience with stampedes as most of those episodes had passed before our time. But I had had some kind of enlightening experiences riding for a couple of years for a cattle buyer back in Alberta, handling bigger bunches than this with only two cowboys and often caught in the dark with them on the trail. So we quietened down and worked up to the wild-eyed milling herd and we just milled around with them for a spell letting them wear their fear off, holding them in a tight circle. The young stock were plumb willing to settle down but there were lots of four- and five-year-old steers in the bunch and they were really spooked.

Gradually we worked right into them in different places. None of us were musical, so the best we could do was call quietly, "Co Bossy," "Yea Bossy," "Easy cows," or any regular cattle calls that are used on the feed ground and on drives. A lot of the stock in those days still packed their horns. The big steers and cows were a pretty formidable-looking outfit to mix into, riled as they were with such lethal weapons on the head end of them in the dark.

I couldn't help but wish I had a real top horse instead of this old Indian pony that had been kind of used and abused as a kid's pony all summer. It was mostly excitement that was keeping him going. I don't recall what horses the other boys picked up but I doubt if any of them had horses which would be recommended for getting into a stampeding herd of cattle at night. Just let one stumble and fall down, and his rider would be in a pretty tough spot. But they all came through and in a little while we got the herd slowed to a near halt.

167

Wherever they started to move again, one of us would work in ahead and slow them down again.

Then, very slowly, with three riders ahead and two along the side away from the river, we started working them down along the river. We tried to hold them to a walk, but it was practically impossible. However, we did keep them under control and when we got them opposite the stockyards we just swung the leaders around and into the herd and started a milling circle again. We held the mill in bounds till they quieted down and the young stock were weary enough to bed down right away.

By this time we all commenced to feel like our stomachs had gone right up into the chest cavity. So we held a council of war and decided Art, Pierre and Bill would hurry over to town to eat, then come back and hold the herd till daylight. Joe and I were to hold them while the boys were away.

Everything was quiet. Shorty had come down and bawled hell out of the trainmen for shunting around in the middle of the night and they had completely shut down operations. But as soon as the boys rode away the big steers got uneasy and started to work up to a trot and everything up and followed them. Joe and I would have to ride like the devil to get ahead of the leaders, and turn them back into the bunch. But there weren't riders enough to hold them to a mill and the big steers would work right through to the other end of the bunch and start out on a trot again. We turned them time and time again all to no avail and I knew our horses would play out at this fast pace after all they had done already.

As we rode I told Joe the best we could do was try to corral them. I got him to go up and open the gate and come back on the inside next to the corrals. When they started to line out up the river, instead of turning them around and back in on themselves, I cut straight through the bunch and got on the river side of them and worked up close on the leaders, then beat my chaps and hollered, not too loudly to scare them but just enough to make them pay attention. I swung my horse right in against the leaders and bent them up towards the corral. I would have to fall back and out a little to keep any leaders close behind from swinging away and up the flats, then quickly ahead again to hold the top leaders at the right angle. Everything on a tight gallop and everything following the leaders. I never swung them too far over to Joe's side. I don't think I could have ridden that old pony fast enough to do that if I'd wanted to. Joe didn't have a thing to do but just be there in case they swung too far, to straighten them back out and, if and when we got them in, to beat it to the hole in the fence and hold it in spite of hell, any way he could.

Neither of us could have crossed through the bunch again to help the other as, by the time they got over halfway to the gate, it was a full-blown stampede again but this time under some control in the right direction, if we could just keep it that way.

It worked. The leaders hit the gate on a high lope and went right on in and every last one followed all the way. I had to swing back and ahead as fast as I could right to the last to keep the outside in line. My pony was in a white lather and starting to stumble from sheer exhaustion, but he made the grade and we got the gate slammed shut before the milling leaders got back to it again. Nothing would have held them back if those big steers had found the gate open again. The break in the fence was different. They hadn't been driven in either time that way and in their fright it would still seem like the original fence they had gone back and forth along before breaking through. Joe was there now hollering and beating pieces of plank on the fence and I joined him right quickly, and inside a few minutes Art, Bill and Pierre came back. We built a huge bonfire right away and they kept it going strong the rest of the night.

The boys had rustled up a bottle of bootleg whiskey for their vigil of night herding. They had figured to be in the saddle the rest of the night but all they had to do was sit alongside the campfire and nurse the bottle. Joe and I gave them a helping hand on the whiskey, blanketed and fed our horses, and then, mission accomplished, we headed over to town. Joe was so tickled he was just like a puppy with a new toy. He said he never thought it possible that just the two of us, or even all of us, could have gotten that wild stampeding herd into the stockyards in the dark. "I gonna get you drunk," he says. I was all for it. I'd caught up on plenty of excitement and thrills that night to make up for all the long lonely years back in the sticks.

You can get quite a thrill running a steep hill on skis, and many other ways, but riding the lead wing on a stampeding herd of cattle in the dark was all the thrill I ever wanted.

We both needed a few drinks to settle down to anywhere near normal after that excitement. Old Joe knew right where to go even at three in the morning and had us a mickey quicker than if it had been high noon. But it looked pretty small to him and he craved bright lights anyway, having the party spirit strong on him by now. He knew of a joint where we could get whiskey by the glass (for a price) and drink right up to the table. Joe was apparently no stranger around Quesnel in those days. We didn't get to town often enough to be interested that-away and didn't have the price either. But this was on Joe and thus plumb different.

So we had a couple of glasses and had had one over at the yards. This on stomachs that had been filled at 6 a.m. breakfast the day before was plenty for Joe. He started to lean over in his chair first one way and then the other. I saw he was going to pass out and talked him into figuring it would be best to get to his room where we could finish up. He was willing but needing help. Before I got him upstairs to his room I was half dragging and half carrying him. I laid him out on the bed, took his boots off and threw a blanket over him. Cowboys always bury their dead! I had a notion to take the bottle but Joe was clutching it like a baby to his breast, and I hated to disturb the peace.

Excitement wouldn't die down in me that fast. The odd drink had taken all thought of eats or sleep away. I was primed for more action and went downstairs and out on the street to see what was doing. The boys had told me that Paley and Quanstrom were guarding the Fraser Bridge, Shorty was up guarding the highway north of town, and Julius Wohl was over on Quesnel River Bridge.

So I lined out to see Alec and Julius. They were shivering and miserable. I told them I figured we had all the cattle in but they doubted if we could hold them, so aimed to stay on guard till we got the herd tallied. I left them to their own devices. Shorty was too far away and so I headed back over to the stockyards to see how the boys were doing. They were doing fine. Their bottle was about lapped up and they had a nice rosy glow on and a nice fire to sit by. So, no eats, no drinks. All we could do was make with the chin music till daylight when restaurants opened up. Man, was I ready for a stack of hotcakes, bacon, eggs, mush, and dinner on top of it. We saved room rent that night anyway and they do say "save money and buy whiskey."

Roannie, Art's saddle horse, had apparently been in the direct path of the stampede. We found him away up the flats with about ten feet of splintered plank on the end of his hackamore shank rope. He was all scarred and bruised, and looked like he probably had been down under the bunch of stampeding cattle for awhile. It scared him so badly that he never got over it, and was no good working cattle in a corral again. He had been a fairly good stock horse before but from then on he just seemed to be petrified with fear when he was in a bunch of cattle, and was plumb useless for that kind of work.

170

CHAPTER XVII

Meadow Cabin and Barns —
Cutting Short-cut Trail

Tony came back into the picture during the summer and winter after we got him. In the summer he would get in the lead with the fastest horse in the bunch, generally Roannie at that time, and away they would go leaving the bunch behind for a quarter or half mile. Then they would race back to the bunch, circle them and away again almost as though they were saying, "Come on, you slowpokes, let's run; it's lots of fun!"

Tony got a lot smoother that summer as he filled out but kept on growing taller. The following winter his playing in the barnyard got to be quite a problem. We had other colts and we turned him out in the barnyard with them. He ran them ragged and played them out nipping them all over just to try to make them play and run with him. Tony decided to work on old Madeline. She was long-legged for a cow and full of fight. She bluffed him for awhile except when he caught her by surprise and came up on her too fast for her to face and do battle. But as soon as he learned how to get the run on her he made her plumb miserable for awhile till we saw we had to put both her and the other colts in the other corral.

That left Tony with just two playmates. One was our work horse stud, Duke, and the other was a neighbour's bull we were wintering. Tony and Duke played by the hour, but always Duke tired first and got too rough. Then Tony transferred his attentions to the old bull, a big long-horned whiteface who figured everything was a little afraid of him. That was the way he aimed to keep it.

Tony was pretty wary of him, knowing that everything seemed to detour around him. But he had to get a run out of something and persisted. He would gallop up to the bull's rear end and get in a quick nip and away, then back in for another nip from another angle. On the second try the old bull was generally prepared and would have wheeled to face the onrush. Tony knew those wide-spread horns were bad medicine for him so he'd pass that one and shy off, then let the old bull settle down before trying the flying tackle again. We decided that this pair was about a standoff. Tony wasn't doing the bull any harm and the bull wasn't apt to get in a blow either. But it did seem that they both got a little fun out of it.

The following spring Tony was a two-year-old stud. We needed saddle horse colts badly so decided he was good enough to be the daddy of them and didn't cut him. But this was not to be. He did sire one colt but then he got with an old Chilcotin mare, and together they went back across country to the Riske Creek range on the Chilcotin River.

We never found time to hunt them up till the following year and I rode for over a month before locating them. When I found them, Tony was no longer a stallion. But he was still the makings of a fine saddle horse and three years old. He was rangy and a little awkward with his long gangling legs but I needed a change of horses to head back for home so clamped my saddle down on him and stepped aboard. Tony was agin it and he showed plenty of action in protest. But, being only a three-year-old colt, he wasn't too tough for me to stay with. I worked him around quite a little in the big corral with some fifty or sixty head of horses in it, and then got Leonard Palmateer who was with me to turn me outside. I got Tony to neckreining fairly well and tied my saddle horse and pack horse onto his tail, and started the long ride home to our range. I only rode him about ten miles to where I made camp. I always figure working a colt too young makes them lazy. Tony was to be my top saddle horse and I sure didn't want him to be lazy so didn't ride him any more that trip or that year.

Having hay at the Baker meadow, we had to have a set of buildings and corrals there to use it. So in the middle of the winter of '37-'38 Art and I got set to go to building. Art was pretty well tied up with stock to feed but aimed to help me all he could. We gathered up a pack of grub and winter camp outfit and packed it on Klooch, then started out as early in the morning as we could get away. We had picked a mild spell to move from cabin to camp but it started to snow quite heavily. We had traps all along the road and we found that a marten had just been at one. Instead of going into the pen from the ground he had climbed the tree and gone back down into the pen, stolen the bait and gone back up the tree and then run away. The tracks were right fresh in the new snow.

Lexie had told us that Indians run all kinds of fur on saddle horse, so we tied Klooch up with her pack on and took after the marten. We followed him this way and that all day. We were always close but couldn't catch up. My little Shorty helped a lot but snow was too deep for his short legs. We saw it was close to dark so had to give up the chase and go back to Klooch. That was still three miles from the Baker

Creek meadow where we proposed to set up camp and we were both soaking wet. Art would have to ride back to Ramsay Creek seven miles if we went on. However, if we didn't go on, it would likely be some time before we'd break away from the cabin again. So we went on in the dark. When we got there we wished we had gone the other way. It was black dark and hard to find wood. The snow was still falling and we had no tent set up. We were cold, wet and terribly hungry. However, we set to work. We had a pile of hay fenced in where we aimed to put the barn, so we unpacked there and fed the horses.

I got a fire going and went to cooking. Art got busy setting up a tent, put hay on the floor, heaved grub and blankets in and, in a little while, we had a home away from home and feed under our belts. Things looked better by the minute except for Art having to ride home. I crawled in right away but Art had an hour and a half in the cold before he got to Ramsay Creek cabin.

I cut logs and skidded them in, then cleared a building site and got the first round set and squared. I had no cement foundation or even rocks and did not even clear the snow out of the middle before building. I got a few rounds up before Art got back down to help me. He got down early one morning. We really highballed that day, got the walls all notched in and a start on gables and ridge logs before Art had to go back.

The next day Lexie came along with his partner, Henry. I talked them into staying over a day and we got the roof pieces split out and laid on.

They went up the trapline promising to help me on their way back in about four days. So I plugged the roof with moss, then thawed out a patch of ground to get dirt out of, and got a layer of dirt on top of the moss. That was enough for the cabin for the winter. Then I cut and skidded a set of barn logs and was all ready to start laying up the barn walls when Lexie and Henry came back. Art made it down the same day so all four of us went to work on it. We got the walls up on an eight-horse barn that day.

Henry came back on the trapline when I was there and stayed with me overnight. I was short of matches and was using strips of kindling to light cigarettes. Before we went out to the barn to fix up the horses for the night I must have lit a cigarette and put the piece of shaving back on top of the heater. We had only been out a little while when we smelled smoke. We hit for the cabin on a high lope and found it full of smoke. When we opened the door, flames broke out in the hay at the foot of the bed by the heater. I figured that when the shaving got hot enough to burn, it curled up and rolled off the heater down into the dry hay. It had burned quite a hole in the old tent which was under the blankets, a chunk out of the Hudson's Bay blanket, and the same out of a heavy wool quilt. The cabin was too green to burn, but nearly losing my blanket roll and tent in February scared me quite a little. I sure watched my kindling after that.

We didn't tackle building at the Sandy meadow till a year or so later. We couldn't get at it early enough and snow got awfully deep to tackle that big a job. But we did move down there and set up another winter camp, as we wanted a corral with open water inside so we could leave a team there. We located the ideal spot with a spring head in it, cut logs for about ten panels of log fence, and set it up. Then we cut timber and skidded it in to build an A fence for a drift fence right across the meadow and a little way up the hill on each side. This was so we could feed young stock on one side and grown stock on the other side. It was all tough work with deep snow to buck and we figured that would do for the winter.

We had set up a camp on my new homestead in the fall so we could get started working on building up our home ranch. We had to cut about four miles of road into it too, then later on some eight more miles of road in from the other side. We hauled several loads of hay the whole seventeen miles from Ramsay Creek meadow. This was no snap. Even with a flat rack only six feet wide and fifteen feet long, and the hay tied down tightly with ropes, it was quite a feat to get by some places without upsetting. On at least three long sidehills that weren't graded, the skinner had to hang out as far as he could on the top side to keep the load from upsetting.

The next important step was to get a barn built. So every trip around the trapline I would lay over a day or so and cut logs, skid them, and later haul them in. I got a little too enthusiastic on the building and neglected my end of the trapline. Once I got a load of logs in I just couldn't keep from starting building. I didn't bother levelling the site or doing any foundation work. I just went to laying up logs every moment I could steal. I was making good time till it got too high for me to roll logs up easily alone, so then I concentrated on getting the rest of the material in.

Hughie Wilkinson stayed with us part of that winter, and another project we were concentrating on was getting a shortcut pack trail across the mountains through from Ramsay Creek. This would cut off about six miles on the trip from Ramsay Creek to home ranch. I had ridden down this trail from Ramsay Creek and from up in the mountain tops the pass looked to be a mile deep. I figured it would be a wonderful runway for fur animals.

Hugh and Art came down and we finished the barn walls and put the flat pole roof on in one day and part of a night. This made our winter establishment one hundred per cent better. Then we switched back to the shortcut pack trail. I found a direct course and had blazed enough from Ramsay Creek out for about five miles so that Art and Hugh could follow it, and they got that end cut out. But I couldn't seem to locate the line I travelled again. I was working up into the mountains from the home ranch end. I got a couple of miles lined out okay, blazed and cut out. But from there I ran into coulees, going up into the mountain range between them. I would follow a coulee going my direction and soon it would branch either way off to left or right. Timber was so thick in the coulees and sides so steep, I was literally fenced in and wouldn't realize I was heading away off before I had gone a mile or two. Two of these coulees I blazed and cut pack trail a mile or so to a dead end before finding they had led me astray.

One day I fought my way out of a coulee and right up over the top of a mountain. The timber was so thick I had to cut two trees instead of one to get a horse through. It was just small jack pine but I figured I'd cut a million of them by dark and where was I? It had turned stormy and I had been so intent on hacking my way through I didn't know where I was. I had a set of saddle pockets on my saddle and they got ripped off and lost squeezing through. Also my lass rope got tangled up and pulled the rope strap out. I had a lynx trap hung on the saddle horn and I had to use the trap chain to tie my rope on. I had no grub, blankets or horse feed and was desperately tired and hungry. My clothes were wringing wet from sweat and now it was raining and snowing by turns and getting blacker by the minute. I was on top of a mountain with coulees going down in all directions. Any sensible person would have headed back the way they had come. The horse would have followed it, no matter how dark it was, and the path was hacked out enough that I could squeeze through.

But I was like the bear. I had to see the other side. I started down the handiest coulee hoping for the best. I struck somewhat bigger timber and at least most of the trees were far enough apart that I could ooze through. Down in the coulee bottom there was a moose trail and the pony took to that. The moose sure hadn't done much of a job of chunking the trail out! They either go over or under windfalls and, being narrower than a horse, they go through where a horse cannot. So I had to cut some more. Even a minimum of whittling in the dark slowed things down pretty badly and I almost gave up and made a camp. Had there been a good spruce I probably would have, but all I could see was jack pine and all green.

175

So I pushed on and finally came out on the main stem of Baker Creek. I had hoped all the time that I was closer to Ramsay Creek but now I knew I had veered off too far west and was still only about halfway, and it was well past midnight. There was a horse trail across the creek from me, but in the dark it was a long time before I could find a crossing. About an hour from then I hit the road and finally got into Ramsay Creek at 3 a.m.

That was a good lesson to me. Now that I was on the Ramsay Creek end I headed down the other way to try to find any straight trail. There was nothing to it coming from that direction, and having snow on the ground I had my tracks for blazes. I went back over it right soon and cut off a few corners, blazed it a little and cut out some of the tightest spots so that we could travel it with a narrow pack horse load. Before we finished cutting it out, the timber got loaded with snow and we had some miserable sessions, but we got our Short Cut Pack Trail through the pass in the mountains, a distance of about eleven miles. Some of it was pretty steep up and down and you couldn't make fast time travelling on it, but it made a circle on the trapline. We figured that thick jungle up in the mountains would be the home of fur and I got a string of traps out right quick.

In this assumption we were a mite optimistic. It never produced a great amount of fur. It seemed to be off the beat for lynx and marten. There were mink at two lakes we went between, only two miles from Ramsay Creek. Other than that there seemed to be only fox. There were lots of foxes in there but cutting that new trail through seemed to scare them so badly they would run away like the devil was after them every time. It was the end of the trapping season before they got bold enough to investigate the horse track or the new ski trail they kept running into around their old home.

We found a wonderful lookout up in the mountains near the trail which goes through between two peaks. We climbed one and climbed trees to get to see out. We could see a huge scope of country; most of it was our trapline and our range. We made some pretty nice catches of fur some winters. To us most of it was just something to sell for all we could get out of it. But fox furs were different. We had ten of them in the cabin one time, all different shades and patterns. There were light and dark reds, but not so much variety in them as in the silvers which ranged from almost black, through a quarter, half and full silver.

The cross fox were the prime beauties to us. No two were alike. Such lovely soft, long, silky fur, some having quite strong silver patterns, some having double crosses, and such beautiful shading from one

176

colour to another. We brushed and stroked them and stood back and admired them and wondered why they weren't worth much more than silvers, or especially straight black which had been the highest priced of all before fur dyeing brought them down to the level of reds. Some of the cross foxes looked far more picturesque to us and we agreed that, had we been women, we sure would have worn cross fox.

However, the top price we got for any of them was thirty-five dollars and an odd silver brought us up to sixty dollars at that time. Only a few years before, top silvers had been over five hundred dollars. Alex Paley got caught badly when they slumped. He had paid the high prices during the winter and when he came out to market them in the spring, found they had dropped from around four or five hundred, to seventy-five dollars. He held some of his best for a couple of years, thinking they would go back up in price. But they went down still further and never did go back up. For several years fox wouldn't pay the royalty, selling commission and expenses.

R. L. Marsh shipped a really nice prime dark cross fox to a fur auction sale in the '50s and his final return: a bill for seventy-five cents!

Almost every time a chinook came in the winter, one of us would take a notion to hunt up some new patch of territory which, in our fond hopes or dreams, was just loaded with every kind of fur. A trap set for lynx would be sure to catch marten, fisher, fox, or coyote, in abundance all around. We never located this Shangri-la but kept looking. On one of those trips, I was riding old Roannie and had been breaking trail all day in around three feet of soft, wet snow. I still hadn't found the oasis of fur-bearing animals, and it was getting towards evening with around eight miles to go home and the trail to break all the way. I had small traps for mink and marten, and about three large ones for lynx, fox or coyote. I was travelling along the shore of a lake and finally saw enough tracks to make it look worthwhile to set traps.

The wind had blown the snow off the edge enough to bare some grass. I was riding Roannie with a hackamore and no bridle, so I turned him loose on the far side of me and went to work setting traps. I got about four set when all of a sudden Roannie decided good hay in the barn at home was far better than rustling old dried-up slough grass, and away he went on a tight gallop right from scratch.

The smart old devil knew if he didn't go fast I would intercept him. I saw right away that I didn't have a chance. He was by me before I could get halfway to stop him. I went right on setting traps till I had them all set so as to make it worthwhile to come back. Then

I took my chaps and spurs off, hung them over my shoulder and started the long walk home. It was nearly dark, snow soaking wet and trees dripping wet from the thaw, and I only had that one saddle horse track on the trail. A horse's tracks are too long for a man and one track in that much snow is very little help, anyway. It was going to be a mighty long, tough trip. I had had an early breakfast which had pretty well faded away.

I walked pretty steadily for the first two miles. By then I was wet to the belt from wet snow and wet from sweat from there up. My ambition was giving out. I had to sit awhile and take a rest, not too long, or I would get chilled and stiffen and take awhile to limber up again. The stops got closer together and it was harder and harder to start up again. By midnight I had made over halfway and a lot of it uphill. Now I had a down grade for nearly a mile but even that encouragement hardly seemed to help. I could only push a hundred and fifty to two hundred yards without a rest. If I could have found a dry stick I would have built a fire and rested up and dried out, but it was all green timber and soaking wet. In the dark and being so tired, it looked hopeless to find anything dry enough to make a fire and I despaired of going further. I was afraid to stop long enough to get the rest I needed or I would get chilled so badly I could hardly move. I commenced to get pretty panicky and thought morning was apt to find me frozen stiff.

Art had gone out to do the night chores and found Roannie at the gate with the saddle on. He had to guess from which way I was coming in, and guessed right, so for some time help had been on the way. Before I got to the bottom of the hill Art hove into sight leading my truant saddle horse. I've never been more thankful in my life to see someone coming. Art had to help me on and I shivered plenty before we got to the cabin. Home, grub, heat and a bed were all ready for me and I needed them badly. One of my nine lives shot.

Art had a bout with bad teeth when we were feeding cattle at the Sandy meadow seventy-five miles from town, doctor or dentist. Snow was pretty deep, too. We did have a sleigh trail broken through, but that doesn't help a saddle horse much without a lot of traffic. Art stalled it off about three days, then turned the feeding over to me and saddled up for the long trip out. He made it to the barn and tent camp at the home place and laid up for a few hours, but couldn't sleep so made it on down to the Tibbles', another fifteen miles. There he rested and fed his horse for a few hours before starting out again on the last thirty-five miles. He stopped in at Cocky Evans' to rest and feed his horse, and went on again for the last seventeen-mile lap. On the whole

178

trip he took just over twenty hours riding and about ten resting and feeding. He had had three days and nights without sleep before the ride. It is no wonder a man dreads a toothache back in the sticks.

The youngsters in the neighbourhood had been growing up all this time and some were getting old enough to ride around on their own hook quite a little. Our place got to be pretty popular with the elder Cooper and Paley youngsters as well as the Tibbles. These families had stock on the range between our place and theirs and any excuse was good enough to ride the range. Then they would come in and stay overnight or longer with us. There was always some activity going on up our way that they could work up a sweat on, if only for the novelty of it. We hired them at times, particularly for haying.

They generally came in pairs, sometimes bringing a friend and occasionally some of the girls for a visit. There was often a bit of guesswork figuring which place we would be at, particularly in the winter. But we always left grub in all the cabins so that no matter who came, or when, they knew they were welcome to stay anywhere and use grub and horse feed. Sometimes we would be up at the far meadows when travelling would be bad in deep snow and they would have to stay overnight. There was never a locked door; we didn't have a lock. To make the travellers welcome whether anyone was there or not we used to leave notes in the cabins. The following are a few samples:

CABIN NOTES

Home sweet home and the fire is out and the lady of the house is long gone.

I've bin told variety is the spice of life in wine, women and grub. Here you only have variety in grub.

You can cook hotcakes *or* biscuits for breakfast accompanied by tea *or* coffee.

For dinner you can cook beans *or* rice.

For supper you can cook rice *or* beans.

Coffee *or* tea *or* water at *all meals.*

So help yourself and don't go away mad.

CABIN RULES

Help yourself to what you need — meat in safe or in cooler, spuds, etc., in cellar — grub in cupboard.

Feed for horses in barn.

Don't be afraid to use the bedroll. It ain't lousy and I hope it's warm enough.

Be careful of fire and be sure to shut off all drafts in heater and stove before leaving.

Leave kindling and wood enough for overnight at least.

Shut all windows and doors.

Leave gates open or closed — as you find them.

Wash all dishes and throw out any cooked grub that will spoil before anyone else comes around.

Thanks for bringing the mail and damn you if you didn't.

Sign the register and tell all you know.

If you don't care to abide my these rules, you can always camp out. We don't mind.

Use but don't abuse.

Thanks from the owner and manager.

Don't steal my woman while I'm gone.

Dude Lavington

CHAPTER XVIII

Cowboy Wedding — Winter of the Blue Snow

Emma Cooper was the oldest girl in the Cooper family and Elsie Tibbles, her cousin, was only a little older. It was quite something for us to get a couple of girl visitors and we really did ourselves proud building high-toned bannocks and such like. When night came we'd turn the cabin and the best of the bedroll over to them and take our blanket rolls out to the barn or tent, or in the wide open if weather was good.

It wasn't too long before I noticed Art would cut Emma out and take her for a ride or they would get off by themselves and make plenty of chin music. That stage didn't last long either. Art must have been a fast worker because in just a little while he up and tells me he and Emma aimed to get spliced. He'd had his fill of batching; cooking, patching underwear, darning socks, washing dishes and general house-keeping. Besides there wasn't any point in building a big ranch unless a man had a family to pass it on to. So why not start the family now and let 'em all help with the building.

We had got past the worst stages of pioneering, having wagon road clean through to enough layouts to put up hay enough for five hundred head. Then we had buildings enough we hardly needed to camp out to any extent. We hadn't many cattle yet but with trapping and feeding cattle for neighbours we could all get by while the ranch was growing, and one of us could get out to work for wages whenever there was any work available. All these angles and a few more had to be taken into account. Emma was a whole lot younger than Art. Would that work out okay? Would we all be able to get along and work together as we had been doing? Emma had been raised in the sticks and had very little benefit from schooling, while Art had gone quite a ways in school, had had a business course and had moved around quite a little. Emma had never been away from Baker Creek settlement and seldom even to town. How would that work out? Would she be able to be happy away back here on a dead-end road seeing no one but Art and me for long stretches?

Apparently the pros outweighed the cons quite a little and the plans for a wedding in November 1938 got underway. This wasn't to be a stylish wedding, none of us having any amount of money. The honeymoon wasn't even planned as, by that time of year, they had to set up housekeeping in the sticks for the winter before snow got too deep to move in.

Elsie Tibbles was to be bridesmaid and I best man, and the wedding to take place in the Anglican church with a reception at the Quesnel Hotel afterwards. All travelling was done by team and wagon or saddle horse and pack horse as none of us had cars. Most of the roads in the area didn't pass for car roads except for the odd outfit that could work its way in and out in the driest part of the summer.

There was quite a gathering of the clan after the wedding and some of the guests at the reception imbibed not wisely but too well. Among these was the minister who had tied the knot.

Alec Paley and Shorty Harrington had a favourite drink for their celebrating, "Swedish Punch." It was a little sweet and so smooth to take that one could hardly guess that it packed a powerful wallop. Art had laid in a bottle or so of this high-powered white mule and the minister had a couple of drinks of it. He apparently wasn't acquainted with the stuff and figured it was a nice light wine, plumb tasty, and so he drank hearty. Then the good man wished them all the best, bade us farewell and took his departure. But before he got far, his feet got to tangling up and he was in real trouble before some good Samaritan helped him on his way.

Up until '38-'39 we still had only a tent camp at the home place. The summer one was up close to the site we figured to build on, and the one for winter trapping was down in a hollow. Now that Art and Emma were married, and we had a barn built and time enough, we decided we would start work in earnest on this layout.

We moved down with a couple of pack horse loads and set up housekeeping in the tent camps. First we did a lot of looking before even unloading the packs, to make sure that this was the best building site. There were several possible ones, and one for later to build a really good house. I think we took a couple of hours sizing up the layout before deciding that the one we had tentatively figured on by the tent camp would be the best. Then we flew at it and cut logs and hauled them in before the snow was gone in the timber so we could haul on a sleigh.

Once we had the logs ready it didn't take too many days to put the walls up and the gables and ridge logs on. Then we were ready for roofing. The first roof was made of split logs, about eight- to ten-inch stuff mostly. This was laid split side down. Then we put moss on; lots this time. Next operation was to haul dirt and shovel it up on top of the moss approximately eight inches to a foot deep on the top and tapered down to about four or five inches at the eaves. This time we made the roof complete right away. We put a set of ridge logs on top of the dirt roof, and put scoops on top of them. This was a much more particular job than the meadow cabins. For this we used logs with an approximate fifteen- to eighteen-inch face.

Having the exterior done we had to go to work building table and chairs, beds and cupboards. Then we constructed a road across the field to high ground in the timber on the other side. Some of this was a never-ending job. There is a creek just before reaching the timber and it had to be bridged. The water level is pretty high at times and the gravel we put on the road each year near that creek seemed to sink out of sight every spring and need a new layer of gravel to hold traffic. But we finally got a car road built across and could haul in anything we needed, as long as we could get the rest of the way to it.

Towards the end of the first winter of their marriage it became evident that Art and Emma were having an addition to the family. Around the middle of June, Art took Emma into town in the wagon to stay with Lennie and Bernice Torgerson and on July 13th, 1939, Emma had a baby girl. She was named Eva after our mother.

Quite soon after her birth Eva had her first ride in an iron-tired wagon out home to the ranch. This was a few years before we aspired to a "Bennett Buggy," which was much more comfortable to ride in. They were made basically from old car frames and wheels by the addition of a tongue and neck-yoke and eveners, so they could be pulled by horses rather than driven by an engine. The rubber-tired wheels were a big help on any road but particularly on a rough "stick road," with all the rocks, stumps and roots left in.

Art had made a crib for Eva. He built a frame and laced it with moose rawhide strings to lay the little mattress on and the sides were made of peeled poles a half inch in diameter. They were strong enough yet had some flexibility, and were spaced close enough that they made a real good playpen and crib combined. Sure changed our way of life to have a baby in the house.

The summer of 1940 I worked as range rider on the Batnuni for the Frontier Cattle Company. I talked them into letting me take thirty head of cows and a bull back with me to run on shares at our ranch.

All summer and fall I had done my camp cooking without a hat on and, until real cold, barefooted. But getting into November it started getting too cold and snowy for bare feet. I stayed bareheaded too late and caught my first cold of the year. It nearly developed into pneumonia.

We had weaned the calves off the cows that I was to take back home to run on shares. I was heading for home about November 15th and had two of their ranch hands helping me to a camp by Dry Lake. By then it had dipped well below zero and none of us had our winter riggin'. I made it to Hill's with my bunch the first night from Dry Lake. It went down to 40 below that night. They were very hospitable and rigged me out with old socks to shove into my gloves and boots, but my cold was getting ahead of the cure. I had sent word out to Art as to about when I was coming back and that I was bringing cattle, but I didn't figure any on his coming to meet me on the trail. So I had a mighty pleasant surprise to meet him on my way out from Hill's. He had ridden in from Flem Harrington's that morning, and although Flem had had to go out to town he had told Art where he cached his house key. It was a temptation to hole up at Joe Spehar's, but the whole outfit was on an island with big ice blocks all around from the ice jam flooding the river, so we worked our way on up to Flem's.

Art had forgotten where Flem had cached the key! He scratched his head and looked and looked but no luck. It was dark and 40 below and cattle were too tired to go any further, so we had to camp out alongside his blacksmith shop and woodshed. When the weather is good it is real nice camping out. But when it's 40 below and you are all set to be holed up in a warm house, it's just plain hell to have to brave the elements outside.

We made it up to old Major Franklin's for noon next day and sat up to the table inside for awhile. Major was plumb concerned about me almost having pneumonia. So he made up a cough medicine he claimed his daddy had invented years and years back. I forget the ingredients, but I believe he started out with a "Hudson's Bay Tea" brew and added onions, vinegar, mustard, ginger and garlic, maybe a little chewing tobacco for good measure. Man, that was a powerful conglomeration when boiled up awhile. There was no cough that wouldn't be affected by it, and I was on the road to recovery from there on in.

One more outside camp at Summit meadow in the Nazko Mountains and then on to Alec Paley's at Baker Creek where I seemed to be back on home ground. It was good to get to see the folks again and they were very curious about the new outfit away out west so I had lots to tell them. The cattle wandered quite a little during that night hunting meadows, but there was good tracking snow and the weather had moderated a little by then. We made it to our home ranch by dark.

Meanwhile Emma had been in hospital in Quesnel, having a baby. Jack Fraser had volunteered to bring her and Billy, the new baby, out as he was bringing a load of groceries out to Paley's in the John A. Fraser store truck. The road was terrible and had got badly rutted, some ruts with a lot of water in them and mud below. There was too much snow on top to tell where to drive and Jack got high centred and spun out. He was stuck between Nazko road and Cooper's with mother and babe; it was still nearly 20 below and neighbours a long way apart. He had to walk several miles in to Tibbles' and Paley's to get help to get the outfit out of the hole.

Emma and baby stayed with her mother until Art could get back to bring them on home in the sleigh. This was to be the winter of the "Blue Snow," the most severe I have ever experienced. It had already started early with this cold snap in November.

We moved right up to Ramsay Creek with all the stock, Emma and the two babies. We put cattle out on meadows to rustle as long as snow wasn't too deep or crusted, but it was a short rustling period in comparison to many other years. However, Art had put lots of hay up. I had sent money back to help pay wages and they had had a good haying season.

We got traps out while the cattle were rustling. Every few days we had to bring some more cattle in to put on hay. Calves had been weaned as soon as we got to Ramsay Creek.

Early in the New Year the weatherman lowered the boom and the colour in the thermometer dropped out of sight. Our thermometer only went to 50 below and, for more than six weeks, most nights it went down as far as it could go and didn't come back up till noon in the daytime. On sunny days it got up to 20 below occasionally but many days it was 40 below all day and some lower. We heard it had dipped to 72 below at Redstone, where they had a weather station, a hundred miles west of us.

So trapping was pretty much neglected and stock care was the prime objective. We fed everything at Ramsay Creek, waiting for a decent day to move. Finally we moved to Baker meadow anyway with most of the grown stock. I fed there till hay was about gone and then we moved back to Ramsay Creek for a few days. The move to Sandy meadow was next on the schedule. We hated moving in the severe cold; tough on stock and cowboys. The move to Baker meadow wasn't bad. Snow wasn't too deep and stock travelled well, figuring they were really getting somewhere. But the move to Sandy meadow was bad.

185

A lot of the cattle didn't know it as well as the other meadows, and by then snow was pretty deep. We hadn't kept a trail open. We stalled the move off as long as possible hoping for a break in the cold. But we had to leave at least two days' feed at both Baker meadow and Ramsay Creek for moving back through.

The time came we had to go. It was cold, damn cold. Art and I took a whole string of horses and sleighs and broke trail out, almost a mile an hour for the seven miles. We had fed everything at Ramsay Creek and then put out feed in another place for the next day, and Emma was to open a gate in the morning to let them through and open a water hole or so if she could. When we got to Sandy meadow we found we really had a job. We had a stack of hay and stack corral adjoining the barn on the edge of the meadow. The meadow is like a funnel. Wind either blows up or down, and continually day and night in winter. Anyway, it had drifted from away on our side of the barn right over the top of barn and haystack and on down the far side to where it tapered off. So we had to dig a tunnel into the barn door; then, from a hundred feet out, into and through the stack yard and out the other side. If we had about ten men — or far better, a "cat" — and had started at the beginning of the day instead of after feeding three hundred and fifty head for two days, done all the attending chores and then the seven-hour trail-breaking, it wouldn't have been bad. But that was the lay of the land and we had to call on all our reserves. It was an all-night job. We broke trail to the house and took grub in and got fires going, then broke trail to water and put on the nosebag. Then we really went to work. We worked in about two-hour shifts. We had thoughtfully put in a bottle of rum, as an antidote for chills after the long trail-breaking. That was worth its weight in gold through the night. After the first heat of digging in and getting horses into the barn, and enough hay to feed them, we went up and put on the nosebag with lots of hot coffee.

In the breaks after that we weren't so hungry, just dead tired. That was where the good, stiff hot rum came in. It seemed to put new life into us and after a half-hour rest we hit her again. We got it all opened up by daylight. We were scared to go to bed for fear of sleeping all day. So we harnessed a four-up and broke trail for feeding, then loaded hay on and scattered about three loads out. Then we rode for Ramsay Creek.

On our way out the day before, we had scattered the last hay load right to the timber on the edge of the meadow, and scattered wisps of hay for nearly a mile further on the road. It had worked. We met the leaders nearly a mile from the meadow, and we shoo-shooed them on in little bunches as we came to them. We started the whole works when we got to the buildings at Ramsay Creek, and took them to the edge of the meadow. Then we hurried back, put saddle horses in the barn, had a quick dinner and went out after the bunch before they changed their minds and came back. There were stragglers after the first mile but the main bunch had strung right out for five miles, and were probably entering Sandy meadow by the time we got to the tail end of the bunch. So the cattle moving wasn't bad. But when we got to the feed ground we found that the big stuff had trampled two calves to death in the deep snow where they couldn't get out of the way. Lesson No. 1 is to make sure all small stock are behind in deep snow. With the feeding done ahead we didn't have much to do before we could eat and hit the sack for the night. We didn't need any lullabies to put us to sleep. Emma and the babies didn't move down till the weather moderated; too risky in that severe cold. She had lots of wood and an open spring for water, and nothing to do but look after herself and the babies. One of us rode up every day to see that all was okay and get wood and water in.

Our big project was to build a shed right quickly as there was no shelter, not even spruce trees on the side of the meadow. Cattle just wandered all night up the sidehill looking for bedground and trying to keep warm. We located a steep-sided coulee and cut the tops off trees in it. We laid trees for stringers on the stumps and onto the coulee sides, and then piled brush tops on the stringers. We worked like hell on it as we knew it was too rough for young stock with no sheltered bedgrounds. Got it finished the second day and figured we'd really got her beat.

Next morning we found two more calves trampled to death. So we had to put bars up so nothing but yearlings, calves or quite small stock could get in. All was okay from then on except that one cow had frozen solid standing up alongside the barn and another further up the meadow leaning against two trees. Neither had fallen down and their legs hadn't even bent. Many had their ears, tails, hocks and knees frozen. I'd never seen anything like it before or since and hope I never do.

Finally we got a chinook, a real good one, and it seemed to break the back of that winter. The temperature rose from 40 below to 40 above in a very short time. It seemed like summer. We left our coats and mitts off and worked in our shirt sleeves, enjoying it thoroughly. So did the cattle. They didn't eat nearly as much either. Takes a lot of hay to keep a cow critter warm in severe weather. Stock which started in good shape took it well, calves were fat and stood it well. But anything on the thin side showed signs of having had a tough battle.

We fed the Sandy meadow out then moved back through the meadows, with a couple of days' stop at Ramsay Creek and at Baker meadow, then on down to home ranch where we combined hay from the Cooper meadow with the tame hay for spring feeding.

CHAPTER XIX

Bear Hunt in the Dark

It was quite an experience for Art and me to have the two babies to watch. Neither of us had been around babies to amount to anything before, and were mighty ignorant of what went on. We were just fascinated; watched them playing in their baths and by then Eva was making fairly intelligible chatter and getting around on her own steam and into mischief quite a little. We knew about calves and colts but had a lot to learn about kids. I baby-sat every little bit to give Emma a chance to go out riding with Art. One session they were out for too long and Bill was a little upset in his tummy. By the time they got back I'd used up all his riggin' and done a washing. While it was drying I'd penned him up naked in a play pen by the stove. He was happy as a clam, but I was pretty worried.

The following fall in haying time we were moving down to the Sandy meadow with a full course haying outfit. This time we had been busy packing and loading riggin' all day getting ready and didn't get finished till away late in the afternoon. I had a four-up on the old iron-wheeled wagon loaded with haying machinery and stacking outfit. Emma came next with a sweep collapsed and loaded on the Bennett Buggy and a lot of household riggin'. That outfit needed a wide load sign on it!

Art was trailing behind with a team of broncs on an extra mower. We made it halfway in daylight. It had clouded over and, before we got much further, got blacker than a stack of black cats. All I could see of my outfit was the shiny hames on my leaders flashing occasionally. I had a wonderful leader. She was out of Black Tiny and Baldy and was the best leader I ever drew a line over. Nettie was her name and she swung Jim, her mate, right where she figured they should go. She would go as far out on the corner as she could and then across to the other side as quickly as a flash to give you every inch there was and then some. We would have had to leave the outfit till morning if she hadn't guided it through. The others followed and we made it okay.

While we were haying at the Sandy meadow one fall, Emma's sister May came up. We were using a two-pole derrick, guyed front and back. When you pulled a load up the poles swung ahead and tightened the back guy. When the load was high enough the poles swung back and hung the load in the middle of the stack. This tightened the front guy, and the back guy line was loose and lay part way on the ground. May was carrying Eva in front of her on her saddle horse and rode over the back guy line when it was slack, but just when they were starting to raise the load the guy line flipped up and tightened right under the horse's belly. Sure got action! The horse tried to buck but its feet were off the ground and it couldn't get into high gear at all. I saw what was happening as I was up on the stack and hollered like hell to get the skinner to back the hoist team down. May's horse nearly upset when it hit the ground, but was scared badly enough it forgot to try to buck or kick and nobody got hurt. Art was so scared at what might have happened that he got pretty peeved at May.

After we finished haying at the Sandy meadow that fall we got an early start aiming to make the twenty-five miles back to the home ranch. We had three men working for us, Tom Cooper, Bernard Cold-well and Walter Merz. They rode down on saddle horse and took the shortcut pack trail from Ramsay Creek to the home place. Tom and Bernard had quite a time with Walt. He was mounted on Baldy and they would slap Baldy with a switch and make him just about jump out from under Walt. Before Walt rode home from our place they painted Baldy's hooves with fingernail polish they got hold of from May. Real bright scarlet. Walt didn't notice till he got too far on his way to turn back. He was a bit leary he'd lose his happy home trying to explain it all to his missus. Walt was one hell of a good work-ing man at most any job, but riding was not his long suit and I guess he walked a lot of the way, preferring it to riding. We had some real good horseshoe games that fall too, as we had quite a bit of wet weather. We kept Walt guessing pretty steadily. Every time we moved to another meadow he would ask us, "How many more?" We would tell him we'd lost track but "The snow ball meadow is the last one." To his queries about that, we were pretty vague but the general idea was that when the snow balls hit you in the ass, that was the last meadow to hay.

Art, Emma and the kids went in the Bennett Buggy with blanket rolls and cook outfit. I brought up the rear with a four-horse load of haying machinery in the freight wagon. The others got in quite a bit ahead of me. It was pitch dark when I got in and I wanted to let the folks know I was a-comin' so as to get help and lights to unhook the outfit. The horses were used to all the racket the old iron-tired wagon made on the rocks and roots but they hadn't heard a word out of me for a long time. I let a good hefty holler out of me as I came out of the creek crossing some two hundred and fifty yards from the house. I got action and plenty, but not the kind I had hollered for. The ponies woke up with a bang and lit out of there like a coyote being woke up with a charge of buckshot.

The ground was rough with old beaver workings, dams and ditches, and I lost my balance and was heaved out so quickly it would make your head swim. In the daylight I might have made it either to hang on or jump clear, but in the dark I got thrown down in front of the wagon and a front and rear wheel bounced right over me with a full load of mowers, rakes, stacking outfit and tools. But I think the speed must have helped. I got the wind knocked out of me and was dazed a bit, but nary a broken bone. The boys heard all the commotion and came out in all directions to see where was hell breaking loose. They located the team piled up in a thick little timber, no damage done, and then I got my wind back enough to get a little holler out and they packed me in.

We had killed a moose at the Cooper meadow just before finishing haying there. As it was late enough in the fall, we had hung the meat on the side of the house till we finished the meadow, intending to move it down to our home place to put in the meat safe. Pate Booth was working for us.

One evening we heard something heavy bump against the side of the cabin. We had no flashlight so I peered around the corner of the cabin holding a kerosene lamp above my head. I could just make out the vague outline of a big black object and the dogs went ki-yiing after it. We guessed it was a bear so got the rifles ready and figured out a lighting plan.

We hadn't long to wait. We kept the dogs in the house this time and soon heard the bumping. I took the rifle, Art held the kerosene light over my right shoulder and we sneaked around the corner all set to do battle. But the light must have scared him and we couldn't get a shot the first time. Next time Emma brought the kerosene lantern as well and I did see enough to get in a shot but didn't see the sights clearly enough to know if I had been on target.

However, the dogs took off barking their best. They only went to the top of the hill and then barked madly in one spot, so we were sure I had wounded the bear and the dogs had him treed. Art and I beat it up the hill towards the barking with the kerosene lantern and two rifles. Emma and Pate came right along behind. But before we got to the barking the whole works moved on, and the same thing happened again, so we all went that way.

This went on time after time. Apparently the bear wasn't being treed, but stopped and stood the dogs off making them bark furiously. Had they gone a long distance we would never have followed what we supposed was a furious wounded bear in pitch darkness. But his going such short distances and standing at bay till we could almost see him enough to get in a shot, led us on and on, this way and that way. Then it started to drizzle rain. Suddenly we thought of the babies back in the cabin, in bed asleep but all alone. We decided we must leave the chase and get back as quickly as possible. But which direction was home? None of us knew! Going this way and that in the dim circle of light shown by an old kerosene lantern in the blackness of a stormy night, intent on stalking a wounded bear, we had completely lost our sense of direction.

Each of us would have gone different routes except Pate. He admitted that one direction was the same as another to him. Art, Emma and I were so familiar with the country this close to home, that the fact that each of us would go different directions seemed to prove to me we could all be wrong. I argued that out and then suggested we string out in a straight line with the lantern in the middle. The idea was to find out the slope of the land. If we went straight far enough we were sure to go either up or down hill or strike a creek or coulee, I figured. Should we find a creek or coulee we just had to find the slope and follow down. A coulee would lead to the creek and creek to the meadow. If we found we were going uphill we must about-face and go down. Nobody seemed to have a better plan and Pate said he was all in favour, so Art and Emma reluctantly agreed to give up their ideas of the sure ways of getting home (in opposite directions) and we started off about halfway between the directions they wanted to go. The man behind did the lining up to keep the others headed straight and in about two hours we struck a definite downward slope. We veered to follow this slope down and came out to a small creek which we were sure ran into the meadow. Following that down, at about 3 a.m. we arrived home.

The youngsters were sound asleep, the old kerosene lamp keeping its lonely vigil. There were some pretty hefty sighs of relief and the coffee pot got quite a workout before we could relax enough to sleep, even tired as we were. We had learned our lesson the hard way again.

It was several days before the bear came back again, but when it did next it came in the late afternoon. Art had just finished raking and was unhooking the team off the rake when he spotted it. He quickly tied the team up, sneaked into the cabin and got a rifle. His big yellow collie dog took after it as soon as he came out again, and the bear went up a tree right in front of the cabin. Art shot him and he fell out of the tree. The dog went right in after him. In his dying struggles the bear locked jaws with the dog, and broke the collie's lower jaw.

So now we had a doctoring job. We made some splints to fit along the jawbone, set the bone the best we could and tied on the splints. We made an inside splint out of heavy poplar bark. I had seen this done on a dog's broken leg back home in Alberta and, as the bark dried, it set to the shape of the leg and hardened like a clamp. We bandaged the dog's jaws together, figuring to feed him soup till we were pretty sure the broken bones were set. It worked out pretty well except that it was a little crooked and he couldn't shut his jaws quite tight, and the teeth didn't match perfectly. But this could have been the saving of his life a short time later when he mixed into a bunch of wolves.

CHAPTER XX

Eight-Horse Plough Outfit — Cow Business on Shares — Breaking Tony

In the spring of '41, Fred Gilbert and his dad came riding into our place and stayed over a couple of nights. The old man knew a lot about farming brush and gave us a few pointers. He told us he had an old brush breaker plough which, although twenty-four inches, could be offset to turn a thirty-inch furrow heavy enough to hold the brush down. He wanted a cow and calf for it. We made the trade. The cow was to be delivered when we brought the beef drive down in the fall. He told us we could easily produce four hundred tons of hay on the home place.

I was breaking a little brown gelding we named Brown Jug and took him on this beef drive although only half broken. The beef drive started with the Paleys coming up to our place to round up, as at that time our cattle ran together a lot. We rounded up east of our layout first and got most of what we wanted, then took them down to Bradley Flats to join up with what Paley wanted.

The cattle drive from Shorty's was seventy-eight miles to Quesnel, and from Joe's over one hundred. Travel was at about an average of two miles per hour. The big three- and four-year-old steers and dry cows would travel quite a bit faster and had to be held back. There weren't many calves sold in those days as they were worth so little, but there were always cripples and naturally slow travellers which held up progress. The drive from Shorty's First Creek meadow to the Summit meadow was about the longest with no feed. There was not enough feed there to hold a large bunch over, which meant too long a drive the next day.

The next day, after we joined the others, the whole drive made it from Quanstrom's to Cocky Evans', close to fifteen miles. The boys helped Brown Jug and me cut the cow out of the herd and headed her for Gilberts'. She was agin the idea and I had to dab a rope on her, Brown Jug's first experience breaking a cow critter to lead. He and the cow learned a lot in the first while and I did a lot of work educating them. We finally got the cow to lead okay, but the calf didn't think much of the idea and dropped away behind. Had to tie the cow up and go back and get the calf; then the cow balked. So I turned the cow loose and roped the calf and broke it to lead ahead. No problem then as the cow wouldn't leave her calf.

Cocky Evans entertained us all in his inimitable manner, as usual. "Bloody bunch of cowboys, probably not house broke, but you can use the other cabin if there's room enough. It there isn't, yer'll bloody well 'ave ter camp outdoors," he said, in his strong Cockney accent. Well, we shacked up in the cabin but by morning several of us wished we'd found a level spot outside. Cocky's cabin was built to fit the side-hill and it was a pretty steep sidehill, so the floor sloped at a mighty steep angle. If you parked up hill with your feet braced against the lower wall, your knees buckled when you relaxed and you piled up agin the wall. If you started sideways, you all rolled into each other and down against the wall. So there was more rolling around, trying new positions, talking and smoking than sleeping. We sometimes by-passed Cocky's on the drive and made the longer drive to Jack Wilkinson's.

So it was kind of a long visit and lots of chin music at nights. During the day we were spaced out with one or two cowboys to the twenty-five or thirty cattle in the lead and bigger bunches all the way back also with one or two cowboys, all extra riders bringing up the drag herd. Occasionally, we had trouble with bulls herding or fighting and one cowboy would have him an ornery bull all by himself. Bulling cows always cause a lot of trouble in the drive and have to be watched constantly. A bunch of steers or bull or so, follow right up through the herd and then off into the timber where they stand and hope to be missed and left to their own devices. With so many different owners there were always lots of cowboys, albeit some not too efficient. Shorty usually went ahead with his truck, making arrangements and getting feed hauled for night camps. Julius Wohl always took a wagon with grub and outfit for some Nazko cowboys. I always got into the cooking act on these sessions, being pretty handy making mulligan with limited facilities.

Our last stop before town was usually at the old Holt place, which is now the golf course and only four miles from town. We always tried to get an early start out of there to dodge daytime traffic and too many spectators. Cow critters from the sticks are mighty leary of people on foot.

Paved roads, traffic and too many people have pretty well shut down trail driving. We always had to get police to stop traffic on the old Fraser River Bridge. That was one of the arrangements Shorty had to make in advance.

195

Prices were very low in those days; so low, that a three-year-old steer some years was only worth forty dollars. We all had an idea that the cattle buyers were ganging up beforehand. They would come up the night before and stay in the same hotel (Cariboo or Quesnel hotels) and we figured they planned their strategy over a few drinks. This buyer wanted so many cows and so many steers. He wouldn't bid more than so high against the other guys as long as they wouldn't bid against him. Quite a few shipped to Vancouver before the auction sales started in Quesnel. They were okay for fat stock ready to butcher if the market didn't get plugged. But it was no good for stocker cattle as there were practically no feeder buyers in the Fraser Valley then, and this type of stock was apt to be bought up and shipped back to Williams Lake with only the railway making anything on the deal. This type of deal led to forming of cattlemen's associations all over the province and also to the B.C. Livestock Co-op auction marketing.

One year Alec Paley's meadows got badly flooded and he had practically no hay, so decided to ship everything to Vancouver yards where Tom Baird was manager. Tom managed to get rid of the beef stock fairly soon at rock-bottom prices, but there was just no sale for stockers and feeders. It wound up that Paley got a bill for feed out of the deal! Quite a lot of belt tightening that year as many ranchers were in about the same boat.

This particular fall, the market was picking up owing to war and we all shipped to Vancouver. I was on my way down to enlist and had a few loose ends to tie up: arranging to get my saddle horse taken back, gathering my junk off the bed wagon, and saying good-bye to the girl friend. I just about missed the train and had to run and catch it on the move at the crossing by the old Quesnel River Bridge. The old P.G.E. wasn't much for speed so it wasn't hard to catch. I shinnied up a ladder to the top and started down the train, hoping to find a hole down into the caboose. But right quickly I had to flatten down as we went across the Quesnel Railway Bridge, where the top riggin' was about to cut me down to size. After that, I moseyed from car to car till I got over the cook shack and could see a hole down to the cook stove. I saw the cook down below.

I hollered down and asked him how to get on the inside. He said to come down the ladder and he'd let me in. I must say it was nicer riding inside, listening to Shorty's jokes. They had even made preparations for the long ride by having a bottle of whiskey. I thought old Joe Spehar was going to get the best of it on the first round. He'd take the bottle in both hands and guzzle, guzzle, guzzle, take the bottle down for a breath and do it again three more times before passing on the bottle. But he went to sleep pretty quick. Shorty, Paley and I had the rest of it for the night. We got to Squamish and cars were unloaded onto barges and headed across the pond quite a ways before we hit solid ground again. Finally we got unloaded in the stockyards and, after giving Tom Baird instructions to feed and water, we were free to hit up town. Vancouver being a pretty sizeable town with lots of hotels and such, nobody had thought to arrange for accommodation ahead. We found that Vancouver was a boom town that year and accommodation was practically non-existent. Paley and Shorty had usually stayed at the Beacon Hotel and that's where we headed. It didn't have a square foot of space available for a month and we were told we'd likely find the same situation all over town. However, the manager said he would phone rooming houses, much less plush layouts, and see if he could find anything for us. Old Joe went out and hired a taxi to find accommodation. Finally the manager hit pay dirt and booked rooms for us at the old Europa Hotel down in the skid row part of town and we got located about midnight. Imagine our surprise to find old Joe just across the hall from us! It cost him a hell of a lot more to find the only accommodation in town by taxi though.

We had to take a taxi down to the yards next day to cut out different owners' stock. Then I headed up to see what the armed forces could do with a part cripple. I didn't get far. First look at me naked, the doctor says, "What's the trouble with that knee?" I told him I had a bog spavin. It was swollen up pretty badly and he says right away, "You best go back to raising cows. That knee won't let you into any of the services." So I got an honourable discharge inside of two days or less and was on my own and headed back to the Europa Hotel.

We got in touch with Alec and Gertrude Fraser and they came over. We found out some loggers and girl friends could play music and dance, so proceeded to drum up quite a party right there in the hotel. We sure made use of the facilities that night.

Another year, old Joe went on his own hook and got located in a rooming house. He proceeded to get loaded and wound up getting rolled for nine thousand bucks. Still another time he wound up in real trouble. Some gal got wind of his having a cattle cheque and more coming. She roped him in, married him and proceeded to strip him year by year without living up to her obligations, as a good wife should. So instead of packing his bankroll in his sock, Joe buried what he could get away with out behind the barn in the manure pile. So the story goes. Old Joe went over the divide a few years back, so no more marital troubles!

Still another year Alec Paley and I made arrangements to get new outfits of teeth to wind up the cattle drive. "Painless Parker" was the outfit. Sounded good anyway. They took impressions on Monday morning and we were told to come back Friday for extractions and new teeth. We went to a lot of shows, day or night, and had one bang-up party in a restaurant/cabaret kind of layout. Pan, his wife "Shorty" and Ron Kolterman joined Shorty Harrington, Alec and me there. Art had got acquainted with Koltermans while he was going to school and logging on the coast. We all got pretty well lubricated and let our hair down, and some hopped around a little with the gals without too much riggin' on.

Last I can remember going out of there, Ronnie Kolterman reached up and stuck a twenty-dollar bill above the door frame for a tip. A twenty-dollar bill in those days was quite something, and I'd a liked to have stayed and watched the waitresses trying to get up to reach it. Back to the quiet life in the sticks again, but this time Alec and I sure had plenty to remember the trip by. The new teeth on raw gums didn't seem to be a good idea for a few days. However, if I had to do it over, I'd do it that way again.

On one of these trips, Shorty wanted to do some shopping in Great West Saddlery Wholesale building and made arrangements to do it on a Saturday when most of the staff was off. Shorty sold quite a little riding gear to the Indians in his store. Alec and I accompanied him and found some kind of old-fashioned do-it-yourself elevator. Well, we got in and got the door closed, but it had no light! With matches we found a lot of buttons and tried some of them without finding one to either go up or down or open the door. We started to get a bit panicky before Shorty located a foot pedal that did something and then a button worked, or we'd likely been there yet. Another trip we saw the Ice Capades and I sure remember that as being an outstanding event. The things those little short-skirted gals did on skates I had to see to believe and hardly believe it yet.

Back at our own operation we did a whole lot of fencing. We built all the fence with A posts and rails from seven to ten axe handles long. First we fenced the horse pasture. That was where we experimented most with rail lengths. We started with ten axe handle rails and then realized they would need a stay in the middle or would sag too much. Seven axe handles would have been best as many trees would make two rails. But that would take a lot more spikes, so we settled on eight axe handles and hoped they wouldn't sag too much. After the horse pasture, we built a house pasture for wrangle horse, milk cows, or calving heifers out in spring. The next year we started on the big project, fencing the big tame hayfield-to-be. We worked all summer on that, just Art and I alone. First it rained every day, then we had about the hottest dry spell on record. It cooked some grass and the willow leaves brown. It about cooked me where we were working in reflected heat under a sidehill. I got a touch of sunstroke and passed out — across the creek nearly a mile from the house and no wagon road to it. Art hauled and dragged me to a shady spot, then dipped water out of the creek with his hat to revive me. He finally got me on my feet and we got back to the cabin. I was pretty shaky for a few days but when weather cooled off we flew at it again. Altogether, with cross fences, we built over seven miles of fence. We did get the haying crew to help with the last two hundred yards before starting haying. Some of it is standing yet today but getting pretty shaky and rotten.

We now had a big old brush breaker walking plough and enough grown-up colts from the two Duke studs to start operations. We rigged up an eight-horse team outfit for the plough and a four-horse team for disc and harrow, and went to work tearing up the home place to make a tame hayfield.

That spring, when we were branding colts, we had thrown one and when I went to jump the rope to get down on his head, my haywire knee buckled. I was in bed about a week and pretty much on crutches all summer, so was pretty helpless around these horse outfits. We got Harold Paley to run the four-up on the disc and harrows. That started out as quite a joke. Harold had never done anything like that before and he circled the ploughed patch a few times and came in saying he was all finished. What to do now? I knew plumb well he hadn't been at it long enough to work it down, so went down and showed him that the real idea was not just to be able to say he had been over it all once, but to keep going over it every which way till it was all chopped up and smoothed down to a well-worked seed bed that could be mowed, raked and, hopefully, have a sweep work on it. That was a horse of a different colour, and the enthusiasm had faded quite a little as the novelty wore off for a twelve- or thirteen-year-old boy, but he was a good skinner and did a good job before claiming it was all finished again.

Art was having a great time with the old brush breaker. We were a little short of broke horses, so every little bit we put a raw bronc or so into the eight-horse outfit. Art didn't aim to use this as a walking outfit and stood up with one foot on the old hardwood beam and the other perched on a three-eighths-inch brace rod for awhile. Then we built a kind of seat on the outfit as his haywire back and old broken leg started to give too much trouble. This seat was built mainly for skookum. It sure was no hell for comfort, but made a big difference. He got bucked off every little bit. Since it was built as a walking plough, he had to get off at every corner, tip the plough out of the ground, follow it around the corner, tip it back up, and jump back onto it when straightened around. It was hell for finishing a field with lots of corners close together, so mostly we ploughed long strips out to begin with. A lot of the field was very rough with brush humps three feet high and hollows between them with brush as high as the horses on most of it; almost too rough to ride over with a saddle horse. We hung a log chain on the plough so it would tuck the brush in under the furrow. Of course some heavy willows, ten or twelve feet high, didn't tuck in and had to be pulled out and piled and burnt later. But it turned a furrow nearly thirty inches wide and that was heavy enough to hold the lighter brush down pretty flat. With heavier brush the furrow would stand on edge and be hell to work down.

I think about the second or third year Art was running the plough outfit he hit a hump that had frost under it, in early July yet. He got bucked off and broke a finger. I was still too crippled in my knee to run the outfit. Some time later I tried it with a six-horse team, as on one haywire leg it seemed by the time I got an eight-up ready to go it would be time to quit for dinner.

We sure got some huge crops off the layout. Usually we put oats in for cover crop. Some years it must have made eight-feet high and was hell to handle. One year it was too wet to cure and we tied it by hand with strings made from straw. Old Bill Stednyck, an Austrian I think, was working for us and he showed us how to make these straw ties to tie bundles. We hauled them into a huge stackyard we built and then stacked them in long rows the full length of the stackyard. The moose sure loved that stuff and did right well that winter on it. The drier ground we sowed into a mixture of brome, timothy, clover and crested wheat. A whole lot was sub-irrigated ground and that part we planted to a mixture of tame red top, timothy, clover, a little Reed's canary grass and some Orchard grass.

Now we were more than ready for cattle and had demonstrated that we could put up hay for over four hundred head. The problem was to get into cattle. The packing and freighting hadn't made us more than mighty short eating-money. Fur business was very uncertain and prices had gone very low. So wintering stock for money and cattle, or running stock on share deals looked like the best bet. Several winters we wintered stock for the Paleys and Prossers and then we got the little bunch of Frontier Cattle Company stock to run on shares. But we were still a long way short.

We got quite a surprise one day around 1942 when a couple of visitors walked in. One of them was Ronnie Kolterman. Ronnie's dad, Percy, had been raised only three or four miles from Dad's place in Alberta but his folks had moved to the coast when Percy was around eight years old. They knew we lived in the Cariboo around Quesnel and had come to Quesnel to locate us. They had to leave their car about eight miles out and had walked in from there. They stayed about a week and enjoyed it so much that Ronnie and his dad started coming up pretty regularly. They had a pretty good business established in New Westminster. Percy was a mechanic and Ronnie a body man and they found that they could buy up wrecked cars pretty cheaply, take them to their shop and remake them. Percy worked on the engine and Ronnie did the body and paint work and they turned out practically a new car.

They also built the odd house for sale and by this time had reached the stage of looking for something in which to invest their savings. They had a hankering to get into the cow business and soon we were away buying cattle all over and driving them home across country; and later hunting all over hell's half acre to find where they went during summer and fall, and also trying to keep timber wolves from taking all the profit off the top.

Building roads, turning moose pastures into hay meadows, building cabins, barns, stackyards, pastures and all such like had kept us plenty busy but there was no income whatever from any of it. So it wasn't too many visits from Koltermans before we got into the cow business on shares. They both loved to hunt and so took their holidays mostly in the hunting season. They came up time and again, worked their way in on fall roundups, and got in on whatever hunting they could, either birds or big game. Also, it was good for them both as they had been keeping their noses too close to the grindstone for too long and both had slight tendencies towards lung trouble. Ronnie was especially affected this way. Later he came and stayed with us most of three years and cured all his troubles. He also found the girl that lived next door to his folks in Westminster and married her.

By the summer of '42 several of our colts had grown up big enough and old enough to break. Some were big enough and bred for work stock, but we had four or five out of Baldy that were the makings of good saddle stock. Art broke one, a real nice looking dark bay he called "Slim," and he proved to be a top horse for a good many years. Tony was ready too and I hoped I was ready for him.

By now there was a lot of horse wrapped up in that big black hide. He had a very intelligent head and a fairly good eye but we guessed that it wasn't all kindness in those eyes and that that craving to play was bound to call for a buck jump pretty regularly.

I always figure a horse learns to buck better and better with practice and that a colt has quite a lot to learn to start with. So I wasn't too shaky when I tied the riggin' on again. Also having ridden him ten miles after his first little buck jump gave me quite a little confidence.

Well, I needed it all! Ronnie and Percy were on hand with cameras and got some nice pictures.

Tony started working on me right from scratch. He was no three-year-old colt now but a seventeen-hand, full-grown horse, with all kinds of life and action, and a fully developed set of muscles, hardened like steel coil springs. But there was more play and run in his makeup than meanness and I won that battle fairly soon. After I'd had time to get my wind back again I set to work in that little corral to make him neckrein and handle real well. I slapped my chaps and petted him all over as he ran and shook my rope out and trailed it and then coiled it again and again, let him know I had spurs, and that they were a guide to him as much as bridle lines. Then I educated him to sidle up to a gate so I could open it off him. That was something that seemed pretty necessary as I had to ride a lot alone and I didn't want to have to get off too often.

Tony got a lot of education that day and I've an idea we both slept right well that night.

It takes a lot of riding and stock work to make a good saddle horse. Tony had the intelligence, and I had quite a little of the know-how to educate him, but we didn't really have enough stock at that time to give a horse like him the work he needed.

I had only made three or four more rides on him when he just about got the best of me. We had rounded up our cattle to take from our home ranch up to the meadows, but we were several head short. We decided to take the main bunch up to the Cooper meadow and Art was going right up up with a sleigh load of grub to the Ramsay Creek meadow. I drove the cattle riding Tony with Art ahead of the herd in the sleigh. When I got the cattle to the meadow I told Art I would go back to the home ranch and hunt for the missing cattle till I found them. He was going right on up with the sleigh and aimed to start November trapping.

I made a short ride for the missing cattle on the way home that night. It was bright moonlight by the time I got in. I edged Tony up to the gate and reached away down for the gate plug. Then hell broke loose! Tony shied away from my outstretched hand and lit into bucking. Well, I was off balance too far to get back in the saddle and just fell sprawled out underneath him.

He was headed into a fence corner and didn't bother to look for a way out of it but just kept on bucking right on top of me. He was sharpshod and weighed around eleven hundred pounds, and he just pounded the devil right out of me. Two bats, one on the head and one under my left arm, were really bad ones. This seemed to go on forever! It probably wasn't as long as it seemed before he moved away and left me to my own devices.

I nearly blacked out. All my left side was paralyzed and I couldn't raise up without going out completely. But I seemed to know I had to get inside or I would freeze to death. Somehow I forced myself to raise up enough to reach the gate plug and then I crawled the fifty yards to the house and rose up again enough to open the door.

Self-preservation is quite a thing. It gave me a seeming obsession that I had to do so many things before I could pass out. It just seemed to command me to light a fire, get water, and cook enough grub for several days so I could take it to bed and then let myself pass out. I seemed to know I would get too stiff to do anything once I lay down.

The cabin was cold and my first necessity was fire. I tried and tried and tried to light that fire but every time I got up high enough to reach the top of the stove, the blackness stole over me and I got helpless and had to flop down again. Temporarily I gave up, but the obsession was still with me. I crawled to the bed and got on it with all my clothes and chaps still on and pulled the blankets over me. But even there I wouldn't let myself go and held onto consciousness. Three times I got up again and tried to start the fire. Finally I succeeded. The rest seemed to have cleared my head enough that I could rise up enough to do things without blacking out.

Having the fire, the urgency speeded me on to crawl over to the creek to get water. On my way, I saw Tony right where I had left him, waiting to be fed and watered. I knew I must get him into the barnyard. Some way I might be able to tie him up and get on him to ride out of there for help, if I wasn't in too bad shape. He had watched me crawling around enough so he wasn't scared of me. I talked to him and he knew me; he was hungry so he let me catch him and crawl to the barn where I opened the door and turned him loose to fend for himself. There was hay for a day or so in the mangers and that was all I could do. He could get to the creek for water. I would like to have taken off his saddle and bridle but no way could I make it.

Then I headed for the creek for the bucket of water and getting that to the house seemed to take days. I finally made it. Time seemed to mean nothing to me as long as I got these things done. I mixed up a bannock and cooked it and took it and some raisins to bed with me, along with lots of water. It was daylight before I got it all done to my satisfaction. At last I took my riggin' off and got into bed.

Then, and only then, did I let myself go. Later I figured out I had slept that day and night and the next day and night without getting up. Time just passed and I knew nothing of it. But when I woke up I was not as stiff as I had feared. Just one side was paralyzed. I hadn't eaten any of what I had prepared but now was hungry as hell and very thirsty. My next move after eating was to get out and look after Tony. It was a real job to get the saddle off but I made it and fed him and then got back to my bannock and raisins and bed again.

I was laid up for about five days but getting better all the time. The cattle I had been looking for came to the gate. I let them in and so was ready to go on up to the meadows except that I was still grounded and paralyzed too much to saddle Tony and get on. I became impatient, being alone and still so helpless.

A bad snowstorm came one afternoon and evening and nearly a foot of snow came with it. I was reading that evening but I couldn't enjoy it. There was little hope of anyone coming to look for me for a week yet and I was worried. A bad storm in circumstances like mine seems to put fear into a person and I was constantly listening but not daring to hope that anyone would come, when suddenly I heard a yell out of the darkness outside. Ronnie Kolterman had come up from New Westminster to winter with us on account of his health. He had broken a leg that summer and had a silver plate and screw in his ankle and the walk of fifteen miles through the storm and soft snow had nearly been too much for him. Paleys had tried to stake him to a saddle horse but he was sure he could make it walking and then wouldn't have to take a horse back. He had very little hope of our being at the home cabin, figuring that we would be at the Ramsay Creek meadow. So we both really had something to be tickled about and I guess I talked the poor guy to sleep telling all my story.

We laid up and rested the next day, planning the next move. Handling colts was right out of Ronnie's class and I couldn't walk anyway. Either he had to walk on up and let Art know my predicament so he could come after me in the sleigh or we would both try it together if I felt well enough to tackle it.

I didn't want to stay alone any more so, next morning, I got up nerve enough to tackle the big pony again. He was okay to lead and handle on foot so we led him in between an open gate and the fence which formed a sort of chute, very narrow at the head and wide at the back. We tied Tony to the gatepost with a rope across behind him.

Ronnie climbed up the gate with the saddle and dumped it on him and very carefully cinched it up. Tony showed signs of being a "cinch-binder" — a horse that has to be cinched tight very slowly or he will blow up and buck.

Then I tied his shank rope and hackamore so he couldn't buck. I had never used this system before and wasn't too sure of it working a hundred per cent. But I guessed at least it would slow him down a lot. Ronnie put the bridle on and we tied a spare pair of socks and a chunk of bannock on the back of the saddle and all was ready.

I was scared to death to tackle it. My knees shook so Ronnie had to help me up the gate and over onto the saddle. I sat and talked to Tony and petted him all over for ten minutes before I let Ronnie swing the gate and let him go.

That was just what old Longboat was waiting for. He hadn't liked all that monkeying around with him tied helpless in a chute. He dived his bead in between his front legs and got the big bow in his back but — "whoa, babe" — there was something all wrong. He couldn't get his head down right. The buckshank gripped his neck and the top of his head and over his nose so hard when he got his neck bent that he just had to straighten up again. I could draw a breath of relief. The system was going to work. He tried it steadily for an hour, and then every time he thought about it for several miles before giving up and lining out. I rounded up the five or six cattle and we started up the hill. When Tony lined out okay, I threw Ronnie my lass rope for a towline and that way we made it up to the Baker meadow cabin, nine miles away, where we stayed the night.

Tony tried the riggin' next morning again but a jerk or so on the hackamore and bridle, and the feel of the sore spots from the day before, soon changed his mind and we got up to Ramsay Creek early in the afternoon. Art insisted on my taking to the bed roll after hearing all the details. I definitely was not agin it! There I stayed for all of one week and most of the next.

It had been quite an ordeal for me. We figured I had three broken ribs under my arm and a shoe print there that showed for nearly three years. My left side was partially paralyzed for the rest of that winter so I couldn't get around much on the trapline and what little travelling I did had to be on a gentle horse. That was another of my nine lives shot to hell!

CHAPTER XXI

Buying Cattle — Cattle Drives Across Country — Another of My Nine

Getting cattle from Moon's was our first venture in cattle buying. First we drove down and they took us out and showed us some on the range that were for sale. Then they were to round them up. We were to put on a sort of company brand: LK on the right hip to indicate Lavington-Kolterman stock. Moon also vented in two places to very clearly indicate that these cattle had been sold. They built a huge log fire but didn't seem to be able to keep their irons hot. We just had one iron but we pulled a little of the best wood to one side, and kept our iron red hot all the time. Mel commented, "You fellers sure know how to run a brand fire."

Now the big job remained — to get them home. We went home to get a pack and camp outfit, and horses for the job. Art couldn't be away for the time it would take. However, Wallace Paley was working down at the Gang Ranch and figuring to come home and Bob Paley was visiting his aunt and uncle, the Jim Scallons of Big Creek, and he was also coming home. Wallace had his own saddle horse but I had to take one for Bob and a couple of pack horses for camp outfit. Bob and Wallace were to meet me at Moon's. I headed across country with the sun and a map to guide me. I knew where I had to go and had three days till the meeting time. I needed every minute of it.

For a long ways there were no roads or trails. Then I first started running into meadow roads and trails near Irvin Twan's. No markers on any roads, so when I hit a road I followed it if it was going anywhere close to my direction. Nobody was at home at their swamp meadows. My second day was the bad one. I got into an awful mess of rocks and windfalls with no feed for miles and miles. It looked like I was to have a barren camp that night. At dark I was still in it. There were little potholes with feed in them, but also too much water and bog. Finally around midnight I came to the edge of the Kinlock meadows that had once been owned by the Yorstons. From there I seemed to be fairly lucky. I had a little trouble getting around Eric Collier's layout with it being so badly flooded by beavers. I made it into Mel Moon's on Meldrum Creek about 2 a.m. the next morning.

I got up to where I was to meet the Paley boys and we picked up the cattle we got from Chas. Moon next morning. We started the drive back to Mel's and from there to home. Mel talked us into picking up Freddie Johnnie to show us the best way to drive up the Fraser River for a couple of days' drive. That worked out fine but that was as far as he knew, and we were on our own guesswork from there. There were pretty fair trails and roads till we got up to Lee's on the Fraser at Marguerite. Flies were very bad, it being early in July. We would break camp early and drive pretty steadily till it got hot, then just drift them very slowly to keep them under control, feeding some till the flies went down at night. By that time we had to hope that they were played out enough to stay put. It worked pretty well, except for the morning we were leaving the river around Lee's, headed up to Eddie Boyd's layout. We got a little too late a start and flies got the jump on us and we lost one in thick, small fir timber. We lost a big chunk of the day and nearly lost the bunch, trying to get that one hunted up — with no luck. So not much mileage that day. We stayed overnight at Eddie Boyd's and he helped us figure the best way to travel across country to our lower Ramsay Creek range. Cattle were well trail broken by then, but we had no trails, so I lined out ahead with the pack horses and let the boys do the cowboying. Weather was clear so we had no problems with directions; but we would come to swamps we had to detour, windfall patches or thick timber that were almost impossible to get through and creeks that it was quite a little job to find crossings on. Heifers followed the pack outfit well though, and we progressed about eight to twelve miles a day.

Whenever I was out with a pack horse or any other horses, I'd turn Tony plumb loose at camp and stake the other horse. The first time this failed was on that trip. It was somewhere halfway between our place and Riske Creek that Tony quit me. Somehow my pack horse got loose and she headed out with Tony following. A nicker woke me about three in the morning and I guessed that the horses were leaving right away. I grabbed Bob's or Wallace's horse and went in pursuit. As it was in mid-July, it wasn't too dark to ride through the sticks but it would be some time before I could tell if my saddle horse was on tracks. I wasn't too far behind them but they were making as good time as I was. When the sun got up a little, they stopped to feed in a pothole meadow they were crossing and I caught up. I went around the far side as carefully and quickly as I could, then got off and called Tony and walked up on him. Was I ever tickled to get my riggin' on him again! Two horses to three men with a big kitchen and blanket pack and fifty head of yearling heifers fifty or sixty miles from any known spot wasn't a nice picture, and in the worst of flytime at that. I always hobbled Tony after that in camp, whether he needed it or not.

Somewhere in this area we noticed we had got to itching and scratching a lot, and it wasn't long before we found out we were lousy as pet coons. Wallace had brought a load of the livestock from the Gang Ranch with him. With us all sleeping in the same blanket outfit, the livestock had dispersed, so we could share and share alike. We had no louse dope with us and no kettle big enough to boil our clothes or take anything but a cold bath in the creeks, so we just had to carry our pets along with us right home. I had got into bedbugs a time or so in my travels and one other time I got loused up, as the saying goes. But ordinarily it wasn't too big a problem to delouse. This time we had to scratch and bear it for more than a week. We weren't a bit sorry to get into Ramsay Creek, drop the cattle and hit for our home ranch and a big clean-up.

That fall we bought a bunch of Staebler's calves, and a bunch of Pan Phillip's yearlings out of Quesnel stockyards. These calves had been loaded onto trucks at Staebler's four miles north of Quesnel, right off their mothers, and were not fully weaned. Pan's yearlings had made the long drive close to two hundred miles from his ranch to Quesnel so were trail weary. Not a good combination to drive together and we knew it. Again we got Bob and Wallace Paley, and also Charlie Forrester. Charlie's main responsibility was to trail along behind with the yearlings. We knew it would be practically impossible to keep the two bunches together. We had to trail the works right through town and across the Fraser bridge. The calves had never seen a saddle horse before. They went out on a high lope and caught up and passed the yearlings in nothing flat, but we managed to keep them circled back to the yearlings every little bit till we got through town and across the bridge.

Then we decided to let Charlie handle the yearlings and let the calves get their run over and get used to being handled, hopefully before we passed Staebler's where cows were still bawling just down below the road. It seemed to be working and we very nearly made it by lining up on the lower side and keeping them moving pretty fast. But cows heard the odd bawl and a whole lot answered. One calf broke away down over the steep bank. Before we could get it back, others broke and we saw we had lost the battle. A few got through fences and in to their mothers, but we got the main bunch into the corrals and shut them up. We roped the others and got them in, and decided to let them bawl a night and a day. Charlie took the yearlings

208

up to Merz's about eight miles from town. We held up production next day, and then we lined up for battle again. This time we drove the calves up a narrow coulee road straight away from the ranch and their mothers to the main Nazko road and on up to join the yearlings at Merz's. We heard afterwards that this was the first bunch that had ever been driven out of there. Staebler didn't ride and his cattle had practically never seen a saddle horse. He handled them on foot with salt to bait them into corrals, and butchered there or trucked them out. We never claimed to be very good foot cowboys! No problems from there home.

After that we bought two more bunches of calves on the ranches up in the Blackwater area, Ron Callis' on Swan Lake and Vandenbergs' on Mud River. The Vandenbergs brought the Mud River calves down with their beef drive and we took them over at Ron's, held them a day or two to wean, and then drove the fifty head or so across country with no trail till we came out at Paley's McDonnell meadow. We had to cross over quite a mountain range, fairly thick timber and windfalls. That held us up just enough so we couldn't make it to Paley's meadow to camp before dark. We struck a little pothole with quite a bit of feed in it and since it was too dark to have any hope of finding better, we decided to try to hold them and camp there. Horses stayed okay, but the calves decided very early in the morning that it wasn't good enough food and no mamas around. We had an idea they were leaving, but it was pitch dark and not much hope of holding them. They sure covered a lot of country before we tracked them down. They went across a swamp we couldn't cross with horses, then wandered out in the timber awhile, gradually about-faced and lined out in the opposite direction and went as far as they could into a patch of high windfalls. Once we got them rounded up it wasn't too difficult to get to the McDonnell meadow and we held them there overnight, then to Paley's and home in two days' drive with no more troubles.

By now we were into the cow business, also into debt, and also into one hell of a lot of riding to range break all this young stock. Some got away. One got back as far as Charlie Moon's and he was shipping it with his when Joe Smith, the brand inspector, spotted it. Wayne and Bob Paley rode with Art and me rounding up at different times that fall. Bob and I picked up three head at Mel Moon's, about seven head at Webster's and one at Lee's. Another year some worked out to Duke Martin's at Alexis Creek, and some to Pelican Lake north of Alexis Creek, twenty miles or so. Some we didn't find till on into January. We sure got to know a lot of country.

The young stock purchased from all over led to another incident with Tony that almost laid me low. We had put most of this new stock on lower Ramsay Creek but not being range broke to the area, they scattered out quite a little. We rode for weeks that fall rounding up. One black, stormy night when Art, Wayne and I were gathering, we were pretty late getting to a meadow big enough to hold what stock we had rounded up.

It was late enough in the fall that we figured we would get snow, or anyway plenty of moisture, so we wanted to get lots of wood to make a big fire, partly for light and partly to keep dry. It was all brush quite a ways out into the meadow so we made camp some distance from the wood supply on the edge of the timber. Art and Wayne got a fire going and I headed back to the timber, tied my rope onto some good wood trees, and snaked them into the campfire. Tony didn't appreciate this deal in the dark at all but I got the wood in and figured all was okay. There was one spruce tree in camp we were throwing all our riggin' under to keep it as dry as possible. I led Tony up to it, took my saddle off and threw it under the tree.

Anyone who has camped out knows how the campfire light blinds you when you are away from it. Anyway I went to walk back to go alongside Tony. I guess he had turned some and I was headed straight for his hind end and I guess he figured it was those wood trees coming up behind him again. In any case he let me have it, square on, with both hind feet in the chest right about the solar plexus and far enough away so I got the full force of the drive.

Well, I figured that was curtains for me. I had been hurt much worse the time before when he bucked over me, but this time it gave me the certain feeling that I was going to die. Wayne and Art said I gasped and groaned all night long and it was daylight before I got my breath coming normal without gasping like a dying critter. They were scared out of their wits; scared to move me for fear my whole chest was caved in and they thought they might do more damage. It was too black dark to see to go anywhere and forty miles to get to any kind of vehicle on a road.

Art should have got grey-haired before me after that long night, but I beat him to the draw in spite of it.

They figured to haul me out on a travois, dead or alive, in the morning. With lass ropes and saddle blankets they could rig one up easily. I've an idea it would have been a mighty rough ride. Other than that, they just didn't know what to do. When the gasps started to die down, they figured sure I was leaving this cruel old world and Art was watching steadily to feel if I kept on breathing. Then I began to breathe easier and rest more normally. They guessed the crisis was over to some extent, and Art got Wayne to take a little rest. I came alive about nine o'clock in the morning and, like the man told about one of the old-time "Uncle Josh" records, "I picked myself up and shook off the dirt, and found after all I warn't much hurt." I felt myself all over and tried breathing a little deeper. I couldn't hear or feel any ribs grating together and found I was hungry as a bear. No supper the night before and no dinner on the roundup the day before. So we cooked up the mulligan and I took on a real feed and felt good enough to tackle a saddle horse.

They helped me load on. I had to hold my breath and even gasp a little but jarred the old pony loose and we made it in to one of our meadow cabins that night. I sure didn't bend easily either that day or for a good many days afterwards. It was quite a job to get under limbs. I would have to get one of the boys to hold the limb up so I could ride straight up under it. Whenever I tried to lean forward to duck under, I'd about pass out with the pain and it was sure good to get to the cabin where I could unload and rest up. So Tony didn't get his man that time either. But another of my nine lives . . . !

In the spring we had to take about two hundred head away down Ramsay Creek. Art was tied up at home with calving and farming, so I got Harold Paley, who must have been about twelve at the time, to help me. We had to break Tiddy Bits out for the job. She was only three or four years old and really small for either Art or me to ride enough to break her out well. But she had the ancestry to be a top saddle horse for a light person, so Art and I rough broke her and started her out on the job. Harold and Tiddy Bits got on famously and by the time we got back she was pretty reliable, and a natural stock horse. Harold had learnt a lot too. We took a pack horse along with a pretty light load as we had to travel a lot where there were no trails. We took extra rice along in case the schedule was upset any.

Art helped us get the outfit on the road and we drove up through our meadows; first stop at Baker meadow cabin; second stop, Ramsay Creek cabin; third, Sandy meadow and from there on, camps. We made it to "Jackknife Flats" where we had to castrate a few calves we hadn't done before leaving. One of them kicked the jackknife out of my hand and we never found it. From then on the flats were called by that name. We had called the area "Timber Wolf Hills" or "Timber Wolf Flats" before. They were the home of wolves and there must have been several dens in the area. We had tried at times to thin them out without much luck. Most of the ones I trapped had broken loose and got away with the traps.

We left part of the bunch on these flats and then started on down the creek on unknown, unmade trails, with very little feed for long distances till we got quite a few miles further down.

We tried to make too far the last day to get to good feed, and we had a hell of a time, landing up at dark at a sort of horseshoe-shaped bend in the creek where springs broke out of sidehills and in the bottom. There was rank green feed in these springs but they were boggy and fairly deep. We tried to keep the cattle up on top and go around this spot, but they were hungry and tired and before we could beat them a bunch got down into the bottom. This was trouble in a big way. They bogged down in the springs in bunches. I had to rope about twenty head and pull them out in the dark, and have Harold try to keep more from getting in and chase anything we pulled out further away. There were still six in the bog in the morning. We yanked them out and then tried to make a fast roundup and get everything we could away from there. Most of what we missed were in the springs when we got back. When we got them all out and a couple of hours drive down the creek to good feed we had a chance to get back and fill out the wrinkles in our hides, then make a decent camp and rest up. We hadn't had time to cook anything but coffee and eat a chunk of meat each till then.

I figured we'd best try to build a brush fence around this patch of territory. All I had was a small camp axe but I flew at it, and sent Harold out to try to get anything he could for meat as by now all we had was coffee and rice. We had coffee and rice, and rice and coffee for eight days! Harold only managed to locate one chicken to go with the rice. Harold asked me if I knew how to make rice hotcakes. His mother often put a little precooked rice into the hotcake batter and it worked out pretty well. That worked fine while we had flour but it got to be plain fried rice when we ran out of flour and all other mixings. Sure lucky we threw the extra rice into the pack.

We did get a pretty fair brush barricade fence built around the danger area before leaving. Cattle settled down fine with lots of feed and were happy as clams, so we high-tailed it back to the ranch for a decent wash and feed. Creeks and springs were still too cold to bathe in and we only had a coffee bucket, rice kettle and fry pan. Harold talks about that trip yet and I think he embellishes it a little. It was quite an event for a twelve-year-old who had been well fed and looked after up to then.

I believe that the next spring someone must have let a campfire get away or set fire to a pothole to make clean feed. The fire burnt up all our brush fence. It did improve the feed for both game and livestock though.

212

CHAPTER XXII

We Split the Blankets

Art and Emma and I weren't getting along too well. We had always had arguments and some pretty serious. But we went to work building up the ranch and forgot them soon. So far as finances went, we had none to argue about. But now there was a difference in too many of our attitudes. I was very conservative and a little frightened of going into what seemed to be too much debt. Actually, we weren't carrying any amount of debt load as most of the cattle were on a share basis, but we seemed to be working too much for someone else and our rewards were pretty small for the years we had worked from sunup to sundown. I was looking at it very selfishly. It looked as though it would be a long, long time before I would have anything I could call my own. Somewhere in my subconscious I guess I had visions of meeting the gal I would want to marry, and I wanted to be able to tell her that I had this and that, and that we could, on our own, make the grade and have a family.

The family co-op deal didn't seem to fit that nebulous vision. I wanted to be a separate individual, do things my own way even if it was wrong.

Every time we argued over anything, there was talk of splitting the blankets. I had quite a definite idea of taking up some meadows down on Narcosli Creek, south of Jackknife Flats, and starting my own outfit. There were an awful lot of disadvantages though. Art and I made a real good working team. We each had our specialties. Even shoeing horses, he was the blacksmith to make the shoes up to fit, and I put them on. We both pulled our weight mighty well. Alone I would have to do everything, and couldn't afford to hire. But I was full of ambition and could still work like a horse, even with my haywire knee and a hip injury that was bothering me some. Nothing came to a head till we decided we needed a stud to breed more saddle horses. Art decided to go over to Mulvihills in Chezakut to try to get one. He stopped at Shorty Harrington's both ways. Shorty was about fed up with ranching. Profits were very small at the price of stock then, and he was getting fed up with the partnership with his brother Flem. Shorty figured by selling everything he could retire or at least retire to something better. He had made enough tough trips over that old Nazko Mountain, with bad roads most of the year and impassable at times.

So he propositioned Art to buy the layout; cattle, horses, machinery and all, and at a price that Art couldn't turn down. Art was really hepped with the idea when he got back. He still figured we could work together a certain amount, and yet be more independent and individualistic. He had a big pow wow with Koltermans and they agreed to finance the deal, and also to buy quite a bunch of yearling steers from Pan Phillips. The upshot was he bought the old Harrington ranch in 1945, also Flem's McFarlane meadow twelve miles away. We sold nearly all the share stock that fall.

The split was made and the move was on. We were pretty handy at moving. Every fall we moved back and forth to meadows for haying and then later for feeding. None of us had anything much. I let Art take the bulk of the stock we had, as he was a family man and I was just a bachelor. Besides, he couldn't take any of the layout with all the improvements he had worked on.

We couldn't split the land, and it would have been practically impossible to sell any of it then anyway. Art wouldn't need much of the machinery as he bought a complete outfit with the layout. He had also bought a used army truck that helped a lot with the moving. There were cattle and horses to drive and several loads to haul. By then it was haying time, and I helped Art quite a bit to get organized and started. But I had to put my own hay up, and alone now, so had to get back on the job.

It sure was lonely. I had to do the organizing. Lexie Long Johnnie had once said that Art was the "figuring man," I was the "foreman" and Emma the "straw boss." Now I was the whole works and for awhile I went around like a chicken with its head cut off. Finally I got organized though, and got my hay up.

Our 13-year unwritten partnership drew to a close. We had done many kinds of work to beat the Depression and make the few dollars necessary to live while building roads, trails, cabins, barns and fences with little but double-bitted axes, strong backs and the sweat of our brows. Each of us had faced death right up close and used up a few of our nine lives, and come up raring to go again. Art had a family and we each had a small nucleus herd of cattle. But we were to go our separate ways for the most part.

Our pioneering was by no means over. Both our layouts were isolated stick ranches and we were carrying on with the pioneering traditions of our folks.

Glossary

Bender: More than an evening's drinking.

Brakes: Where the upper flats and hills brake steeply in coulees and ridges down to a river.

Break-up: When snow melts away and frost comes out of the ground in spring.

Buckpole: A sort of homemade sweep consisting of a squared log with an upright frame and swinging arms built onto it. With a team on the end of each arm it was used for bunching hay in the field, taking it to the stackyard and up a slide onto the haystack.

Chicken: Grouse.

Dallies: Wraps around the saddle horn to hold the critter on the end of the rope.

Forked hand: A good rider on a rough horse.

Go-devil: A stone boat or sled.

Green: Blissfully ignorant of ranching methods.

Ground-staked: See "tied to the ground."

Henskin blanket: A very light, inadequate blanket.

Hogs-back: A natural ridge.

Hogging: Bucking.

Hi-yuh: An Indian word meaning lots; e.g., hi-yu snow (spell it any way you like to get the hi u sound).

Jawbone: Credit.

Klooch: Indian woman.

Muck a muck: The "come and eat" call.

Necking them together: Tying animals together by the neck.

Parbuckle: Putting a cable, etc., round the middle of a log. Somebody balances one end while it is pulled up.

Poofing: Sort of grunting.

Range broke: Accustomed to a particular area or range.

Reach: What joins the front and back of a wagon.

Remittance men: The ne'er-do-well sons (and sometimes drunkards) of well-to-do families who had been sent over to the Colonies to keep them from ruining the family reputation with their philandering. They received an allowance or remittance fairly regularly to keep them from returning.

Russell fence: Posts in X formation with a wire stirrup for rails.

Rustling: When cows do it, it means eating grass out on fall or winter range.

Skinning: Driving a team or several teams of horses.

Tied to the ground: Dropped bridle lines tie a horse to the ground.

Turkey: Bedroll.

Vented: Put a registered brand, called a vent, in a different position from the original brand to show the cattle had been sold.

Wind-puff: A soft swelling.